PSYCHIATRY - THEORY, APPLICATIONS AND TREATMENTS

AF838720

VICTIMHOOD, VENGEFULNESS, AND THE CULTURE OF FORGIVENESS

To Earl

with appreciation

and friendship

Miriam

PSYCHIATRY - THEORY, APPLICATIONS AND TREATMENTS

Additional books in this series can be found on Nova's website under the Series tab.

Additional e-books in this series can be found on Nova's website under the e-book tab.

PSYCHIATRY - THEORY, APPLICATIONS AND TREATMENTS

VICTIMHOOD, VENGEFULNESS, AND THE CULTURE OF FORGIVENESS

IVAN URLIĆ
MIRIAM BERGER
AND
AVI BERMAN

NOVINKA

New York

Copyright © 2013 by Nova Science Publishers, Inc.

All rights reserved. No part of this book may be reproduced, stored in a retrieval system or transmitted in any form or by any means: electronic, electrostatic, magnetic, tape, mechanical photocopying, recording or otherwise without the written permission of the Publisher.

For permission to use material from this book please contact us:
Telephone 631-231-7269; Fax 631-231-8175
Web Site: http://www.novapublishers.com

NOTICE TO THE READER

The Publisher has taken reasonable care in the preparation of this book, but makes no expressed or implied warranty of any kind and assumes no responsibility for any errors or omissions. No liability is assumed for incidental or consequential damages in connection with or arising out of information contained in this book. The Publisher shall not be liable for any special, consequential, or exemplary damages resulting, in whole or in part, from the readers' use of, or reliance upon, this material. Any parts of this book based on government reports are so indicated and copyright is claimed for those parts to the extent applicable to compilations of such works.

Independent verification should be sought for any data, advice or recommendations contained in this book. In addition, no responsibility is assumed by the publisher for any injury and/or damage to persons or property arising from any methods, products, instructions, ideas or otherwise contained in this publication.

This publication is designed to provide accurate and authoritative information with regard to the subject matter covered herein. It is sold with the clear understanding that the Publisher is not engaged in rendering legal or any other professional services. If legal or any other expert assistance is required, the services of a competent person should be sought. FROM A DECLARATION OF PARTICIPANTS JOINTLY ADOPTED BY A COMMITTEE OF THE AMERICAN BAR ASSOCIATION AND A COMMITTEE OF PUBLISHERS.

Additional color graphics may be available in the e-book version of this book.

Library of Congress Cataloging-in-Publication Data

Victimhood, vengefulness, and the culture of forgiveness / editors, Ivan Urlic, Miriam Berger, Avi Berman.
216 p. ; 27 cm.
Includes bibliographical references and index.
ISBN: 978-1-62257-781-1 (soft cover)
1. Victims of crimes --Psychology. 2. Revenge. 3. Forgiveness. 4. Crime Victims --psychology. 5. Psychoanalysis. 6. Stress Disorders, Post-Traumatic --psychology. I. Urlic, Ivan II. Berger, Miriam III. Berman, Avi
HV6250.25 .V4845 2010
362.88

Published by Nova Science Publishers, Inc. † New York

CONTENTS

FOREWORD

Malcolm Pines

Readers of this powerful, important book are drawn to becoming witnesses of some of the worst outrages of this "dark century" (Mazower): Holocaust, Balkan wars, which followed the disintegration of Yugoslavia, the country patched together after World War One. The three authors all trained in the group analytic method, which originated from the teaching of S H Foulkes.

Foulkes had lived through World War One and Two, World War One in a communication unit of the German army and World War Two as a psychiatrist in the British army. It was from that experience, likewise to W R Bion, that group therapy and group understanding of war trauma originated, though Bion had been a fighting soldier in a tank regiment during World War One. Assertions have been made (Nitsun et al.) that Foulkes had not come to terms with his experiences as a German Jew who chose exile to United Kingdom in 1933. This question represented the voice of a younger generation of group analysts who are not as closely tied to Foulkes and his early circle.

After this preamble, we move to the devastating aftermath of the tragic experiences of Jewish survivors of concentration camps who managed to travel to what then was a British protectorate, Palestine, later the State of Israel, which itself was immersed with the surrounding Arab states. Through these struggles, hardened in the fire of war, has emerged the resilient strong profile of the new Israeli citizen.

Two Israeli authors, Avi Berman and Miriam Berger, show us their experiences as psychotherapists encountering subjects who live lives for whom the traumas of persecution, their own and those of previous generations, are always unremittingly present.

Berman describes and elaborates on "post-traumatic victimhood." Berman describes the formation of Post-traumatic Victimhood as a self-state that is created within the post-trauma recovery process.

This self-state focuses on a self-identity of a victim, a wish for compensation and regressive tendencies towards past dependency. An emotional experience of revived anger and vengefulness compromised by fear eventually creates typical victimhood aggression.

Berman suggests four aspects of victimhood self-state.

A. Claiming recognition as a victim. (A need to be recognized as a victim as a request for help and understanding).
B. Displacement of victimhood aggression. (Displacement of anger and vengefulness against a perpetrator from a real past, towards some present, non-threatening people).
C. Transforming personal suffering into influence, domination and control. (Conscious or subconscious use of personal suffering for obtaining powerful priority over other people).
D. Suspension of concern for other people's feelings and rights.
E. Thus, real suffering may be transformed into self-justification, exemption of concern for others, together with the demand for compensation and overpowering. This combination often brings rewards that are emotional, social and economic.

Berman states: "Victimhood self-state may be known to many of us, by experience, as a state of mind. Under certain circumstances of pain, we all seek recognition from people close to us, and try to influence them to stand on our side. We expect an effort of reparation and compensation. We wish for power and domination to re-balance our powerless and under-privileged condition, and we exempt ourselves temporarily from concern for others. By exposing ourselves as victims, we make ourselves better heard and felt. These behavioral patterns are usually effective in directing the attention of those we care about to our feelings of being wronged and inspiring them to make special efforts at providing better attention and reparation. Usually, this behavioral pattern is transient."

However, Berman suggests, in some people, especially the post-traumatic, victimhood self-state might be fixated and become the main explanatory principle especially when dealing with complex or threatening situations. In many cases, over-activation of Victimhood Self-State in one's behavior might cause inter-personal distress and may bring people to turn to psychotherapy. Psychotherapeutic points of view are discussed by Berman in Chapter Three.

In addition, Berman emphasizes that a whole society and even an entire nation can adopt a victimhood identity. According to Berman, Victimhood might become a component of a system of social values and identity. Reminders of national suffering serve to ensure national solidarity. "Social victimhood" is represented in what Berman terms "victimhood ideology." Such ideology is part of an overall national perspective, reflected and disseminated by leaders in public discourse. This phenomenon can be considered as "victimhood leadership."

A social or "national victimhood" may reflect all four aspects of the victimhood syndrome as Berman describes it. Victimhood social identity is based on a collective experience of injustice. In this case, memories of injustice are a central factor in the nation's common history. People come to believe that they are still victims of an injustice done them by a relentless and permanent enemy. Rage that originated with some past injustice is now displaced onto others. In one case, the rage following a trauma in the past is directed towards a group or a nation in the present.

National victimhood might encourage the transformation of victim identity into domination and aggressive use of power. In such cases, it is defined in absolute and ideological terms, making it impossible to achieve reconciliation. The demand for compensation may become fixated and inspire belligerent acts.

Berman claims that the most harmful process within a victimhood society happens when suspension of concern turns into exemption from concern. The exemption from concern for the opposing group might legitimize aggression and can bring about a self-justified takeover of another people's rights as a part of the secondary gain of the victimhood ideology.

Berman, in this fine contribution, gives us his own personality profile and describes how he gradually came to recognize this syndrome. This chapter, as are all the others, is strikingly well written, well researched in the current literature and gives vivid clinical, historical and political examples. Psychotherapy and group therapy of victimhood self-states are discussed through contemporary psychoanalytic and group analytic concepts.

Miriam Berger survived as a hidden child in Poland. She writes powerfully on vengefulness as a discredited emotion. She makes a case for vengefulness, for "hard feelings," as related to uniquely human vulnerability, part of the regular emotional exchanges between people. She points out that in Greek drama, vengefulness fuels the motivations of drama heroes and sets innumerable plots in motion. From the Old Testament, Berger brings out the killing of Abel by his brother Cain, fuelled because God had respected Abel's offering of lands not his, the fruits of the tilling of the soil. For this killing, he was punished by becoming a fugitive and a wanderer. Berger offers a reading of this crime and the redemptive act of accepting God's curse as a "formative myth: the acceptance of personal responsibility." Cain moves from denial to acceptance. "Being part of the human community means being bound to a community of reciprocity. Even God takes it upon himself to rectify his act of non-recognition" (page 66); he protects Cain from being killed by others by giving him a mark, the Mark of Cain. The exiled murderer Cain is credited as the founder of civilization, builder of the first city, the invention of agriculture by this tiller of the soil. Here I remind readers that in ancient China, the worst punishment that could be inflicted was for a mark of shame to be inscribed on the forehead, which exiled him from the citizens.

Berger claims that the desire to exact revenge on another is neither an indication of emotional pathology nor a sign of flaws in one's moral character. On the contrary, vengefulness can be assigned a meaningful relational function. As a restorative/communicative process, it has a double purpose: it informs us about basic relational needs that have been disrupted, while at the same time serving as a self-remedy meant to repair the disruption. Some of the disruptions vengeful wishes summon our attention to are injuries to one's dignity and pride, to one's sovereignty and self-definition as a subject in one's own right, one's sense of justice, one's hope to be counted as a worthy member of one's community, to name just a few of the unconscious messages encoded in vengeful wishes.

These unconscious "messages," when decoded, can serve as part of an emotional regulatory system that point out basic needs or "vital human concerns" that arise when mutual recognition is disrupted and needs repair. Vengeful wishes represent a mirror image of non-recognition: thwarted as they may be, they retrieve reciprocity.

The events that evoke vengefulness as a restorative/communicative process run a continuum, from the mundane frictions permeating everyday human relationships to the most extreme forms of brutality that people can inflict on one another. This continuum of injuries, from the smallest to the largest, evokes a wide range of emotional responses, vengeful wishes included.

The creation, disruption, and repair of mutual recognition constitute a continuous relational process, creating a transformative basis for the making of "subject relations."

Vengefulness as discredited feeling can be transformed into dissociated states of the self: the person sees him/herself as defective and unworthy, therefore hiding such feelings from the self, which results in disruption of reciprocity, detrimental to one's growth in every sense. Vengefulness constitutes a "social feeling": reciprocity is a most meaningful dimension in relationships and personal development. People are utterly connected and dependent on each other. It informs us that the relational matrix has been disrupted, that the water we swim in has become stormy. Vengefulness tells us that something in the processes of reciprocity, mutual acknowledgement and connectedness has been disrupted and needs repair. She claims that the modern de-legitimization of vengeful wishes may result in vengeful acts within relationships and also between groups and communities. She perceives vengefulness as having a meaningful function in restoring a culture of care and mutual recognition between man and others, without which human society cannot exist. Here is the picture of the human personality as laid out by Foulkes with Norbert Elias.

Berger makes an important statement: (72). Mutual recognition entails passion: it's an emotional process of becoming *mindful of each other as separate yet interconnected centers of initiative. Its nature is paradoxical and cyclical: one's need for the "other's" recognition is an acknowledgement that this "other" is indeed a subject whose recognition is valuable; otherwise, it would be pointless to need his recognition.* Miriam Berger gives us strong vignettes from her therapy experiences that persuasively illustrate how she uses her understanding of vengefulness.

In both Avi Berman's and Miriam Berger's writing, we see the respect that they hold out to their patients through their skill and patience, though these can become sorely tried. When we come to Urlic's experience with war veterans, this same respect holds. All our three authors are group analysts, and their work gives us evidence of the value of the group experience as an opportunity to reconnect with the world of others. The group can become the "collective other," which can grant recognition, become a pathway to regain self-esteem, connection and a sense of belonging to a community: hope restored. The ability to perceive vengefulness as part of our personal and social fabric is humanizing; hopefully it contributes to the effort to develop a community of acceptance and mutual concern.

Finally, Ivan Urlic from Croatia opens his contribution to the "impossible" task, to think about un-forgiveness with a poem by a Swiss Catholic priest who organized medical help during the war in Croatia, Bosnia and Herzegovina. This powerful and poignant poem takes us to the heart of darkness.

Urlic first surveys the literature on post-traumatic stress disorder and then gives us the experiences that a team of psychotherapists in the region of Split (Croatia) region to help displaced persons, refugees and soldiers. His clinical vignettes vividly exemplify the deep damage to the psyche of war veterans, which, though pushed out of mind, poignantly reappear in their dreams and in the group dynamics. The writing on "the inability to move beyond the unforgiving attitude," is aimed towards reaching a forgiveness attitude that will enable reconnection processes to unwind towards the relations between self and others. This again is well expressed by a poem from a refugee woman from Croatia. Urlic writes interestingly about the work that is being done in neuroscience and introduces the Enright Forgiveness Inventory (EFI) as an objective measure of the degree to which one person forgives another who has hurt him/her deeply and unfairly. He brings this information together in an integrated neuropsychological model of forgiveness in a table on page 156.

I find his writing on the destruction of "inner innocence" of the war veterans illuminating and moving. As they more fully perceive the wounded parts of the inner-selves, this killing of "inner innocence" has changed them profoundly. There is the possibility to work toward reparation, but not on complete restoration of their good inner objects. He is realistic of how difficult, perhaps impossible, is the process of full recovery. Dramatic experiences lead to the formation of rigid defense mechanisms, which cannot be significantly changed even by long-term group psychotherapy.

Urlic's writing on mourning and forgiveness as parts of a healing process are very important. On some countertransference issues: "speaking from the experience of my own and though I was working with in this field, the war and its aftermath was not only affecting those who became patients but those who entered the role of therapists as well. The arousal of an identificatory experience because of the total war situation endangers therapists and patients alike."

There is an important section "on compassion, empathy, and spirituality during psychotherapy process and in social issue" (173). He introduces writings on forgiveness that I had not known: "When we forgive, our wounds of past grievances are cleansed and healed....forgiveness is letting go of all hopes for a better past." His only experiences confirm that it is necessary to foresee the space for relationships to be offered again. The phenomenon of the collapse of time is the consequence of excessive violence that overwhelms the coping mechanisms that result "as psychic pressure" on social and intimate levels. It is the mourning process that represents the precondition for the space for relationships to be recreated and hopefully filled with forgiving and reconciling dynamics. However, this definition of forgiveness expresses the ideal. People are imperfect; they rarely reach the ideals they strive for; yet genuine forgiveness presents a goal for everyone. It is a goal many will not reach, but without that goal, forgiveness is likely to degenerate into demeaning what any given client or clinician wishes it to mean.

On almost any page of this book, there are statements that illuminate these most painful disturbing experiences for human beings. The writing is masterly, illuminating. My final illustration is from page 199, almost the end of the book.

Whether one prefers to believe that "God made me do it" or "my genes made me do it," the consequences of devaluing personal responsibility can be tragic. What might happen instead if mainstream science began to accept not only that free will exists but also – as is strongly suggested by experiments on anomalous cognition and by the findings of quantum physics – that the mind is an active, interconnecting force, deeply entangled with ourselves and the world, and that the true nature of the universe is fluid, self-organizing and inherently co-operative? Could such an expansive world view lead to improved moral behavior, a greater sense of compassion, and perhaps a reduced fear of myth? The possibilities that the answers might be, "yes," strongly encourages an open mind and continued dialogue.

Page 199: "All too many times we have to rediscover what was already preserved in old wisdom of human genius. Mourning processes and their meanings have been and still are a matter of many disputes of mostly secular or spiritual orientation. All wars finally end when people sit and talk. (War ends with jaw) and there is no emotional need or rational decision to forgive in order to start a dialogue, or the mourning process completed, or the compulsion to restore justice and to reconcile. My experiences have taught me that it is important to bear in mind the possibility and the need to develop the culture of forgiveness, and to enable and foster the necessary intertwined phases of mourning processes to unwind. What will ensue will be the necessity to reconcile with oneself and the other(s) in order to survive, not only existentially but even emotionally and spiritually."

I commend this book as an important step for all to enter into the renewal of a social space for forgiveness.

Introduction: Personal Motivations, or How This Book Came into Being

This book was born out of the dramatic sociopolitical situations to which each of us has been exposed, both as therapists and as human beings. Each of us was subject to traumatic realities of man-made violence, bloody fights, wars, and social enmities in which we were caught without our choice.

The parts of this book came together in a spontaneous yet logical way. Although written in two different countries by three different authors, we feel that they are bound together by a shared and inherently connected spirit; both the subject matter we deal with and our similar perspectives about it are what brought us together.

The topics of victimhood, vengefulness, and the (im)possibility of creating a space for a culture of forgiveness that can lead to the unfolding of processes of reconciliation have been issues of special interest for all three of us.

Coming together from different countries, we tried to focus on what seemed to us to be universal phenomena that transcend the boundaries of any specific society. At the same time, our differences contributed an added perspective about the subject matter. Each of us served as an objective "other" to his colleagues and contributed his share to the ability to understand more fully our respective work.

All three of us are psychotherapists and group analysts who deal with trauma caused by open wars, chronic hostilities, continuous outbursts of violent sightings, and various acts of aggression that have taken many different shapes over the years. Two of us are psychologists from Israel, one a psychiatrist from Croatia. We share with our patients realities of threat, insecurity and strife. Living through the same actualities with our patients enables us to develop a deeper empathic understanding of their emotional pain, their vulnerabilities, their strength, their courage, and their struggle to preserve human dignity in the face of destructiveness and evil. We feel that our commonality with our patients has helped us become more aware of the basic human needs for safety and concern, and more cognizant of the long-term emotional consequences of violence and its widespread personal and relational damage; it has strengthened our belief in the pressing need to prevent violence and seek ways to heal its wounds. While the need to contain horrible facts of injuries and loss is a continuous struggle with despair and unbearable pain in our role as therapists, it has also motivated us to look for ways to promote a culture of reconciliation that might mitigate the cycles of aggression and violence, if not stop them altogether.

Ears alone do not suffice to become sensitized to such emotional realities; one must develop a sense for many hidden, deeply repressed themes that have been encapsulated through dynamic processes of dissociation, denial, projection, and projective identification, and reinforced by feelings of fear, guilt, and, especially, shame. These processes, which are explored in each of the chapters of this book, are characterized by clusters we defined as victimhood and vengefulness (whether in fantasy or in acts) and by great difficulties to open paths for forgiveness and reconciliation. We have become closely acquainted with the various facets of these dynamic clusters through long-term therapeutic relationships with war veterans and with persons who had been severely wounded as a consequence of aggression; these close encounters with the subjective worlds of people hurt by man-made violence have left an indelible mark on our lives as well; at the same time, they have also expanded our capacities to bear witness and to contain suffering without losing hope; they have helped us grow, both personally and professionally.

Owing to those experiences and to the introspection that was part of our work, we claim that victimhood, vengefulness and forgiveness are issues that have a strong presence in the everyday lives of many people but have not been sufficiently explored using psychoanalytic methods.

In the case of victimhood, the claim of having suffered may be abused to the point of exemption from concern for others and may serve as self-justification for causing others to suffer. This form of abuse may arise from disowned guilt and/or anger and in some cases may result in an impasse in which mutual aggression impedes any possibility of reconciliation.

In the case of vengefulness, the desire for revenge may evoke fear, shame, anger, and moral indignation; since this desire is mostly discredited and repudiated, it may eventually push people towards utter loneliness and despair that culminate in acting on their wish for revenge in ways that are destructive to themselves and to others. Thus, cycles of violence may perpetuate themselves hopelessly.

Victims of traumatic histories may suspect that forgiveness is an impossible illusion and resign themselves to an existence in a harsh, hostile world in which one is destined to live chronically by one's sword; such a stance undermines constructive vision, hinders learning from experience, and obstructs healing and renewal.

In writing this book, our goal is to draw attention to Victimhood, Vengefulness and Forgiveness as significant conceptual entities that can enhance our understanding of the dynamic processes involved in their various inner and outer configurations; we hope that being more aware of the subjective meanings of the feelings, thoughts, and behaviors these "clusters" generate would enable therapists to be more empathic and responsive to their patients and make the therapeutic relationship more productive.

From our perspective, victimhood, vengefulness and forgiveness are dynamic processes that evolve all the way from unbearable destructive emotional states, towards prospects of reconciliation. We offer a focused psychoanalytical exploration of these issues, since we believe that such a study opens an additional (much-needed) path towards a humanizing dialogue and contributes to the struggle against senseless violence.

Over the years, we have explored these subjects and developed their various theoretical and clinical aspects in a number of papers that we presented in several professional conferences.

We first presented these ideas during the Group Analytical Society (GAS) Congress in Bologna, Italy in 2002; then, the first combined workshop on all three subjects was hosted at the International Association of Group Psychotherapy (IAGP) Congress in Istanbul in 2003. This was followed by meetings during the European Group Analytic Training Institutes (EGATIN) Study Day on supervision held in Split, Croatia in 2004, and the GAS symposium in Molde, Norway that same year in which the second extended workshop on these issues took place.

In March, 2006, during the "IMAGINE" conference in Tel Aviv, Israel, these topics were presented to an audience comprised chiefly of Israeli and Palestinian participants. The last workshop was organized in June of the same year, at the School of Psycho-trauma in the Inter-University Centre in Dubrovnik, Croatia. Throughout this time, our processing of the workshop topics and our continued discussions of the various issues related to them developed into the material presented in this book.

Thinking back about these presentations and workshops, we have noticed that the reactions of participants was frequently quite similar: the discussion of victimization tended to dominate the discourse, while vengefulness was touched upon rather sparingly; forgiveness and reconciliation were not discussed at all, as "there was no time left."

Since this pattern repeated itself time and again, we conjectured that it may have been indicative of some of the processes inherent in each topic: that is to say, it may have reflected the difficulties to make room for a culture of forgiveness and reconciliation until issues of aggression and other hard feelings have at least partially been processed and resolved. It appears that a tremendous amount of energy is consumed by the struggle to identify, acknowledge, and understand the impact of traumatic experiences and to become aware of their emotional counterparts and of the powerful hold they have on one's relationships with oneself and others. Thus, the repeated phenomena we noticed throughout those occasions may have mirrored the pressing need to undergo an arduous and patient process of working through the traumatic experiences before one opens up to forgiveness and reconciliation and can embrace them as real alternatives to victimhood and to destructive acts of revenge. The reluctance of therapists to touch upon processes of forgiveness and reconciliation and their tendency to concentrate instead on the inner dynamics of aggression may have been an indication in that direction. The need for a third party, a "witness," whether a therapist, a group conductor, a fellow participant in group psychotherapy or a supervisor, seems to be vital in this process. Each such "other" may serve as an essential "witness," lending the attentive human presence without which reconciliation becomes meaningless.

Dealing with victimhood and vengefulness relates to interpersonal and social dynamics in which injury provokes injury and revenge causes counter-revenge, in which victims become perpetrators and generate more victims in turn. These personal and interpersonal cycles are fraught with feelings of fear, helplessness, rage and degradation; they are marked by failures of acknowledgment, lack of mutual recognition, and the tendency of each party to perceive the "other" as the aggressor.

We describe two kinds of recognition that can have the greatest impact on instigating a move towards a culture of forgiveness: One is the aggressor's acknowledgment that he has caused the victim suffering, namely, that he sees himself as accountable and responsible for his own deeds. The other is the victim's acknowledgment of his "victimhood aggression" and vengefulness and his ability to perceive them as an inner emotional state seeking understanding and transformation.

The relational patterns that generate pain and injury take place in a social context in which people prefer victories over cooperation and winning over joint achievements. It seems, however, that the joy of victory is temporary and can easily turn into mourning over losses. Losers and winners thus take turns in a never-ending cycle. It appears to us, then, that perceiving victory as a solution to problems is likely one of the most prevalent and costly human mistakes.

We believe that the culture of forgiveness and reconciliation presents an alternative to these realities. It enhances the ability to disrupt the traumatic cycle of aggression-victimhood-revenge and to replace it with the actualization of human similarities; it provides hope for the renewal of dialogue in the midst of enmity and for promoting a culture of mutual concern.

ABOUT THE AUTHORS

Miriam Berger M. A. is a clinical psychologist, supervisor, and a group analyst. She is a Co-Chairperson of The Israeli Institute of Group Analysis and one of its co-founders and part of its teaching staff. She was the initiator and co - founder of the residency program for clinical psychologists in "Amcha" Tel Aviv (an association for treating holocaust survivors and their families) and its first chief psychologist. She is a supervisor in the post graduate program for psychoanalytical psychotherapy in the school of social work in Bar Ilan University. Her professional experience includes therapy and supervion of post traumatic states in various clinical and sociopolitical settings . She has published a number of papers in psychoanalytical journals and contributed various chapters in books pertaining to areas of the above interests. She is in private practice in Tel Aviv. Contact information: (address) 3 Begin Street, Yehud, 56478, Israel, e-mail: bergerm.miriam.maria@gmail.com.

Avi Berman, Ph. D. is a clinical psychologist, psychoanalyst, and a group analyst. He is a member in Tel- Aviv Institute of Contemporary Psychoanalysis and The Israeli Institute of Group Analysis. He is a co-founder of "Be'Sod Siach" Organization for conflict resolution in Israel. He is the initiator and co-founder of the Israeli Institute of Group Analysis and its former chairperson. He teaches in Tel-Aviv University. His professional experience includes post traumatic therapy and supervision in "Amcha" (an association for treating holocaust survivors and their second generation's siblings. He has published a number of papers in psychoanalytical journals and contributed various chapters in books pertaining to areas of the above interests. Contact information: (address) P.O.B. 1017, Ramat Hasharon, Israel, e-mail : a_berman@012.net.il.

Ivan Urlić, M.D., Ph. D. is neuropsychiatrist, psychoanalytic psychotherapist and group analyst. As professor of psychiatry and psychological medicine, Medical School, University of Split, Croatia, he teaches on several Universities in Croatia, Bosnia and Herzegovina and Italy, as well as internationally. He is founder member of IGA Zagreb and IGA Bologna (Italy), where he is training group analyst, and supervisor. He used to be the chairperson of EGATIN, and Board member of GAS (London) . Now he is Board member of IAGP, and of ISPS Int. He is co-founder and deputy president of the ISPS Croatia.

His special interests: Group psychotherapy for patients with psychosis, and with PTSD. He founded the Regional Center for Psychotrauma, for Dalmatia (Croatia), for treatment of war veterans and their family members.

He participated in the international project named, “The mutual acknowledgement between Israelis and Palestinians project”, founded by Jessica Benjamin.

He published many papers and chapters in books. Besides in Croatian, he is writing and lecturing in Englidsh, Italian and French. Contact information: (home address) Starčevićeva 3, 21000 SPLIT, Croatia, e-mail: ivan.urlic2@gmail.com.

PART ONE

Chapter 1

POST-TRAUMATIC VICTIMHOOD: BETWEEN RECOVERY AND FIXATION

Avi Berman

In this world, there are victims and there are perpetrators who deserve our witnessing, our ability to overcome denial tendencies, our compassion and intervention. Many people have endured traumatic events as a consequence of war, injury, torture, political persecution, physical abuse, or long-term oppression by society or within the family. Others have been wounded psychologically after having witnessed another's suffering. These people live with paralyzing anxiety, a sense of helplessness and intense shame and humiliation. Their lives are often reduced to a debilitating effort to survive. They often suffer from post-traumatic stress disorder (PTSD). These people are victims.

As a result of the trauma, the victim's pain diminishes his sense of inner locus of control. His experience of free will and personal effectiveness are greatly reduced, if not lost altogether. He may feel threatened and helpless weakness, and he becomes more dependent. The person's primary subjective experience is that of suffering, with concomitant feelings of dread, shame, humiliation, and rage.

The term Post-traumatic Victimhood indicates a different condition. I refer to Post-traumatic Victimhood as a self-state that is created within the post-trauma recovery process. This self-state is centered upon self-identity of a victim, a wish for compassion and compensation and regression to hopeful dependency. As a result, reduction of concern for others may occur.

Recovery processes may occur only within an environment that recognizes the suffering the person has endured and is predisposed to enabling the restoration process. This happens when the family and/or the society is recruited for this purpose. Quite often, this social support network contains elements of empathy, compensation, and affirmative action. Sometimes, the perpetrators themselves (or at least some of them) are those who attempt to help the victims through reparation.

Despite a post-traumatic victimhood self-state, the victim may aim at comprehensive restoration of his pre-traumatic personality. When he is moderately successful, restoration of ego-strengths may increase, and concealed inner resources may be re-activated. Energies are renewed, the level of activity increases, and there is a return to benign interpersonal relationships. Hence, feelings of depression and despair become re-balanced with hope, and there is an oscillation between paralyzing feelings of helplessness and revived involvement and activism. From the emotional point of view, this alternative involves the subject partially overcoming his hatred and rage and embarking on a process of mourning and forgiveness. Hence, a past victim may also create a restored self-state within which he may re-experience, at least partly, his pre-traumatic life.

At the same time, however, post-traumatic dissociated and disavowed feelings of humiliation and anger are re-experienced and eventually form an assertive or aggressive behavioral component. While in this state of mind, the post-traumatic person feels re-empowered to transform his feelings into a claim for recognition of his recent suffering and a demand for acknowledgement of physical and mental affliction. The overt expression of pain and anger may lead to complaints, accusations and a demand for compensation.

I suggest that there may be two aspects of a recovery process of trauma: one encourages the restoration of the pre-traumatic personality and its further growth and the other preserves the victim's identity. On one hand, the victim may wish to return to his pre-traumatic personality including restoration of normal life. On the other hand, he may seek to maximize compensation while simultaneously preserving the painful events that justify the community's compensatory efforts. I suggest that these two poles may balance each other up to a point of fixation between compensation and recovery.

Eventually these aspects may integrate into different and dissociated self-states. With increased duration, the victimhood self-state becomes part of the one's personality. This self-state may be dissociated from the other self-states of the personality and may play a primary role in personal and interpersonal relationships with close friends, spouses, children and relatives as well as within the larger social environment. I suggest that restoration of ego strengths and independent functioning need to be dissociated from demanding of recognition and compensation. Restoration processes of independent initiatives and orientation for future personal and interpersonal equalization might be arrested and weakened by a dependent demand for compensation. Past painful memories might set the person back. They need to be disavowed in order to enable new structures.

Post-traumatic victimhood behavior can be distinguished from the more familiar, post-traumatic stress disorder (PTSD). It is important to differentiate between the two patterns. One of the common attitudes and behaviors in the PTSD is avoidance: The PTSD individual tends to avoid places, people, memories and symbols that might remind him of the traumatic event. In certain cases, this involves a loss of interest in any aspect of the event that made him into a victim. This avoidance is accompanied by a major reduction in expression of affect. The breadth of the victim's emotional world is narrowed. He suffers from increased sensitivity to stimuli and reduced tolerance for affects.

As with post-trauma, post-traumatic victimhood includes expressions of pain and suffering. Yet, individuals, while in victimhood self-state, do not manifest social avoidance. They are often highly energetic, regaining vitality and acknowledging their suppressed anger and humiliation. Their behavior indicates the existence of available ego resources. In fact, they often make it a point to publicly proclaim the suffering in their lives through verbal commentary and certain behavior patterns. They demand recognition and recompense, and many times convey anger, accusations and complaint. Within victimhood self-state, there is often a hidden desire to influence people, to gain power over them and (sometimes) a conscious or unconscious goal of acquiring leadership positions.

I refer to "post-traumatic victimhood" as a self-state within the concept of multiple selves (Sullivan, 1950, Mitchell, 1991, Bromberg, 1998). Within this concept, the meaning of human personality is reconsidered: despite our usual experience of one continuous self, each one of us is a composite of different self-states that may or may not be recognized by other self-states. From within any certain self-state, one's personal experience is of authenticity ("this is me" experience), while any sign of any other self-state is experienced as "not me" (Bromberg, 1998). For instance, from within a victimhood self-state, one's normal functioning, or even socially accepted achievements, may be experienced as a social disguise: unavoidable false and placating social behaviors. In many cases, self-states might be dissociated from each other. In post-traumatic cases, dissociation may become a major mechanism of defense. Dissociation enables the injured person to function without the intrusion of his traumatic pain and dread into his everyday life.

Much has been said about the crucial importance of the dissociation as a protection from the overwhelming memory of traumatic events and derivate experience (Bromberg, 1998, Howell, 2002 Davies and Frauley, 1994). A person cannot function while being overloaded with feelings of dismay and helplessness. Dissociation enables him to carry on. The threatened and oppressed post-traumatic self-state and the rehabilitated and partially recovered self-state have to be dissociated from each other in order to enable an organized and efficient functioning (Bromberg, 1998).

Post-traumatic victimhood self-state may serve as an important mechanism of defense. Holding to victim's identity and claiming recognition of it recruits other people's concern but at the same time might contribute to fixation of wishes for dependency and external locus of control. This dependent position is meant to be non-threatening for a possible future aggressor (Frankel, 2002). An over-successful recovery process produces a threat of becoming too attractive to a next potential aggressor. Moreover, the restoration process and self-fulfillment, as a human motive, are most wished for but at the same time, they may result in fear of further abandonment by the benefactor, making him believe that he is not needed anymore.

Victimhood self-state may be known to many of us, by experience, as a state of mind. Under certain circumstances of pain, we all seek recognition from people close to us and try to influence them to stand on our side and ask them to take responsibility for our suffering. We expect an effort of reparation and compensation. We wish for power and domination to re-balance our powerless and under-privileged condition, and we exempt ourselves temporarily from concern for others. By exposing ourselves as victims, we make ourselves better heard and felt. These behavioral patterns are usually effective in directing the attention of those we care about to our feelings of being wronged and inspiring them to make special efforts at providing better attention and reparation. Usually, this behavioral pattern is transient.

In addition, I might emphasize that a whole society and even an entire nation can adopt a victimhood identity. Since victimhood can also be a learned behavior, the socialization process of a community can educate its members to develop a victimhood identity. Children may come to develop victimhood behavior similar to that of a parent through trans-generational transmission. Paradoxically, the socialization process, by itself, can also be accomplished through means of oppression, which strengthen, through experience, the formation of a learned victimhood.

Victimhood is probably first mentioned in psychoanalytic literature by Meissner (1976, 1977, 1979) in his analysis of Freud's Schreber case (Freud, 1922). Meissnner writes:

> The core element in this paranoid system is the organization of the sense of (false) self around the core introject that underlies the identification with the victim—so that victimhood becomes the basis and the motive of the substitutive object involvement. For Schreber, the need for victimhood, along with the narcissistically driven need for acknowledgment and recognition in terms of compensatory grandiosity, were aptly resolved in his special redeeming relation to the father-God.

In other words: victimhood, according to Meissner, is a derivative of a paranoid system organization, where a person's false self is built around identification with a victim. The person seeks recognition in terms of compensation and grandiosity, simultaneously. Later, he adds that the basis of victimhood exists in relation to a sadistic figure. Submission may result in "feminine weakness, vulnerability and victimhood" (Meissner, 1977). Aggression is also introjected beside identification with a victim. Yet the aggressive introjects are more repressed.

Bernstein (1988) adds that victimhood is of a masochistic origin and includes a difficulty in taking responsibility for one's life.

Brandschaft (1988) refers to a feeling of desperation. Hover (2005) suggests that "victim identity enables one to deny that one may also be a perpetrator" and that identification with an aggressor is a hidden aspect of victimhood. Hirsh (2003) emphasizes the passivity and helplessness of victimhood. Schafer (2005) mentions the self-righteousness that accompanies victimhood.

Victimhood is also mentioned as a result of identification with the aggressor (Laub, 2005). Some authors refer to victimhood as having a gender component: victimhood is considered to be more feminine (Bass, 2002, Gartener, 1999).

Many authors deal with the socio-political aspects of victimhood, citing victimhood among Holocaust survivors (Marcus and Wineman, 1985) or international conflicts that are partly based on victimhood attitudes (Montville, 1989, Hogget, 2001). (Others will be discussed in Chapter 2.)

Most of the time, victimhood is mentioned as if the term is self-evident.

Identification with the Aggressor and Post-Traumatic Aggression

The term "Identification with the Aggressor" was suggested by Ferenczi (1932) as one of the main psychological results of abusive traumatic offense. He found that people who experience an inescapable threat may become totally compliant with the aggressor, avoiding any resistance and eliminating significant parts of their own selfhood. Ferenczi refers initially to a dreadful self-adjustment of the victim to the aggressor, including a submissive compliance to the aggressor's wishes and commands. This submissive attitude may include an internalization of the offender's aggression, which may result in self-accusations, "self-victimizations" (Davies and Frauley, 1994) and re-traumatization (Howell, 2002).

A complementary sense of "Identification with the Aggressor" is a sort of imitation of the aggressor's attitudes and behaviors. It seems that victims may adopt aggressive behaviors. Ferenczi mentioned a possible aggressive aspect of victims, terming it "The terror of the suffering"' (Ferenczi, 1932); he did not elaborate on it. The fact that subjects of abuse, despite their own suffering, may become aggressors themselves has inspired some psychoanalytic explanations.

Anna Freud (1936) suggested that the origin of aggression in these cases is basically internal: The aggressor is the person's harsh superego, which threatens the personality and therefore is projected on an external figure (like the analyst sometimes). In her view, the process is based on projection of intra-psychic attack that results in aggression aimed at a real person.[1]

Howell (2002) and Prior (1996) suggest Victim/Aggressor dissociation. Following a traumatic event, two different and dissociated self-states may be formed. The victim and the aggressor self-state may appear under different conditions. The victim may become an aggressor and then return to post-traumatic victim experience while threatened. Yet, according to Howell, the aggressive behavior of victims is a neurological imitation not mediated by symbolic thinking.

Frankel (2002) claims that the victim's aggressive aspect of identification is meant to know the aggressor from within and to foresee his action in advance. Yet, the victim's aggression will never be aimed at the aggressor. Any return of a real threat will cause the victim to submit again without taking further risks.

I would like to suggest that the rage component in victims' experience (Davies and Frauly, 1994) may join authentic vengeful wishes that were created at the traumatic moments but disavowed and dissociated. Many victims become conscious of their vengeful fantasies when the traumatic threat is over. Vengeful wishes' delayed reactions to trauma are not easily recognized in contemporary psychoanalytic writings. It seems that victims are protected from being described in the same terms as their aggressors. In my view, however, during the process of recovery from trauma, restoration of ego strengths and increasing feelings of safety may enhance integration of rage and revenge (Berger, following chapters), resulting in a post-traumatic vengeful aggression.

Many times, the victim himself has to deny or dissociate his vengeful wishes as a defense against "unconscious aggressive libidinal fantasy" (Dickes, 1965), which in my view is created and intensifies during the process of recovery from trauma. Since vengeful wishes may undermine the victim's sense of grievance together with his differentiation between the perpetrator and himself, raw vengeful wishes should be dissociated and/or transformed.

I suggest, therefore, that the post-traumatic victimhood self-state includes a typical "post-traumatic victimhood aggression" that results from identification with an aggressor combined with re-experienced anger and vengefulness. However, unlike borderline personality disorder, post-traumatic victimhood aggression is usually not explosive nor overtly destructive. It seems that in the recovery process, self-inflicted guilt that results from identification with the aggressor process may be transformed into healthier renewed feelings of self-pity and protest (Mitchell, 2000). Usually, rage is self-moderated through self-pity because of the need to present a victim identity that must be differentiated from the aggressor identity. Moreover,

[1] Anna Freud did not recognize real trauma as a factor in the psychodynamics of identification with the aggressor. Moreover, she did not mention Ferenczi's contribution. Ferenczi's protest against the psychoanalytic denial of real traumatic event as a factor of mental disturbances was apparently overlooked by Anna Freud.

aggression is expected to be contained within ongoing stable and restored relations with the benefactor. The post-traumatic victimhood self-state includes a self-presentation in which the "victim" is in the fore, while the "aggressor" is hidden behind. From within post-traumatic victimhood, any expression of aggression may be disowned, experienced as "not me" and referred to other people's offense.

Victimhood's self-state entails "doers and done-to" complementary relations (Benjamin, 2004). Aggressive aspects of post-traumatic victimhood often involve transforming one's personal suffering into domination, control and overpowering of others. Guilt-provoking behaviors that inspire other people's compliant and compensatory responses are common. Often, post-traumatic victimhood includes periods of indifference and lack of empathy and concern towards the suffering of others, including the denial of another person's rights.

Another aspect in the post-traumatic recovery process may be an everlasting fear and alertness of the possible return of aggression and oppression. A sudden change into a state of mind of submissiveness and compliance is always possible in front of a threatening figure. Therefore, victimhood aggression may be displaced from real past (sometimes present) perpetrators to non-threatening, sometimes most devoted, people. In most cases, the person makes a conscious or unconscious differentiation between circumstances and people in the presence of whom victimhood aggression may be expressed and those before whom he will remain cautious and socially accepted.

A Personal Point of View

At a certain point in my life, I discovered that expressions of suffering and vulnerability on the part of those close to me were often deliberately exaggerated and resulted in my giving up aspects of my personal agenda to alleviate their real or alleged suffering. It was a moment of disillusionment that has changed much of my interpersonal perceptions and choices.

I was born to Jewish parents who immigrated to Israel from Europe before WWII. Most of their family—parents, brothers, nephews and nieces—were killed, while my parents managed to rescue themselves and survived. Though they did their utmost to hide their mourning and bereavement, a cloud of a possible disaster, fear of a sudden loss and constant duty of commitment were always present. The family emotional atmosphere oscillated between sadness, anger and rehabilitated vitality. Like many typical "Second Generation" children, I was fated to carry my "amputated" family and bear in my mind the future creation of the next generation. This meant I had to give up the innocent risk-taking that characterizes childhood, understand the suffering of others, make no noise, suppress anger, not surpass my parents' powers, excel in my studies and be happy. To a great extent, I succeeded in carrying out these missions, though I had some difficulties in fulfilling the last one.

People most often internalize the personal stances and relationships to which they are exposed. So it was with me. I realized that the state of mind to which I was subject in my early years had produced in me behaviors and attitudes that I now refer to as a "post-traumatic victimhood self-state." This realization, however, could never have happened in my family nor by myself alone. Interactions with other people, outside my family, contributed to new experiences that I now consider to be disillusionment. Some of those interactions confronted my basic beliefs about closeness, friendship and mutual consideration. Surprisingly, my behaviors had sometimes stirred anger and frustration. My excuses were not accepted. Within those encounters, I often felt hurt and rejected. Upon reflection, I came to see (with a little help from my friends) that occasionally I made use of victimhood myself. My distress gave me a greater sense of entitlement in relations with others and encouraged me to demand compensation. At times, my desire for compensation was greater than my desire for changes in myself. I learned to excuse myself from mutuality in relations through complaints about daily hardships, bad moods and over-work. Eventually, I realized both how well victimhood works and its price of creating frustration and distance within people I cherished. Yet, at certain moments, breaking out of the victimhood self-state and identifying with different points of view was hard, strange and sometimes frightening, as if I had to give away my home and my language.

Switching of self-states seems never to end. The victimhood self-state is always ready and available. Yet, expanding my experience to other self-states was also liberating. I discovered that sometimes expressions of pain and suffering that stir other people's efforts are subject to choice, either consciously or subconsciously. I realized that expressions of weakness and vulnerability, often accompanied by complaints, may serve as a source of interpersonal power and influence. Powerlessness may become forceful. The more I observed and thought about it, the more it seemed that certain people choose to present themselves as victims as a part of their identities.

As a counterpoint, I have noticed that people who suffer greatly are often invisible. They don't make themselves heard. They may remain closed up in their houses, alone with those who are close to them, particularly when they are low in energy, sad, withdrawn and feel ineffective. They tend to isolate themselves socially.

My own experience contributed its share to the following discussion of post-traumatic victimhood. These impressions finally led me to an examination of some of my most basic assumptions. Over the years, I have been exposed to the behavior and verbal interaction of many people. I have documented many examples and studied different possibilities of individual and group therapy. Years of social involvement had led me closer to identifying victimhood within social and political situations. I have examined attitudes and interactions of social and political leaders and their ideologies and the relationships between groups and nationalities. All this has led me to suggest the existence of a self-state and a pattern of social behavior that I refer to as "post-traumatic victimhood." In these chapters, I propose to focus and clarify what I mean by this concept in a way that I hope will contribute to some valuable insights concerning clinical, socio-political and psychotherapeutic domains.

THE FOUR INTERPERSONAL ASPECTS OF VICTIMHOOD

I suggest that post-traumatic victimhood self-state is usually formed in people at a certain point of their process of recovery from a real trauma. Yet, as mentioned before, this self-state may be created under certain socio-cultural circumstances as a learned behavior. Post-traumatic victimhood self-states may be activated in relations with non-threatening people and when one is challenged by interpersonal confrontation or a wish to obtain certain advantage or a privileged position. Whenever this self-state is activated, one's personality seems to be taken over by a pattern of beliefs, emotions and interpersonal attitudes and behaviors. In the following description, I would like to emphasize those aspects that are often obscured, or even denied, by our compassion and empathy. They entail overt behavior and explicit personal and interpersonal attitudes. The examples I present are taken from therapeutic sessions, organizational consultations, documentation of political and social activity and personal experience. The people described here have all experienced traumatic events in their pasts that caused genuine suffering, including sexual assault, torture, persecution, social abuse, oppression by parents or siblings, political oppression and social humiliation.

The post-traumatic victimhood self-state has its reasons, its personal inner experience and its interpersonal derived relations. I would like to present four aspects that are typical, in my view, of the “post-traumatic victimhood self-state” in interpersonal relations.

A. *Claiming recognition as a victim.* Post-victimhood self-state contains includes a need to be recognized as a victim as a request for help and understanding. Victimhood identity may become the main explanatory principle especially when dealing with complex or threatening situations. Claiming a victim’s identity draws on past suffering, on feelings of injustice, which are often reenacted in the present,.
B. *Displacement of victimhood aggression.* Post-traumatic victimhood self-state includes the displacement of anger and vengefulness against a perpetrator from a real past towards some present, non-threatening people. Those people are, sometimes, one's most benevolent and available figures.
C. *Transforming personal suffering into influence, domination and control.* Post-traumatic victimhood self-state is characterized by a conscious or subconscious use of personal suffering for obtaining powerful priority over other people. In his interpersonal behavior, the person's reports of suffering are accompanied by expectations for compensation, sometimes underlined by overt accusations of people close to him.
D. *Suspension of concern.* Post-traumatic victimhood self-state includes suspension of concern and empathy towards others. People who are characterized by victimhood syndrome might feel temporarily entitled to ignore other people's rights, due to their own past suffering and present efforts toward recovery. Suspension of concern may be accompanied by non-mutual feelings of entitlement.

Claiming Recognition as a Victim

Claiming a victim’s identity is, first of all, a call for empathy, understanding and support. From within a post-traumatic self-state, victimhood identity may become the main explanatory principle for difficulties, mistakes, fear of failure and low self-esteem. In many cases, people present their victim identity the way they express other aspects of their identity, such as gender, parenthood, profession, education, etc. Through words and behavior, they proclaim their wish to be recognized as victims by their environment. Any other self-states based on more independent and self-sustaining motivation may be felt as enfeebling and therefore rejected and dissociated.

I suggest that the desire to be perceived as a victim becomes interactively significant. It is a feature in relationships with others, who then participate in the interaction in one of two ways: by becoming perpetrators or by becoming empathic and supportive witnesses. They function as supportive witnesses when they listen sympathetically and commiserate with the teller's experiences of injury. If they fail as supportive witnesses, they might become perpetrators themselves, their injurious behavior now a reason for complaint. In psychotherapy, the therapist him/herself may be considered a supportive witness and then, under the influence of transference, an aggressor. I will elaborate on this dynamic in Chapter 2.

Supportive witnessing is based on empathy as an attitude and intention to understand and resonate the post-victim's subjective experience, point of view and behavior. Yet empathy alone might be experienced as being insufficiently supportive. Supportive witnessing requires the witness to clearly stand by the victim's side and prefer his point of view to any other. Moreover, the post-traumatic victimhood self-state occasionally includes unpredictable reactions to the environment's empathy. Usually, we expect that empathy would deepen the discourse of the individual's inner world, bring about some relief or closeness, and promote structural change (Kohut, 1971). I suggest that in a patient, empathic effort is always needed, yet in cases of post-traumatic victimhood self-states, the person often does not respond to empathic efforts, neither by providing additional material from his inner world, nor by self-transformation, nor by transformations in self-object choices. In many cases, from within a post-traumatic self-state, the person perceives empathy as acknowledgment and justification of his complaints. Acknowledgment by justification is needed for maintaining a victim's identity in front of inner and interpersonal challenges. Therefore, the need for empathy and supportive witnessing is often hardly saturated. Being empathically justified, either inter-personally or publicly, might be preferred over bridging self-states and feeling closer to one's benefactors.

I would like to demonstrate this aspect through the following example. Vera is a woman close to 70, a Holocaust survivor (child survivor), who later married, gave birth to a son and daughter and generally re-built her life. Yet, she experiences suffering on a daily basis. This is partly because of ongoing memories of her past but mainly because of the many worries for her large family in the present. Her daughter recently became a widow. One of her grandsons seems to her to be a homosexual, and she is anxious about his future. Another grandson is doing poorly in school, and she is anxious about his grades. When he was in his 20s, her son immigrated to another country and now comes to visit her only once every few years. Vera is tormented. She sees her family's situation as an extension of her own personal suffering.

In her relationship with her husband and her daughter, there is a reversal of roles between aggressor and witness. In the following vignette, for example, in which the daughter is seen as an aggressor, her husband is supportive of her complaint. One evening, her daughter didn't answer her phone calls. Vera became anxious. Later that night, when the daughter finally called, she learned that her daughter had gone to a movie. Vera complained that she had caused her a sleepless night. The daughter had an outburst, declaring, "When Dani (her son) was sick, you only complained how difficult it was for you, but you didn't offer any help with the children. I was the one who was widowed, but you were the one who suffered. Now that I'm finally going out a bit, instead of encouraging me, you complain that I'm making you anxious. I feel as though I don't have a family."

Vera was shocked. In therapy session, she protested, “She doesn’t have a family! *I* don’t have a family. My own daughter is being inconsiderate of my worries.” She felt like her daughter was abusing her. The therapist suggests an alternative: “Maybe you were anxious and also curious to hear where she had gone and how she had spent her evening and did not find words to say it.” Vera becomes quiet and withdrawn. Finally, she says, “You are logically right. But it’s not the way I feel. I feel hurt, and she is shouting at me.” Apparently she did not see her daughter’s outburst as an expression of distress similar to her own and did not resonate to it by empathy. Instead she experienced it as an attack, which reinforced her self-perception as victim.

Vera had lost a lot in her life, and not having been answered by her daughter brought up again her worst worries. Yet, at certain moments of family conflicts, her victimhood identity seemed to be self-invested by her, no less than her identity as a mother, a woman or a spouse. At these moments, she presents herself as the one who suffers more than others. In this case, her daughter turned for her into an aggressor and her therapist turned into a witness. The distress of her daughter and others in the family, instead of arousing empathy, in fact amplified Vera’s suffering. When she proclaimed that "*she* is the one who lacks a family,” she was basically saying that her suffering was worse than that of her daughter. The therapist’s suggestion that she presented her daughter with an alternative interpersonal stance, namely, curiosity, only arouses Vera’s reservations. Curiosity, which is a libidinal expression (of vitality, for instance), as suggested by her therapist, did not represent Vera’s victimhood identity and therefore was overlooked by her.

Displacement of Aggression

When someone’s life is under threat or when he is tortured or oppressed in some other way, feelings of dismay intensify and take over. Feelings of shame, anger and vengefulness, aroused in such situations, also exist but are disavowed and dissociated in order to prevent them from provoking the aggressor. In front of a possible or actual aggressor, he may remain submissive, compliant and appeasing.

Victimhood self-state, as was stated above, is activated in situations in which there is a relative diminishing of the feeling of oppression, especially within a relatively safe environment. The danger of threat and oppression never totally disappears, but it is less immediate. The partial alleviation of the threat permits greater expression of the angry and aggressive self-states.

People who were never traumatized, who feel safe and supported, can often call for help, turn their anger towards the aggressor and fight back. As I will explain more fully in Chapter 2, group and social belonging very much strengthen a person’s sense of self-esteem, safety and ability. In situations where the person feels part of a group, hatred can easily be expressed towards someone who is defined as the enemy.

I suggest that within a process of recovering from traumatic experience, the person develops a different relationship with different people. Some of them are perceived as dangerous to him/her. Others seem much more containing and reliable. Different self-states are activated accordingly towards different people. In many situations, people who appear threatening activate a frightened and submissive self-state. Disavowed anger is re-experienced and enacted in the presence of non-threatening people and actually towards them.

The term "displacement" was offered by Freud (Laplanch and Pontalis, 1988). He suggested that by displacement, over-intensity of an idea (usually of a forbidden sexual content) is reduced and moderated by connecting it to a more detached idea. Later, Ferenczi suggested that displacement is an emotional and interpersonal mechanism that detaches negative emotions from their place of origin to more distant and less dangerous circles (Friedman, 1995). Anna Freud (1965) was the first to suggest that a personal attitude and behavior may be displaced, by projection, from one person to another. Bowlby (1980) added that displacement aims at directing anger away from the person who elicited it and towards some more or less irrelevant person.

I suggest that post-traumatic victimhood displacement is a typical form in which feelings of humiliation, anger and vengefulness are transferred from a threatening figure to non-threatening one. Many times, victimhood-displaced aggression is aimed towards close people who present containing and consoling behavior.

Whenever victimhood self-state is activated, displaced aggression involves intensive complaints and accusations. Those accusations often include reports of mental or physical health damages that are allegedly caused by these people's wrongdoings. Threats of self-mutilation often follow. In these displaced complaints, benevolent people are often accused of causing suffering. Post-traumatic victimhood aggression sometimes may be so direct and painful as to appear to be abusive. However, in other cases, it may be more latent and subtle.

Often, benevolent people in the surroundings of the person who was traumatized are, to a large extent, willing to contain this displaced rage. The decision to contain aggression may be conscious, in order to permit the person to eliminate bad feelings and recover. In many cases, this goal is achieved. Yet, post-traumatic victimhood displacement might be fixated and remain a stable mechanism of defense and discharge, reinforcing the availability and activation of the victimhood self-state. In these cases, the benevolent figure might be included in the victimhood emotional balance system without inducing the desired transformation towards benign mutuality.

It is important to note that what I term as "post-traumatic victimhood displacement" is not experienced by the victim himself as such. Quite the contrary, whenever victimhood self-state is activated, the person may truly feel that he is being abused again and, to his great disappointment, by the people whom he dared to trust. He may feel hurt and betrayed. He may feel that past suffering is being reconstructed in the present. Nevertheless, to a third party, the difference between a past perpetrator and a present benevolent person is quite clear. The benevolent person usually makes an effort to contain, console and appease complaints, and when accused, he seems to try harder.

In the following vignette, I wish to present a young woman who suffered sexual abuse. The rage and vengefulness that were split-off at the height of that difficult period in her past were displaced, years afterwards, to new figures in her life. One of them was her boss, whom she herself described as a pleasant and tolerant person, a "grandfather-type." The other figure was her therapist.

Ms. O (an alias), 35, until recently was employed as a lawyer in a successful firm, after having been unemployed for a year. For the last two years, she had been in psycho-therapy. As a girl, she was sexually harassed by a family member. Encouraged by the school nurse, she told her parents, and the harassment stopped. However, she felt that her parents' reaction was too mild, and their support was hesitant.

Unlike her colleagues in the office, she had a very tense work relationship with her boss, Mr. E, a veteran lawyer and owner of the firm. She felt she had not been adequately recognized for her talents, which had been evident in highly insightful litigations. She had been devoting part of her energy to "office coffee-break complaints," the topics of which included, among other things, gender-based discrimination in the firm and under-compensation. She was trying to garner support for unified demands to be written and delivered to Mr. E.

Eventually her complaints reached Mr. E's ear, and he invited her in for a talk. He was his usual pleasant self, listened, responded and concluded by promising a results-dependent pay increase. Things were quiet for a week.

For few days, it seemed that Ms. O was willing to co-create an interpersonal reality in which different views and interests could coexist. She seemed to accept the advice of her colleagues and friends, all of whom encouraged her to be satisfied with the new arrangements and feel satisfied in her work. She also seemed to cope with what she experienced as an empathic attitude on the part of her therapist.

One day, an important, wealthy client, greatly valued by the firm, was sitting in the waiting room waiting to meet with her boss, who had a reputation for arriving late. Mrs. O. sat outside with the increasingly annoyed client, until he got angry and left. At this point, the fatherly boss came out of his office and panicked.

"Why didn't you tell me he was waiting?" he asked her bitterly. She burst into tears and replied angrily: "You know you are always late. This should be a lesson for you. Besides, you yourself have taught me not to treat the rich any differently from the poor. Why should I come in and notify you for this guy but not for others?" Faced with clear and painful financial damage, Mr. E isolated himself in his office for the remainder of the day. In the evening, he called Ms. O. in and fired her.

In the following session, Ms. O. was absorbed in her memories of her growing in a poor family. Mr. E and his rich client actually were her parents' landlords who came to charge her parents their monthly pay. She remembered how distressed they used to be and how exhausted they felt in their lives. Her therapist had been very empathic to her feelings throughout the session, even though she regretted the loss of hope for better understanding between Ms. O. and her boss. Towards the end of the session, her therapist reminded Ms. O. of the last optimistic talk she had with Mr. E. Ms. O. seemed dumbstruck by her therapist's comment. As far as she was concerned, what the therapist had said totally erased any gains derived from the earlier part of the session.

Hurt and angry, she told the therapist she might not be the right person to treat her, owing to her young age, and accused her of lacking the assertiveness necessary to understand the importance of standing up for her rights in her firm. The therapist felt guilty and ashamed. Towards the next session, she was anxious and nervous. She felt attacked and devaluated. Considering her feelings, she realized that she became emotionally distant from her patient.

In this vignette, I attempted to illustrate how Ms. O. had developed a victimhood pattern of displacing rage and vengefulness onto non-threatening figures. This pattern had its origins in the time she had been abused as a young girl and unprotected by her poor and tired parents. Now, as an adult, Ms. O. feels as if she is being abused and neglected again. Anger and humiliation that were disavowed and dissociated in her childhood were re-experienced and enacted towards benevolent figures in her present life, namely her boss and her therapist. Her boss may have become for her (subconsciously) the abusive man. Her therapist and her boss together may have represented her non-protecting parents. For her, these feelings were present and real. Both her talents and her distresses at the office were responded to with a certain amount of encouragement and tolerant consideration. But this did not change the rigidity of her displaced victimhood aggression. Her boss might have felt that he is paying heavily for other people's wrongdoings.

I suggest that displacement patterns may be contained by benevolent figures up to a certain point. Afterwards, they might exhaust the relations. I will elaborate on the therapeutic considerations in the Chapter 2.

Transforming Personal Suffering into Control, Power and Domination

I suggest that post-traumatic victimhood self-state may include a motivation to transform personal suffering into control, power and domination over others. The will for control and domination are meant, first of all, to anticipate and prevent the potential recurrence of perpetrator aggression.

Many times, post-traumatic victimhood's self-state's basic demand involves compensation for past suffering. The person feels the need for reparation in terms of positive over-discrimination. He may feel partially incapable to cope alone. Compensation by other people may become more important than personal development and self-sustenance.

Identification with a past aggressor may add an aggressive component to the demand. Reports of suffering and overt accusations are meant to enhance other people's efforts and gain support. Victimhood self-state utilizes renewed ego-strengths, which makes it easier for the person to become more demanding, especially when he forms new relations with responsive people. Many people understand the latter's expectation for reparation and compensation and may find themselves acceding to these demands by prioritizing the person who manifests them. They respond with an effort to compensate.

Yet, victimhood's expressions of control, power and domination may switch the roles of victim and aggressor. A past victim may react as a past aggressor (while claiming recognition as a victim). Close people are often intimidated by victimhood over-powering. They become over-vigilant and over-responsive to victimhood and react by patterns of identification with the aggressor, which often result in compliance and over-devotion. Identification with the victim and identification with the aggressor may join together in their relations with the victim.

In some extreme cases, when people find themselves in a victimhood-charged relationship, they are unable to break out and go their own way. Neither are they able to remain in the relationship and work to change it. If they do try ploys, they might be accused of betrayal, abandonment and of acting out of selfish motivation. Thus, their individuation processes might be arrested. Sadly, their denied feeling of oppression may lead to the future manifestation of a post-traumatic Victimhood self-state of their own.

I would like to elaborate this aspect of post-traumatic victimhood self-state through an example from an organizational consultation in which I participated. The client, Mr. G. was a

60-year-old male school principal. Prior to the consultation, an educational reform had been passed, one result of which was to give each principal in the overall network of schools several hours of personal consultation on his/her work. This was the background of my work with Mr. G.

Before I met with him, it was explained to me that Mr. G. was a somewhat old-fashioned authority figure. His school was his kingdom. He earned a good reputation through years of diligence. The school's academic achievements scored high until recent years. Many teachers left over the years, and new methods were not assimilated. Few people expected Mr. G would change and suggested that I should be satisfied if, as a result of the consultation, his ability to work with his young deputy improved.

The latter, Ms. L., was quick-thinking, energetic, and seemed open to any ideas of ways that would improve cooperation with Mr. G. Her academic degree was higher than his, and she had professional and management achievements to her credit, which strengthened her self-confidence.

At the beginning of the consultation period, I took part in faculty meetings run by Mr. G. In these meetings, I saw that his way of exerting power was different from the more directive and confrontational style I had seen in other principals with whom I had worked in the past. He related quietly and courteously to all those present. On the surface, the atmosphere appeared friendly. I noticed that his staff never contradicted him. Later on, I learned that every decision had to be to his liking; otherwise, they would have been changed by him the next day through passive or active support of some of the teachers. They knew better than to openly try and change him or his style. Whoever didn't like it had to either adjust or leave.

Mr. G had come to the one of the next meetings armed with the reform plan and eager to begin. As far as he was concerned, the staff meeting was the place to start implementation. On the agenda was a motion to establish a steering committee, whose purpose was to plan and carry out special annual events. Three teachers, supporters of the deputy, volunteered; the committee began its work right there in the meeting. Or so it appeared. The following day, the deputy found out that Mr. G had dispersed the entire committee. When Ms. L learned of this, she was hurt and enraged. She was encouraged by me to meet Mr. G. before the next meeting. She preferred, however, to bring the subject back to the general meeting where the steering committee was initially initiated.

In the next meeting, she turned to him and in front of everyone demanded he explain his actions. The atmosphere was tense. People were staring at their papers on the table. The faces around the table expressed a general feeling that by directly challenging Mr. G, Ms. L had violated some unspoken rules. Mr. G looked sad and beaten. He said that after the prior meeting, he had been awake and upset the whole night, suffering from what he perceived as a great insult. He spoke about his long and deep investment in improving the school and said that his personal contribution had been greater than that of any steering committee. He claimed that the establishment of a special committee to deal with problems that he himself had always carefully taken care of was highly insulting. He complained that he usually feels lonely in his struggles at school. He mentioned that he had lost his parents at the age of five and had to cope alone as an orphan. He then turned to his deputy, complaining that she had persuaded "her people" to join the committee and accused her of creating factions among the teachers. This was unheard of, he said.

When he finished his long speech, a heavy silence ensued. Ms. L looked shocked, and appeared to be holding back her tears with great effort. The meeting was dispersed. Most of the teachers immediately disappeared. Mrs. L. was in need of my support. She felt wounded. When she could put words to her feelings she said that she felt overruled by Mr. G.'s unfair use of his miserable childhood in order to de-legitimate her motivation. It seemed that my witnessing of Mr. G.'s reaction and his victimhood use of power in his managerial behavior was crucial for her to re-count her own sense of reality.

At the next session of my consultation with the principal Mr. G, I expressed my empathy of his feeling that setting-up a committee that would deal with the very subjects that he himself had always taken care of was a failure to acknowledge his contribution to the school. He responded by expressing sorrow, nearly remorse, for the manner in which he had spoken in the meeting and complimented me in an exaggerated manner. I felt that he was aiming at what he thought I expected him to say. His aggressive criticism in the meeting turned into compliance with me. I could understand that for him I was an outside dangerous observer. I suggested that he may have felt threatened by initiatives that were strange to him and might have missed his deputy's loyalty and cooperative attitude. Mr. G could not accept this. In what seemed paranoid sentiment, he insisted that I did not appreciate the danger he had to deal with and how disappointing it was for him to deal with her initiative.

My brief consultation with Mr. G ended without having achieved its goal. He continued to earn the overt support of most of his staff and remained at his post. The committee never got off the ground, and Mr. G never took back his accusatory words. The reform and the special project faded out, and the school continued in its routine. However, something of importance did happen. The deputy, Ms. L, left for another position in another school where she was highly appreciated for her contribution. One of her supporters left with her. Two others left for personal reasons.

When threatened, Mr. G returned to victimhood self-state and based his leadership on it. His power patterns focused on accusations and his employees' feelings of remorse and guilt-driven submission. The teachers' compliant attitudes towards him were clearly shaped by his expressions of insult. In order to appease him and avoid a guilt-provoking rebuke in public, they obeyed his expectations. He rewarded them afterwards by gestures of closeness and belonging and by complimenting their work. He needed to be recognized as the main talent in his school. He kept his followers close to him and expelled others who displayed independent thinking. His narcissistic needs combined territorial behavior was based on victimhood self-state.

Paradoxically, it seems to me, my particular intervention contributed to the deputy's departure. My witnessing and support of her after the meeting helped her to recover and discharge some of her anger. She distanced herself from the staff's compliant behavior and quit shortly afterward. Other people in other projects could benefit from her talents and motivation.

SUSPENSION OF CONCERN

The term "concern," in its psychoanalytical meaning was elaborated by Winnicott (1963). The human infant is ruthless in his basic demands from his mother. According to Winnicott, the baby's realization that he might instinctually consume his mother too much might result in fear and guilt. In his attempt to repair the damage that he might have caused her, he develops concern for her. Concern then becomes a positive form of guilt. In its most valuable form, concern includes contribution: the baby develops a capacity to contribute to his mother something of his own inner world.

Following Winnicott, I would like to stress that the capacity for concern, in its mature sense, should include cautious attention to the possible over-consumption of the resources of the other, guilt over pain caused to him, willingness to repair through contribution and the establishment of mutuality in relationships. Gradually, the capacity for concern becomes inclusive of many other people to the point of emotional interpersonal position of a person in the world.

I suggest that post-traumatic victimhood includes a regression of the person to his pre-concern, ruthless stage in which basic needs are revived and directed towards close people. The person needs protection, encouragement, containing and patience. He may feel that in order to be able to contribute again, he should be given some priority over others including the giver himself. The person may feel that past suffering, the efforts of new adjustments and coping with every-day obligations exhausts his/her ability to address other people's needs. He may feel that his pain might worsen if any further demands were made on him.

Primo Levi, in his book *The Drowned and the Saved* discloses: "...I had also assimilated the principle rule of the place which made it mandatory that that you should first of all take care of yourself. I never found this rule expressed with as much frankness as in the book entitled *Prisoners of Fear* by Ella Lingens-Reiner (where, however, the sentences are attributed to a woman doctor who, disregarding her own statement, proved to be generous and brave and saved many lives). 'How was I able to survive Aushwitz? My principle is: I come first, second and third. Then nothing, Then again I, and then all the others.'" (Levi,1988, pp. 59).

We can assume that suspension of concern may be assimilated as an attitude of survival and then may be unconsciously fixated for life. This does not mean that while within victimhood self-state the person has given up mutuality and reciprocity. He may believe that concern is only suspended until he recovers. Yet suspension of concern may be fixated. Within post-traumatic self-state, people tend to focus on their suffering as an excuse for their inability to experience concern for others. Many times, they are responded to with compassion. Yet, people who are close to them may, in time, may feel over-burdened and frustrated.

I would like to demonstrate this through the following example. Three years into her supervision, a supervisee told me that her patient owed her an ever-growing amount of money. He used to pay her every few months in drips and drabs. In silence, she accepted his small checks and said nothing about his growing debt.

Her patient, Ron, is a young man who looks vulnerable and sad. He turned to psychotherapy following years of difficulties in satisfactorily interacting with women. He had been repeatedly turned down, without understanding why. He tended to explain his being rejected as a result of, what he thought, his innate poor physical appearance.

Over time, the therapist came to feel very compassionate towards the patient. She felt sorry for him and shared his pain after having been refused again by another woman. Gradually, she had been losing more and more of her professional confidence. In fact, she started self-critically wondering to herself, "Am I of any real use to him?" "Do I deserve this money?" Eventually, she felt she was such a disappointment for him that she saw her expectation for reimbursement as aggression towards a vulnerable, suffering person. This affected her ability to insist he meet his financial obligations. Thereby, she had to contain financial hardships as a newly married and young mother.

The more time passed, the more it became clear to me, as a supervisor, that a certain self-state in the patient's personality and behavior had not been touched on in therapy. I suggested to her to turn to her feeling as a woman in the transference relations with him. When she did, it became clearer to her that his demanding, poor attitude made her very compassionate but totally indifferent to him as a man. She could imagine him with other women and understand more the reasons for the unsuccessful interactions he had been reporting. For example, upon reflection of what he had been telling her, she found that he put pressure on the women he met when, after they tried to pull away from him, he expressed great hurt and neediness. He made it clear he expected special consideration from them. Yet, he did not treat them with mutuality of consideration or gratitude.

The timing of her telling me that he had accumulated a large debt was of special importance. It was shortly after she passed her final certification exam and had become a recognized clinical psychologist. I viewed her decision to finally bring up the money matter as relating to being recognized as professional, reviving her self-worth and her feelings of "entitlement." Now, from this new position of strength, she could examine the whole monetary position between her and her patient. For the first time, she could differentiate herself from his needs and reconnect to hers. Once there was a mutual agreement between them, these reflections led her to bring this material to supervision.

Ron, in the above case, wishes for financial alleviation. In this case, the patient does not pay his fees for many months, while his therapist suffers from financial difficulties, but is unable—emotionally—to demand her due.

However, this strategy is only partially successful. It helps him gain compassion; but it does not get him love. He acquires special "passes" but never real and mutual partnership in his intimate relationships. It seems that suspension of concern for others on his side put a heavy burden on his efforts to create satisfactory and mutual relationship with women.

Suspension of concern may become a stable aspect of the post-traumatic victimhood self-state. It entails a non-mutual sense of entitlement. Injury may cause narcissistic self-absorption about one's needs and deficiencies. Regression to a dependent position in relations may follow. Compassionate, patient and supportive reactions from close people may be encouraging and helpful. This, in fact, is how people help each other throughout mishaps and troubles. For a while, the injured person may relax and feel protected and exempt from anxiety-provoking challenges.

While this experience is usually transient, victimhood's suspension of concern may be fixated in a stable self-state in which extra efforts and protection from others and equivalent reduction of one's own efforts and obligations are prioritized over mutual and balanced relations. In some cases, close people adjust themselves to what they consider the victim's helpless inability to restore mutuality. They may tend to establish complementary relations with other people. In other cases (as I will demonstrate in Chapter 2), people may just leave.

SUMMARY

It is possible to describe the formation of post-traumatic victimhood self-state as a stage in the post-trauma recovery process. In this condition, there is a process of restoration of ego-strengths and reactivation of concealed inner resources. The post-traumatic victimhood self-state, however, preserves the victim identity alongside the restoration of the pre-traumatic personality and its further growth.

During the traumatic event, the victim adopts the attitude and the behavior of the perpetrator as part of the condition known in psychoanalysis as "identification with the aggressor." This may lead to a formation of "post-traumatic victimhood aggression."

The experience of real suffering may be transformed also into self-justification and the suspension of concern for others, together with a demand for compensation. This combination often rewards the person emotionally, socially and economically.

Recovery and past suffering may form a new stable personality aspect that I term "post-traumatic victimhood self-state." With increased duration, the victimhood identity becomes part of the person's self. This self could be dissociated from the other self-states of the personality and could play a primary role in personal and interpersonal relationships with close friends, spouses, children and relatives as well as in the large social environment.

BIBLIOGRAPHY

Bass, G. (2002). "Something Is Happening Here: Thoughts and Clinical Material Regarding Multip..." *Psychoanal. Dial.* 12: 809-826.

Benjamin, J. (2004). "Beyond Doer and Done to: An Intersubjective View of Thirdness." *Psychoanalytic Quarterly* 73: (1): 5-46.

Bernstein, P. P. (1988). "Psychotherapy and the Paranoid Process." *Psychoanal Q.* 57: 443-447.

Bowlby, J. (1980). Attachment and Loss: Volume III: Loss, Sadness and Depression. London, *The Hogarth Press.*

Brandchaft, B. (1988). "Chapter 10 A Case of Intractable Depression." *Progress in Self Psychology* 4: 133-154.

Bromberg, P. M. (1998). Standing in the Spaces: Essays on Clinical Processes, trauma and Dissociation. Hillside NJ & London, *The Analytic press.*

Davies, J. M. and M. G. Frauly (1994). treating *the Adult Survivor of Childhood Sexual Abuse.* New York NJ, Basic books.

Dickes, R. (1965). "The defensive functions of an altered state of consciousness." *Journal of American Psychoanalytic Association* 13: 356-403.

Ferenczi, S. (1933). Confusion of tongues between adults and the child. *Final Contributions to the Problems and Methods of Psycho-analysis.* M. Balint. London, Karnac Books: 156-167.

Frankel, J. (2002). "Exploring Ferenczi's Concept of Identification with the Aggressor." *Psychoanal. Dial.* 12(1): 101-139.

Freud, A. (1936). *The Ego and the Mechanisms of Defence* (rev.). New York, Int. Uni. Press.

Freud, A. (1965). *Normality and Pathology in Childhood: Assessments of Development*. New York, International Universities Press.

Freud, S. (1922 (1955)). *Some neurotic mechanisms in jealousy, paranoia, and homosexuality*. Standard Edition. London, Hogarth Press. 18: 221-232.

Gartner, R. B. (*1999). "Cinematic Depictions of Boyhood Sexual Victimization." Gender* and Psychoanalysis 4: 253-289.

Hirsch, I. (2003). "Reflections on Clinical Issues in the Context of the National Trauma of..." Contemp. *Psychoanal*. 39: 665-681.

Hoggett, P. (2001). "The Love That Thinks." *Free Associations* 9(A): 1-23.

Hoover, S. R. (2005). "Discussion of Barbara S. Kane's "Transforming Trauma into Tragedy&#..." *Psychoanal. Rev* 92: 957-962.

Howell, E. F. (2002). "Back to the "States."" *Psychoanalytic Dialogues* 12: 921-957.

Kohut, H. (1971). *The Analysis of The Self: A Systematic Approach to the Psychoanalytic Treatment of Narcissistic Personality Disorder*. Medison & Connecticut, International University Press.

Kohut, H. (1971). *The Analysis of The Self: A Systematic Approach to the Psychoanalytic Treatment of Narcissistic Personality Disorder*. Medison & Connecticut, International University Press.

Kohut, H. (1984). How Does Analysis Cure? A. Goldberg, University of Chicago Press.

Laplanche, J. and J. B. Pontalis (1988). The Language of Psychoanalysis. London, Karnac Books.

Laub, D. (2005). "traumatic Shutdown of Narrative and Symbolization: A Death Instinct Deriv..." *Contemp. Psychoanal*. 41: 307-326.

Levi, P. (1988). *The drowned and the saved*. London, Abacus.

Marcus, P. and I. Wineman (1985). "Psychoanalysis Encountering the Holocaust." *Psychoanal. Inq*. 5: 85-98.

Meissner, W. W. (1976). "Schreber and the Paranoid Process." *Ann. Psychoanal*. 4: 3-40.

Meissner, W. W. (1977). "A Case in Point." *Ann. Psychoanal*. 5: 405-436.

Mitchell, S. A. (1991). "Contemporary perspectives on self: Toward an integration." *Psychoanalytic Dialogue* 1: 121-147.

Mitchell, S. A. (2000). "You've Got to Suffer if You Want to Sing the Blues: Psychoanalytic Reflections on Guilt and Self-Pity." *Psychoanalytic Dialogues* 10: 713-733.

Montville, J. V. (1986). "A Diplomat among Psychoanalysts." *Psychoanal. Inq* 6: 247-250.

Prior, S. (1996). *Object Relations in Severe Trauma*. Northvale, NJ:, Aronson.

Rodman, F. R., Ed. (1987). *The Spontaneous Gesture* (selected letters). Cambridge, Harvard University Press.

Schafer, R. (2005). "Cordelia, Lear, and Forgiveness." *J. Amer. Psychoanal.* Assn. 53: 389-409.

Sullivan, H. (1950 (1964)). the Illusion of Personal Individuality. *the fusion of Psychiatry and the Social Sciences*. New York, W. W. Norton.

Winnicott, D. W. (1963). "The development of the Capacity for Concern." *Bulletin of the Menninger Clinic* 2:167: 73-82.

Chapter 2

POST-TRAUMATIC VICTIMHOOD: PSYCHOANALYTIC PERSPECTIVE

Avi Berman

Many people with post-traumatic victimhood patterns seek psychotherapy. Although they have been given help and support by those in close relationships with them and basically maintain normal everyday lives, they, nonetheless, often feel depressed, unloved and emotionally isolated. Furthermore, they tend to feel a gap between their potential and their actual self-realization and are frustrated by their lack of independence and their ongoing anxiety.

We can assume that a victimhood self-state may become moderated through psychotherapy. Psychotherapy may provide the patient with an environment in which the analyst constitutes an “all-good” empathic and understanding figure. If the psychotherapy is successful, there will be a reduction of anxiety and loneliness. When the patient feels safe enough, he can explore his relations with others and acknowledge expectations for reciprocity. Restoration of benign relations with devoted and loving objects in one's life may be achieved sometimes through self-containing and moderation of the excessive expressions of victimhood.

Psychotherapy may be successful when the patient's other self-states become concurrently accessible to him, bridging dissociations. The patient's ability to "stand in spaces" (Bromberg, 1998) between the victimhood self-state and more libidinal self-states may help him empower processes of self-fulfillment, which aim at actualizing his future vision of his life. Inner locus of control may consciously contradict passive wishes for compensation. Self-identity of a victim may be confronted by an empathic self-state that includes objects of love and concern.

Hidden behind the behaviors associated with the post-traumatic victimhood self-state, there is yearning and hope for mature, reciprocal intimate and meaningful relations. Despite appearances, mutuality between two people, reflected in love and reciprocal contributions, continues to be a desired goal. The suspension of concern associated with victimhood behavior may be transient. It may reflect a wish for “reparative discrimination” through which the person who sees himself as victim hopes to restore his self-esteem and again be an equal among equals. The accusations he hurls at the people closest to him are often a request for recognition of the extent to which he/she is suffering. His striving for power and dominance is his attempt to regain control and establish an alternative to the familiar positions of compliance, submission and humiliation.

Periods of time during which a person feels totally helpless may have an undermining influence on him for the rest of his life. Aside from the feeling of terror for not being able to protect himself and that another person can abuse him again, the feeling of helplessness creates a serious blow to his belief that he is the master of his destiny. He may experience debilitating despair when faced with challenges in later life.

Experiences of helplessness hinder the person's inner locus of control. He may find it harder to believe that a person's fate is in his own hands. That points to the importance of supportive people in the life of a person who struggles with helplessness. The presence of compassionate people, who are willing to offer assistance, constitutes a great source of hope for rehabilitation and sometimes for his mere existence. However, the need to preserve the object as someone who is totally supportive may cause one to dominate and control those around him. Feelings of helplessness may enhance the person's needs for compensation. He may expect family members, friends or even society at large to prefer his needs to their own, to favor him with a kind of positive discrimination, support his position in confrontations and to renounce their own needs when they are in conflict with his.

In psychotherapy, the analyst may become the subject of the wish for compensation. Within victimhood self-state, the person may well understand the rules of psychotherapy in the sense that the analyst is a person from whom he will not receive material compensation. Nevertheless, in many cases, the patient expects some special and personal gestures from the analyst that have a symbolic value of compensation. The analyst's consent to the patient's special demands, like some extra time, another appointment, changes of physical condition, serve as symbolic acts of compensation and correspond with the patient's sense of his injured narcissistic entitlement.[1]

All the people involved in this dynamic, including the suffering person himself, honestly believe that this positive discrimination is temporary and will cease when the suffering recedes or when his emotional hunger is satiated.

Empathic Witnessing, Sameness and Otherness

Even though we cannot always expect transformation of victimhood to take place through witnessing and empathy alone, it is nonetheless essential that they will always remain a safe home for psychotherapy. By being with the patient in his painful memories as they appear in the "here and now," the analyst becomes a witness. Empathic witnessing is more committed and affirmative than empathy in its traditional meaning. The patient's wish is for the other to recognize his suffering. Often, the patient needs to be acknowledged specifically as someone who was severely injured by someone else. The analyst who acknowledges the victim's suffering and its harmful implications becomes regarded as significantly different (and better) than the past persecutor, someone who empathically confirms his suffering and its results and justifies his point of view. By witnessing and acknowledging the victim's pain (and the

[1] This kind of transference may be similar to Balint's concept of "malignant regression" (Balint, 1969).

perpetrator's evil responsibility), the analyst constitutes living proof that there is still human goodness in a world that until then had failed to show it. The existence of a witness always represents hope for change. The witness is an alternative to bitter solitude or the despair of belonging to groups that ignore or deny his painful experiences. The unbearable situation in which evil can be done to him in complete isolation and helplessness is eliminated when an empathic witness joins him. This mirrors his need to feel again his self-worth and hopeful entitlement.

The role of the analyst as witness has been discussed in psychoanalytic literature. Miller has coined the term "enlightened witness" (Miller, 1990). According to Miller, in a life filled with stress, threats and pain, the meeting with an analyst, as an enlightened witness, constitutes a source of comfort and security for the victim. Felman and Laub (1992) suggest, following Freud (1917), that it takes two people to unravel the unconscious. They stress the role of the witness to experience a personal crisis while witnessing and to regain authenticity. The patient needs witnessing as confirmation. Such confirmation serves as a specific kind of mirroring in which the patient is recognized as an innocent victim of other people's wrongdoings (Orange, 2003). Ullman (2006) adds that witnessing allows the return of the "I" into the dialogue, placing the "I" in the midst of the trauma. This begins the process of erosion of the dissociative barriers, enabling a psychic transformation. Grand (2002) suggests that empathic witnessing resumes human recognition and mutuality in contrast to the bystander's position. Poland (2000) suggests an analytic attitude of "witnessing" in front of "otherness" of the patient and. According to this idea of "witnessing," the analyst respects the patient's otherness and his painful biography, which may be very different from the analyst's own, and the resulting behaviors and attitudes form the patient's otherness. "Witnessing," as Poland suggests, offers safety and receptivity, together with separation "without the promise of magical union" (pp. 26). Actually, the analyst's witnessing is "a profound nonverbal communication of recognition" (pp 32).

As an empathic witness, the analyst is idealized and expected to have an omnipotent ability to understand, express unreserved agreement, support, containing and stand by the suffering person through any and all conflicts between him and those around him. The analyst is a powerful source of compassion and compensation. In therapy, when the patient senses the analyst as willing to stand on his side in total understanding and support, he may experience the analyst as a "twin soul,"[2] someone who would feel and react exactly the same as he does, had he undergone what he himself has been through. In this way, the patient experiences sameness with his analyst. The experience of sameness with his analyst may become a therapeutic factor. It enhances the patient's trust in a stable and consistent supportive figure who can be referred to in reality and in fantasy whenever needed. Once the patient's experience of sameness is formed, the analyst is expected to be in total congruence with the patient in order to maintain it. The analyst may remain a listener, sometimes even nonverbal, and he is still assumed to totally agree with the patient's point of view.

Oscillations between sameness and otherness are basic and archaic aspects of human relations. In healthy normal human psychic states, experiences of sameness and otherness form relations of complementarity and co-creation (Benjamin, 1988, Ogden, 1986). Healthy tension between sameness and otherness is crucial for intimacy and love (Bersani & Philips,

[2] Feelings of sameness may take part in forming twinship transference (Kohut, 1971, 1984) in which the other (the analyst) is experiencing twin self-object who understands through being the same. Twinship transference may have the benefit of gradually enhancing ego strengths.

2008; Benjamin, 1991). A "delicate balance" between sameness and differences is crucial for interpersonal processes (Mitchell, 1992).[3]

Ogden suggests that "Even at the very beginning of life, the infant has some sense of otherness that he bumps against. At the same time, there is an aspect of consciousness in which the infant and mother are one. These understandings do not represent contradictory statements. Instead, they represent attempts to describe the coexistence of multiple states of consciousness" (Ogden, 1991).[4]

In this chapter, "Otherness" is defined as any deviation from the expected experience of sameness that is provided by an empathic witnessing. The term "otherness" refers to the presence of any person as a distinct other human being, including his own gestures, rhythm, attunements, attitudes, values, feelings and behavior. Within the subject's need for sameness, otherness might be felt as a frustration or even as a form of confrontation and impingement into the realm of the subject's safety going on being.

Until recent decades, many psychoanalytic approaches assumed that the analyst's needs and personal agenda should be reduced and kept out of the therapeutic process as much as possible. In his attempt to join with the patient, the analyst may try to minimize the expressions of "otherness" between himself and the patient. According to Kohut, for example, the analyst tries not to interfere with the patient's need for the analyst as a self-object. Through empathy, as a therapeutic attitude, the analyst dedicates his own ability for self-observation to his patient as a vicarious introspection. The analyst explores his patient's inner world restricting his own. Optimal frustration derives of the analyst's inevitable empathic failures and happen despite his best efforts (Kohut, 1984).

People who have experienced severe injury or oppression may suffer from an excessive exhaustion of their ability to contain tensions in the relationships with other people. They seem to need joining through empathic witnessing, understanding and expressed agreement with them. Often, the patient needs clear justifications for his feelings, behaviors, misbehaviors and motivations. In some cases, any environmental expression of otherness might be felt as a threat to the restoration of their self-structure and even as a recurrence of a traumatic event. In many other cases, expressions of otherness might be felt as an attack on their rehabilitated trust, which makes them feel lonely and deserted. The emotionally exhausted person responds to another person's needs and interests with frustration and disappointment. In these moments, the other's expectation for mutual relations seems to be unrealistic.

I suggest that in dealing with post-traumatic victimhood self-states, it may be necessary to first of all establish the analyst as an empathic witness before expressing any kind of otherness. The patient may react to the analyst's otherness with fear, desperation, resentment or anger. He may get silent and distant or protesting and confrontational. Yet the first thing the analyst should bear in his mind is the patient's unconscious compliance with the analyst's expression of otherness.

Following Ferenczi (1933), I suggest that premature expressions of otherness on the side of the analyst (interpretations of defense mechanisms in particular) can lead to premature

[3] Other meanings of otherness deal with the other as an excluded victim of one's rejected attributes (the mad, the Jew) and the foundation of ethics in Levinas writings (Bersani & Philips, 2008).

[4] According to Ogden's view, the most devastating experience of otherness might occur during the "Autistic – contiguous" stage of early infancy. Otherness, at that stage, might be an intrusion into the infant going on being and a threat to his early self's structure (Ogden, 1986).

consent with the analyst, which might be basically a form of compliance derived from identification with the aggressor rather than the inner growth of some genuinely new position. Premature agreement with the analyst's positions should be suspected. We may presume that while in the post-traumatic victimhood self-state, the patient may be experiencing the analyst as a persecuting object without even realizing it. This may be particularly so when the patient is readily willing to accept harsh interpretations from the analyst.

I would like to demonstrate a patient's compliant behavior that may be the result of identification with the aggressor through the following example. The patient is a retired academic, approaching 70 years of age. He is a broad-minded, eloquent person. He sought treatment after his daughter had stopped responding to his telephone calls. His son had broken their relations years ago. He understood, in retrospect, that in a recent encounter she had been hurt (again) by something he had said.

As a child, the patient received a strict and abusive education. His parents would punish him for minor mistakes and any sign of a falling-off of achievement. He remembers himself as a submissive son, careful not to provoke their anger.

As an adult, he changed but had nonetheless internalized his aggressive parent's impact on him. As an adult in the new family, he had become an authoritarian parent himself. He had often been distant and rejecting. His children's demands interfered with his after-work recreation time, which he needed so badly. He stopped them from behaving in this way. He used to be critical of his wife's needs and saw her as inconsiderate. He explained himself to her in a very efficient manner or so he used to think. Eventually, he learned through difficult experiences that they were terrified by him. He learned to loosen up only when they rebelled. He was assisted in this process by a therapy of several years' duration.

During his first months in therapy, he tried to avoid any difference of opinions between us. In his effort to repair his relationship with his daughter, I had pointed out his willingness to learn from his personal experience and to try different approaches in reaching out to her. At one time, I pointed out that his attitude towards whoever was considered stronger than him was different and more conciliatory than that towards those he considered weaker. I suggested that his daughter was a target of complaints because she belonged, in his mind, to those who do not threaten him. This interpretation proved to be too early. In response, he said, “What doesn't hurt, does not bring forth fruit.” I imagined that he was referring to me, saying in a somewhat flattering way that he was hurt but understood that I hurt him for his own sake. At that moment, I thought that I was getting acquainted with his submissive self-state. He was not about to express opinions that differed significantly from mine, nor should I expect him to, at least at that point. As far as he was concerned, I became at that moment an external source of evaluation and criticism. Moreover, I might have been transformed into his past oppressive figures. He was adopting my alleged belief in painful learning in order to keep me as a good object, while submitting to my "attitude of education," as he understood it based on his early experience with his punishing parents.[5]

I tried to resonate with his fears and help him back to feeling safe with me. I said that maybe he was hurt by my description of his father-daughter relationship as based on power and threat. I further remarked that it seemed he wished to share my point of view in order to avoid disagreements between us. He immediately agreed and thanked me for that, too. Yet,

[5] Fairbairn (1940) has pointed out that people may attribute badness to themselves and goodness to the object in order to be able to believe that they may be rescued within relation with a good object.

his expression of gratitude towards me might have been resulted from fear in the transference and presented further compliance. Any agreement with me at this point could not been differentiated from identification with the aggressor.

At that point, his positive perception served, from his point of view, to build a necessary, harmonious relationship with me. More important than being able to disagree with me, he needed me as a empathic witness only. It would have been premature to interpret, even if I were right, that his relationships with people are determined by the extent of threat he feels from them. He did not yet need me to intervene with suggestions as to how he might repair some of these relationships.[6] Only much later we could refer to his early transference in a more balanced way.

The analyst, who just a moment before was basking in the feeling of being an empathic witness for his/her patient may suddenly find him/herself related to as a persecutor, now having to deal with the patient's defenses. The patient's expressions of compliance, over-agreement and exaggerated pleasantness can serve to conceal fear of the analyst's anger, criticism and power. Identifying with the aggressor and subordinating himself to the analyst's point of view may be a way of calming down the analyst's possible threatening position.

Shifting Empathic Attunements

In many cases, the analyst's recognition and empathy resonate with the patient's need for witnessing. The analyst, as a witness, mirrors the patient's claim for victim identity. The patient feels heard, understood, supported and encouraged by having an idealized good object on his/her side. The patient may expect an undisturbed all-good attitude from his analyst. The analyst may, consciously or unconsciously, approximate this expectation, and provide the patient with an environment in which the analyst constitutes an "all-good" empathic and understanding figure. As mentioned, if this therapeutic investment is successful, there will be a reduction of feelings of anxiety and loneliness. When the patient feels safe enough, he can explore his relations with others and acknowledge expectations for reciprocity.

However, in other cases of post-traumatic victimhood self-state, recognition and empathy alone are not enough to promote transformation. Many times, empathy does not contribute to transformation but serves simply to strengthen the patient's claim for victim's identity and his sense of entitlement for compensation without further changes in his personal attitudes and interpersonal behaviors.

The analyst's empathy, by itself, carries with it the risk of achieving positive transference in isolation from the patient's overall life. The patient's victimhood self-state will join the analyst's supportive self-state, but other self-states of both patient and analyst may remain outside the therapy, dissociated and inaccessible. Indeed, post-traumatic victimhood self-states in which the patient expresses post-traumatic victimhood aggression towards the people close to him may not be brought into the therapy at all. Reports from the patient may be

[6] In many ways, the split between a beneficial object and a persecuting one is reminiscent of the paranoid/schizoid position of Melanie Klein (1946). There is a partial resemblance between post-traumatic victimhood and Klein's PS position. However, forming a post-traumatic victimhood self-state should be considered as a result of real life experience that stems directly from real damage and injury in reality and not just an inner world position. Specifically, a real aggressor from the person's past has left sharp memories of persecution and threat. Memories from a painful past time may return any time.

limited to describing how people close to him have caused him to suffer or at the very least have turned a blind eye on him by maintaining their own agendas. When the analyst's attitude is based on empathic witnessing alone, eliminating any expression of otherness, post-traumatic victimhood aggression may never emerge in the transference. The patient's feeling of sameness may postpone (split off) fear and frustration in transference.

I have presented a treatment approach for people in an over-active post-traumatic victimhood self-state in which the establishment of trust in relationships with a supportive object is particularly vital. I also suggest that if such patients perceive the slightest possibility of violation of this trust, there may be a rapid transition of the self-state, from feeling safe to feeling persecuted and isolated. In the eyes of the patient, the analyst may suddenly change from an empathic witness to a persecuting other, and this may jeopardize the therapeutic alliance.

I suggest that at a certain moment, while exploring the patient's point of view, the analyst may become preoccupied by the patient's avoidance of concern for people in his life. The more the analyst is open to experiencing his own feelings and images within his reverie (Ogden, 1997a, 1997b; Fonagy and Target, 1995), the more he may become aware of this issue in the patient's everyday life relations. This may be the moment when split-off victimhood aspects in the patient become evident. The analyst's subjectivity, including emotions that are stirred within them, may crack his comprehensive empathic witnessing[7].

During the psychotherapeutic process, the analyst may even come to identify momentarily with a person he has only heard about from the patient, such as a spouse, children, parents, boss, etc. Racker's concept of "complementary identification" (1957) may be relevant here. Through complementary identification, the analyst may get to know the rejected parts of the patient. For example, the patient's rejected aggressive parts may be projected onto the analyst and become included in the analyst's counter-transference. He might feel aggression or anger towards the patient when this kind of complementary identification is activated (Gabard, 2003).

I suggest that in these moments, spontaneous shifts of empathic attunements[8] interfere with the analyst's empathic witnessing. In other words, the analyst may spontaneously shift his empathic attunement from the patient to other people in the patient's life who are subject to his post-traumatic victimhood behavior and may represent a form of personification of the unrecognized parts of the patient. The analyst may find himself identifying with their points of view, which may differ from those reported by the patient.

"Switching empathic attunement" means holding in mind different points of view and different self-states of the patient. The ability to switch empathic attunements can lead to new perspectives, enabling the analyst to see things from outside the immediate therapeutic relationship. From this new position, the analyst is better able to contain the various views, as well as keep a certain distance from them. In my view, shifting of empathic attunement is the

---

[7]. Fonagy and Target suggest that the analyst's ability to listen to himself is a crucial factor in effective therapy: "One dimension of the analyst's listening stance should therefore be dedicated to his ongoing experience of the here and now at the same time his focal attention may be elsewhere. That is, no matter how 'important' the manifest verbal content appears to be at a given moment, the analyst should try to remain simultaneously attuned to his subjective experience of the relationship and its shifting quality" (1995, pp 498). I would like to add that attunement to one's subjective experience may result in experiencing denied relevant aspects of the patient's interpersonal world.

[8] The term is mentioned also by Meissner (1985) and in Bromberg (2004).

therapeutic equivalent of "standing in spaces" (Bromberg, 1993).[9] Even when the analyst acquires an empathic understanding of the patient, it nonetheless makes a difference whether this attitude is built on “switching empathic attunements” or on a single attunement only. Therefore, I suggest that switching attunements can strengthen the validity of a therapeutic intervention and increase its effectiveness.

The patient's avoidance of concern for close people in his life, together with the manifestation of victimhood aggression, may result in a reserved and distancing reaction by others. Through shifting empathic attunements, the analyst may be acquainted with the toll of ambivalence and exclusion his patient is subjected to in his life and understand better his feeling of loneliness and dissatisfaction.

From the perspective of different and dissociated self-states, the analyst's empathy with the patient's report of being a constant subject of other people's abuse may result in empathic failure for another self-state that yearns for intimacy and reciprocity. Therefore, I do not consider shifting empathic attunement as a form of an empathic failure in its original sense (Kohut, 1984). The analyst who understands better causes and effects in his patient's interpersonal relations may eventually be more understanding and serve better his patient's therapeutic needs.

The analyst's inability to experience those difficult feelings and to shift empathic attunements will leave him trapped within the patient’s current dominant self-state and his epistemological and emotional world. I have seen situations in which the analyst and the patient joined together in total understanding until the patient was suddenly deserted by someone close to him, someone who had been feeling misunderstood or even persecuted for a long time due to the patient's victimhood behavior, without being heard enough or dealt with in therapy. In such cases, it is possible that shifting attunements might have saved these relationships from being destroyed. Therefore, it is important to understand that the early experience of idealized harmony between analyst and patient does not and should not remain exclusive.

Shifting empathic attunement may lead the analyst to let his otherness show, consciously or not. While in post-traumatic victimhood self-state, the patient may react to the “otherness,” detecting changes in tone of voice and body language, attitudes towards punctuality, and response or non-response to small requests. The patient may see in any or all of these behaviors on the part of the other a failure of relatedness and react with fear, disappointment and anger.

Yet in many cases, transformation may be achieved only by including the experience of otherness in the therapy. One might ask, then, how and when including the experience of otherness becomes part of a common agenda of patient and analyst alike. Moreover, how can the therapeutic alliance be maintained when empathy is shifted?

It is important to note that many times, these spontaneous moments of shifting empathic attunements in the analyst’s experience represent the readiness of both the patient and the analyst to start dealing with the patient's post-traumatic victimhood self-state from different points of view. I suggest that the analyst's expression of otherness often results out of mutual unconscious enactment of both patient and analyst. We should bear in mind that the analyst's reverie of his patient's deprived self-states reveals the patient's readiness to undergo weaning

[9] Bromberg: “Standing in the Spaces” is a shorthand way of describing a person’s relative capacity to make room at any given moment for subjective reality that is not readily containable by the self he experiences as “me” at that moment” (pp 515).

process out of the exclusiveness of the needs of his victimhood self-state. It is possible that the patient himself enabled the analyst to shift his attunement to other people and, in doing so, to include their experience in the treatment. It is crucial, therefore, that the analyst be emotionally free to experience his own memories, fantasies and feelings (including anger, fear and distress) while listening to the patient.

In time, while the patient does not stop feeling the analyst's empathy, he nonetheless may become aware of two (or more) points of view regarding his interpersonal situations.

One of the most important insights that the patient may gain from this process is that he is an active factor in his interpersonal relations. Many patients, while in a post-traumatic victimhood self-state, are much more familiar with the experience of being passive done-to figures in their lives. Many times, they may be surprised to realize simple facts about the connection between cause and effect. Recognizing themselves as agencies may lead to an ambivalent reaction on their part. On one hand, they might feel rejected and accused and denied rights of self-definition as victims. On the other hand, they may feel motivated to contribute their assets to their most cherished relations.

Other people's experiences correspond with the patient's dissociated self-states. Including more self-states in the therapeutic discourse enhances the relevance of therapy to the patient's life. When the various self-states are experienced together, dissociation may turn into intra-psychic conflict (Bromberg, 1998, pp. 516). More conscious conflicts allow for the patient's choices and efforts to take place.

Transferences and Typical Enactments

I suggest that interacting with post-traumatic victimhood self-states may form some typical enactments (Aron, 2000, 2003; Renik, 1993) in which the patient's need for sameness is resonated by the analyst's compliance, and at the same time the analyst's responsiveness is resonated by a further need for sameness. At this basic stage of forming a therapeutic alliance, both patient and analyst may share hope that the need for sameness can be saturated in time, making room for other self-states to be activated.

I suggest that within this enactment, empathic witnessing includes an unconscious attempt to reduce any interpersonal tension by avoiding any conflicts or disagreements with the patient. The analyst may sense that any disagreement, in effect any expression of different personal feeling and thoughts, may arouse intolerable tension.

There is a risk that the analyst will inadvertently "join" in the patient's denial of "otherness" in their relationship. The analyst may feel the threat in the patient's accusations and complaints through the patient's accounts of his painful and angry reactions towards the people close to him. He may avoid the patient's victimhood aggression towards him. Furthermore, the analyst may feel, at an unconscious level, the very different experiences of the people in the lives of the patient and aspire not to be in their place.

When the patient puts such pressure on the analyst to deny his sense of otherness, the analyst may be tempted to deny his anger or at least have to make a special effort not to let it show. He may resort to the use of reaction formation to control his emotions, becoming overly supportive and devoted (Searls, 1967; Gabbard, 2003). Without realizing it, he may develop a victimhood position himself within his professional personality, in which case he may find himself increasingly overburdened and worn down. These heavy feelings may be carried over into his personal life.

As I suggested above, at a certain moment, while exploring the patient's point of view, the analyst may become preoccupied by the patient's avoidance of concern for people in his life. This may be the moment when split-off victimhood aspects in the patient become evident. Spontaneous shifts of empathic attunement may represent the analyst's authentic experience. He may feel that being empathic with other figures in the patient's life is his "true self" experience. When the analyst does not deny nor oppress his subjectivity, he may find it hard to remain exclusively empathic to his patient's dominating victimhood self-state.

Addressing the patient's denied self-states that are recognized through spontaneous shifting of empathic attunement may meet with a sharp change of emotion and transference on the part of the patient. Even when the therapeutic alliance is well established, the patient may feel, at those moments, painful and frightening expression of otherness on the side of his analyst. He might feel rejected, frightened and ashamed. He may then react with protest and complaint. In some extreme, yet not too rare cases, the patient may react with anger and even retaliation against the analyst for breaking the previous alliance of sameness and empathic witnessing.

The analyst's experience of being an empathic witness is very different from the experience of expressive otherness. However much the analyst feels authentic and therapeutically true to both himself and the patient, he still might be anxious and sometimes shaken, feeling that he has just hurt the patient, adding more to his previous suffering. Hurting his patient may be a guilt-provoking event for the analyst. Moreover, he may feel unsure about his professional contribution and distressed by self-criticism.

I suggest that this transference-counter-transference experience is also formed by enactment that may be typical in the post-traumatic victimhood therapeutic process. The analyst's experience may become a form of projective identification (Ogden, 1986) and serve as an emotional reconstruction of a small traumatic-like event. Roles of victim and persecutor may be switched. The analyst may feel somewhat persecuted (accused) by the patient for causing him more pain and at the same time self-persecuted through his own professional criticism. He may undergo himself an unconscious experience of identification with the aggressor. He may identify himself with the patient accusation expression of psychic injury and become overloaded with immediate and spontaneous feelings of guilt and regret. In some extreme cases, his experience may include disruption of going on being, feeling of threat, fear and loneliness. Guilt feelings, shaken self-confidence and reality testing, followed by (professional) identity crisis may be unconsciously identical to the patient's original trauma and become a form of a relational unconscious (Gerson, 2004).

However shaking the analyst's experience might get at this moment, we can assume that this kind of enactment is of therapeutic value. The experience of the original trauma and the horror of the victim-persecutor relation are unconsciously reconstructed within the patient-analyst relations. The analyst's experience, when elaborated and understood, may draw him closer to the patient's experience. Simultaneously, the analyst may confirm his empathic attunement of the experience of the patient's interpersonal relation.

I ascribe special therapeutic importance to the analyst's expression of otherness. Despite the analyst's jolted professional self-confidence, the patient may benefit from his authentic disagreement with him. As I suggest above, the analyst's expression of otherness often results out of mutual unconscious enactment of both patient and analyst and that the analyst's reverie of his patient's deprived self-states reveals the patient's readiness to undergo weaning process out of the exclusiveness of the needs of his victimhood self-state. Paradoxically, by this enactment, the patient can identify with someone who stands against aggression and keeps to his own mind (Davis and Frauley, 1994). This kind of identification may help the patient believe that eventually he will be able to stand up for himself someday, too. Feeling stronger in this way may contribute to his eventual recovery from trauma. Yet, I would like to add that for the patient, the analyst becomes a real aggressor at those moments. The analyst who is willing to recognize it and own his aggression as a disruption of the patient's exclusive need for empathic witnessing may contribute more to the therapeutic endeavor. He may represent an attitude in which aggression may be recognized and negotiates as a part of benign human relations that sometimes include moments conflicting interests. (Mendelson, 2002).

The patient's recognition of the existence of both an internalized persecutor and post-traumatic victimhood aggression and acknowledging that he might be, in fact, causing pain, fear and suffering to loved ones may be a difficult experience that may lead to anger and protest. After all, a victimhood identity requires the person to ignore (through dissociation) the existence of a parallel identification with the aggressor. For the patient to give up his life-long identity as victim is truly daunting, at least at the start of therapy and even over time.

When the analyst succeeds in contacting these dissociated self-states, containing them together and acknowledging and interpreting them, there is a good chance that fear, anger and frustration will appear in the sessions. These can then be related to increasing the patient's ability to recognize and contain the "otherness" of the persons with whom he has relationships. Hopefully, a supportive basis of therapy, built with patience over a long period of time, can provide for safety and trust in which patient and analyst can work these matters out.

The analyst has different self-states, too. Different self-states may be activated when the analyst is loved and appreciated, when he is the focus of his patient's helpless dependency or when he is feared, accused and feels punished. His ability to "stand in spaces" and move between those self-states is likely to offer a more comprehensive therapeutic attitude to the patient's needs.

Eve

I would like to present a case in which favorable results were achieved through enactments and shifting of empathic attunements.

Eve is a forty-five-year-old woman; she is an artist and maintains an artistic and academic career in a prestigious college. She is married and mother of three children. She grew up in a religious Jewish family. As a child, her physical needs were well taken care of. However, she experienced great emotional neglect, both as a daughter and young girl. She was given less attention by her parents than were her younger brothers and her sisters. At the same time, she used to take care of her aging parents.

As a teenager, she was usually on her own. When she was sixteen, she was seduced and abused by her uncle. When she told her parents about it, they preferred to look the other way; The whole event was denied. This episode of sexual abuse constituted severe emotional trauma for her, which she repressed for many years.

Despite her pain and disappointment, she has coped courageously, pursuing a successful route of self-fulfillment. Her life opened up through early marriage to a young, sensitive and considerate man, who was willing and able to truly listen to her. She told him everything about her early life, and, in turn, he shared with her many of his own misfortunes. They loved each other and became a deeply devoted couple. I believe that this deep connection facilitated the establishment of initial trust in me at the beginning of therapy, though she did put me through tests from time to time.

Eve turned to psychotherapy because of frequent painful misunderstandings with people at her place of work and members of her broader family. These events had a flavor of righteous indignation. Usually, Eve felt hurt and betrayed by friends, colleagues and members of the family. When she spoke of her complaints, usually in the presence of other non-involved people, they would become offended and reserved. She lost contact with some of them.

In therapy, Eve showed courage and uncompromising self-observation. In one therapy session, she said with honesty, "I need to be a victim. If not, I feel I have no right to say anything. By being a victim, I make them listen to me." By voicing this, she seemed to be expressing awareness that a declaration of victimhood may not only be an expression of pain but also a way of asserting herself and gaining influence over others.

However, her growing insight did not prevent further expressions of victimhood. One day, when she felt she could trust me, she blurted out dramatically, "My daughters have betrayed me!" She told me that she had a fight with her youngest daughter and that her daughter threatened her again by expressing suicide wishes. Then, her daughter preferred her aunt's (Eve's sister) company and moved there. Eve's other daughter went there, too, and stayed beside her sister. Her daughter's suicide wishes and the two daughters joining together at Eve's sister's home was what she called "betrayal." She hated the idea that her daughter would expose their intimate conflicts to her sister and maybe the whole family.

Eve could not tolerate this and eventually asked her husband to send their daughters away from home.

As detail after detail unfolded, my distress grew. I became worried that she was re-enacting with her daughter her own parents' withdrawal from her when she had come to them in such intense distress. She was still carrying much anger and fear of rejection from that period of her life; and the more her daughter now expressed her anger and distress, the more these still-existent feelings were aroused. At one point, she could tolerate it no longer and threatened to send her daughter away.

Listening to all this, I found myself experiencing a growing sense of concern for her daughter, towards whom my empathic attunement shifted. I was worried about her, certain she was suffering from feelings of rejection and loneliness and might be at risk of suicide. I also was concerned for Eve, whom I imagined would be extremely over-flooded with feelings of guilt in the future when she would grasp her daughter's true emotional condition.

Trying to control my inner turmoil, I remained reserved and silent. Eventually, aware of the daughter's possible distress and the mother's equally dramatic threat of "exiling" her, I said, "It seems that both you and your daughter communicate by surprising each other and in painful ways." Eve appeared taken aback by my comparison with her daughter and the implication that they communicate with each other in the same disturbing way. I realized, to my distress, that she may have felt she had lost her privileged place with me as she became silent and withdrawn. The meeting ended; and as she went out, I heard her calling her husband on the phone.

The next session was two days later. I thought that what I had said—which was essentially an interpretation of the denial of her aggression towards her daughter—had been too distant. In my reverie, I remembered that years ago my reaction to feeling angry and worried at the same time (towards my parents, for instance) had always led me to restraint and distance. I inferred that my patient could have felt me as being cold and reserved in front of her distress. Maybe in her experience I betrayed her too. I wondered whether my concern and anger were an overreaction. Perhaps she had not actually intended to send her daughter away but rather desperately tried to make me understand how much she needed me to recognize her pain. She had been overlooked for so many years, and she needed to feel privileged by me.

Thinking it over, I realized I was much more bothered by how I had sounded than by what I had said. I really believed she needed to see the similarity and reciprocity between her and her daughter. However, I may have sounded accusing and rejecting. I wondered whether I had become trapped in complementary identification with her disowned aggressor self-state and acted it towards her in a persecuting way. I felt bothered by what I considered as an offensive professional mistake.

We each came to the session somehow transformed. I had regained my attentiveness and empathy without denying my worries for the mother and her daughter alike. She was thoughtful and self-observant again. She told me that she had been shocked and hurt by the way I described the mother-daughter relationship. It had never occurred to her that she was involved in a power struggle with her daughter. Neither had it occurred to her that she had been punishing her daughter in response to the latter's threat of suicide. She had experienced the suicide threat as an attack on her and had felt that asking her husband to have the daughter leave the house was a legitimate way to defend herself. Adding salt to the wound was the fact that in her mind, she was basically alone in the world, while the two sisters had each other. She felt they did not respect her as their mother.

Despite my hope in the prior session that she had not really intended to send her daughter away, she had in fact really meant to do so. But following our session, she had changed her mind. Indeed, she had written her daughter a letter, which she proceeded to read to me. It was a love letter, full of affirmation, inclusion and hope. For the moment, the danger was averted.

Reflective upon this event after two additional years of analysis, my patient's pain of her daughters' betrayal has never been forgotten. She still has tears in her eyes when she recalls it. Yet, she seems to have overcome any vengeful urge. When further crises occurred in their relations, she oscillated between retaliation and devotion and eventually remained faithful to what she wrote in that letter.

I am trying to underline here the importance for the analyst to be able to switch empathic attunements and also to step out of them in order to see the whole system. After several years in which I had been fully empathic with the patient as victim of sexual harassment and parental abandonment, I had suddenly found myself preoccupied with her daughter's suicidal crisis. We can assume that the fact that she brought in this material was not accidental. She was revealing a whole new side of herself. She seemed willing to bring this new material thanks to the trust built up between us. It probably happened on the foundations of my continuing empathy.

A complementary identification had been aroused within me regarding the patient’s daughter. This new identification had caused me to briefly “switch sides.” My initial emotional response to the daughter was intense, surprising and unrestrained. I was very concerned for her and even angry at my patient. I said something that I hoped would sound accurate and relevant. But at the same time, I was threatening her experience of having me as an empathic witness who is always on her side.

Reflecting upon my unconscious interaction in this enactment with my patient following the first session, I realized that I became a threatening person for her. My response may have made her feel rejected and lonely. At that moment, I might have become the perpetrator for her. When I identified with her possible experience with me, I felt professionally unsure and confused, blamed by my patient's distress, self-criticized and in need for assistance. Gradually, recouping my ability to think more clearly, I understood the relevance of this experience to her treatment. Without underestimating my professional doubts, I could refer to my experience as a projective identification stemming from her initial post-traumatic pain. I think I felt her loss of trust, loss of self-confidence and loneliness through reflecting on mine. Switching roles of victim and perpetrator in these moments helped me to understand her better. Eventually, my empathy towards her experience became more deep and effective. In my view, this is the essence of one of the most meaningful enactments in victimhood cases.

Nevertheless, I think I had managed to contain both experiences, that of victim and that of persecutor. My identification with the daughter enabled me to recognize danger in the mother’s plan to reject her, thereby leaving her alone with her distress. I could sense the daughter’s fear and the very real danger of suicide together with her own aggressiveness towards her mother.

Later, upon reflection, it seemed to me that my ability to switch empathic attunements enabled me to arrive at a more independent, therapeutic space, one between both mother and daughter. From here, I could see how they were, in fact, alike in their pain, anger and tendency to feel victimized.

Group Analysis

I have noticed that group therapy is a powerful tool for treating post-traumatic victimhood. Group therapy is a not suitable for all patients, and suggesting to a person that he join group therapy should be done with sensitivity. Some of these patients experience this suggestion as rejection by the therapist. In such cases, it is better not to push it.

On the other hand, I have found that some post-traumatic victimhood patients are intrigued by the idea of joining a group. A group could perhaps contain several people who could serve as empathic witnesses. Some patients imagine it as much safer than being alone in a room with a therapist, who might at any moment suddenly turn into a persecutor, in the way I described above.

For such people, group therapy has particular advantages. For example, the participants' distress is mutually accepted. Furthermore, in comparison with people in the victim’s immediate personal environment, members of the group can often tolerate more behaviors resulting from victimhood self-states and for a longer period of time.

In a group of Holocaust survivors, for example, one of the participants continually complained about her many problems, interrupting other members, while ignoring their needs in the group. She asked participants to keep her regular seat. She had requested small services, such as a glass of water or unlimited time for herself, interrupted other members and insisted that she be allowed to answer phone calls from her sick husband, etc. Without explaining anything, she made it clear that her special needs had to be understood as proper reparation of her past suffering.

And to top it all, she seemed to block any verbal reaction towards her as she would bring in cakes and ask to distribute them to the group during the meeting. She was very insulted when asked by the conductor to wait for the meeting to end. In protest, she stopped speaking; her silence was experienced by everyone as highly accusing. The group conductor, an experienced psychotherapist, was increasingly angry, inside herself, towards the woman, and worried that it might show. She was afraid other members would become upset at the woman's disruptive and egocentric behavior and their benefit hindered. At the same time, she felt worried that the therapeutic value of the group might be damaged because of that patient's non-verbal confusing behavior and the disruption of the group setting. She began to feel blocked by her anger.

As it turned out, the members felt the conductor's anger. It was communicated in facial expressions and her uncharacteristic lack of patience. In one of the meetings, which the participant could not attend, the members addressed the issue and literally calmed the conductor down. They told her, "Don't worry. We can deal with her. She does not bother us. We can understand her. She is not able to behave any differently at this point. Give her time. She'll fit in."

The group conductor herself is a second-generation Holocaust survivor. She had grown up with parents who were extremely preoccupied with their own agenda and could not listen and contain their daughter's separate needs. Furthermore, her mother tried to communicate with her by feeding her whenever she could. The Holocaust member's need to feed everyone in the group with cakes was, therefore, a bit too close to home for the conductor and elicited a countertransference reaction of anger and fear. Now she felt that she had been helped by the group members and that she could accept that. The group's reassuring response helped her reflect on the process and recoup her professional demeanor. She could now contain her anger and better modulate her feeling and functioning towards the woman and other group members. At the same time, her ability to feel angry, without defenses, helped her to communicate her otherness and to gain more understanding for everyone.

It is important to underscore the dimension of time in group therapy (Berman & Weinberg, 1998). While at the first stage, the group is characterized by mutual support; in the next stage, members' feelings towards each other and towards the conductor are more complex and differentiated. There is an increasing ability by some members to accept differences in each other. This includes participants' attitudes towards post-traumatic victimhood self-state's behavior. While it can continue to be tolerated and indeed supported by some of the participants, others may experience increased frustration, insult and anger.

It appears to me that the mutual support characterizing the first stage of group therapy and the increasing acceptance of differences constitute important healing components. A member's inclusion in the group is at the heart of her healing (Foulkes, 1948). The group may form a collective or a temporal society of empathic witnesses. In the first stage, the member who sees himself as a victim is accepted by members who support and defend him and show compassion towards his life situation. Later, however, he begins to encounter different, subjective points of view. He becomes aware of the phenomenon of "otherness" in the group, which may at times be painful and frustrating for him. Mirroring in the group process (Foulkes, 1964, 1964) may reflect how the patient is seen and felt by other members. Moreover, mirroring processes in the group may combine the interpersonal and the intra-psychic.

As I mentioned before, the post-traumatic self-state may become dominant in one's interpersonal behavior, while other self-states may remain dissociated and non-active. Yet, in group therapy, a significant change may occur. I suggest that within ongoing mirroring processes within the group, other group members may represent the patient's own dissociated self-states. Through identification with other members of the group, the patient may recognize aspects of himself that were hidden under the domination of his post-traumatic victimhood self-state. Moreover, other members in the group may demand reciprocity and may ask for his concern and help. They may express love and hate and may pose challenges of coping with complex relations. They may call out for the patient's pre-morbid or restored self-states. I have found it highly encouraging to see post-traumatic patients gain significant positive and healing experiences in group therapy through activating other self-states that were dissociative and inactive until touch upon within the group process.

However, the beginning of this process in the group might be difficult. Individuals in the group may feel confronted by different expressions of otherness; some might become impatient or even angry. When a patient is confronted by anger from others, he may become frightened. Helping him, though, are always some other members, empathic witnesses, who stand on his side and communicate their understanding to others.

I would now like to present a vignette from one of my therapy groups, at the center of which is a participant I shall call Anna. Anna joined the group after a psycho-diagnostic evaluation, in which she was found to have an attention and concentration disorder stemming apparently from both emotional and neurological factors. Her level of education was lower than that of the other group members, which, in addition to her direct and down-to-earth behavior, created a certain gap between her and them. However, she brought with her several assets, including much motivation for self-fulfillment and change and a rich life experience of coping with difficult experiences. She readily found her way into the group and came to be respected by most members.

Anna grew up in a large family, and her life had not been easy. She was sexually abused by her brother for several years. Her parents' small business went bankrupt. Not only wasn't she protected by them, she also had to do whatever she could to help out. She worked as a salesperson, and for years contributed to the family's finances, at the expense of responding to her own needs. Male supervisors often treated her harshly. She felt a second-class citizen most of her life.

In the group, she was occasionally blunt and encountered reactions of disagreement. She easily accused other members for denigrating her for her lower background. However, as time went by, members displayed increasing understanding towards her and tried to contain her in these occasionally difficult moments.

In one session, Anna predicted that the intimate relationship of one of the members would not turn out well. The member, a young woman, responded by saying she was envious and aggressive. Avner, a male member who until then had been supportive of Anna, said that with all due respect, she was being ungrateful and called her "a man-hater." Anna attacked him, and he lost his temper, insulting her and calling her "envious and evil." He said that she was ungrateful towards him and the group and ignorant about proper conduct in human relations.

It was a spontaneous, harsh and out-of-the-ordinary outburst. Group members did not know what to say and looked to me for my response.

It seemed clear to me that her criticism of Avner and his reaction was a re-enactment of situations in which male aggressors had pursued her all her life. I suggested that members relate to what had happened. Most of them expressed reservations about Avner's offensive remarks and defended Anna. Two participants, though, stated that she had been provocative and teasing, goading Avner on.

Anna seemed unsure whether to feel insulted by their criticism or pleased that the others had come to her defense. Avner himself was both frightened and angry. When the meeting was about to end, I spoke briefly, saying this event must have aroused many feelings in members, and Avner and Anna in particular seemed to be experiencing much distress. I concluded by saying we would continue as usual next week.

It is my practice that when I find myself concerned about the welfare of any of my group patients, I make myself available to them between sessions (and make this known when setting rules of group therapy). I clarified this to Anna and Avner, but neither made an appointment to see me.

At the next meeting, everyone showed up. Avner opened by addressing Anna. He said that he got out of his temper because Anna had been so ungrateful towards him and others in the group. After the last session, he had realized that the deep insult he felt had related more to relations with his life partner, who in his view had never appreciated his efforts on her behalf and complained too much about what she was missing in life. In fact, he explained, he shoulders the financial burden of the two of them, while also spending a great deal of time bringing up their young son. Despite his investment, he finds himself always apologizing and trying to please her. After the last session, he went home and an argument broke out between them, in which for the first time ever, he told her he was finished being a pleaser and demanded recognition and mutuality.

When he stopped, Anna spoke. She was calm and organized, telling him that she did not need him to tell her to read more. If she had had the right opportunities in her life, she would have done so, just as he had. But, she continued, she had no intention of giving up and one day would resume her studies. Furthermore, she added, "You were mean to me, and I am angry now. Yet I know from our past sessions in the group that you told me that because basically you care about me. I forgive you now and behave yourself."

Later in the session, she addressed the whole group, telling them, "This group is very difficult for me, but I am trying to work on myself here. The supportive way you all said goodbye to me leaving the last meeting meant a lot. I wouldn't have come back here today had you not treated me as you did. I've been thinking about it all week and have been waiting for tonight." A look of relief appeared on members' faces. The threat of group crisis seemed to have passed.

The group may form a collective or a temporal society of supportive empathic witnesses. This may render a basis for a therapeutic alliance for post-traumatic victimhood self-state that enables any member to withstand feedback about his split-off dissociated aspects. Participants may encounter occasional harsh criticisms; but if they feel basically included, appreciated and loved by members and included in the group, their ability to contain it will strengthen.

Specifically regarding the post-traumatic victimhood self-state, being exposed to different points of view from different members may serve as a therapeutic factor. Members in the group may resonate to many themes, each according to his/her most emotional issues in life. This resonance exposes different identifications from different figures that are brought up in the group. Within mirroring processes in the group, victimhood complaint and behavior may result in unpredictable complementary identifications, which reflect the rejected aspect of the patient. Moreover, the victimhood wish for domination and control of other people's attitudes and behavior is eventually frustrated by the independent, spontaneous discourse in the group. Victimhood wishes for domination are challenged in a way that helps the participants increase their tolerance for insecure interpersonal situations. The patient may experience uncontrolled interactions that are not abusive or evil and even turn out for the better.

Faced with Avner's anger, Anna was actually confronted with someone who disagreed with her victimhood perspective. He turned it upside down. He said that she was the aggressor at that moment and somebody else was now her victim. He complained about her ingratitude towards him. And he was supported by some others. Processes in the group were beyond her control and made it hard for her to continue presenting herself as a victim.

Anna was able to protest against what she saw as Avner's aggressive stance towards her but at the same time see him as a caring figure. She had a hard time in the group, yet she was grateful towards the group and expressed her desire to continue working with them and with me on her personal development. This dual and complex emotional stance was difficult to contain but helped her to reestablish concern, differentiate between past oppressors and present friendly figures and regain their support.

Anna could have insisted on her lifelong demand from others that she be recognized as a victim and have left the group. Or, she could have stayed in the group and changed the way she saw and presented herself to others. She chose the latter. Moreover, in her case, she made a clear choice to turn to her own resources and prefer her way of personal growth to insisting on victimhood short-term gains. Even though this choice was taken by her early in her life, she could conceptualize and validate it at that moment in the group.

For Avner, too, the confrontation between them had been a decisive and turning moment. From that day on, he began to address the issue of his wife's dominance, and there was a gradual change in their relationship.

A group therapist is usually more acquainted with shifting of empathic attunements (Stone, 2003). He shifts his empathic attunement from one patient to another according to the needs of each of them while holding all his group patients in mind. I suggest that the role of the conductor is, first of all, to facilitate a complex, spontaneous interaction like the one described. Interpretations may follow. However, it is important to protect the members who expose themselves in their vulnerability as well as aggressiveness against scapegoating by other members. It is important that the conductor help ward off a group tendency towards scapegoating the patient who sees himself as victim and other participant's potential reactions of anger and frustration. Victimhood is always a group-as-a-whole theme. Other participants may find themselves reflected in the mirror that is provided by the group process. Hence, healing processes of post-trauma and of post-traumatic victimhood are also a group-as-a-whole contribution.

CONCLUSION

It seems to me that psychotherapy can help in the transformation from a post-traumatic victimhood fixation to a fuller way of being in the world, in which the person expands his field of activity and improves relationships with those close to him.

Confusion and resentment can eventually lead to insight and awareness of the various conflicting self-states. This turmoil may arouse feelings of guilt and remorse, which in time can renew the patient's experience of concern. His recognition of the pain he is causing those close to him may lead to more empathic behavior, which may lead to experience with relief. Those close to the patient will now find it easier to express concern and love back to him. The patient's new ability to take part in the joy of others may enable him to become a happier person. In short, there will be more mutuality in his relationships, with more room for forgiveness and rejuvenation of energy. If this can be achieved in therapy, then there is a real possibility that the patient's sense of personal agency (Slavin, 1997) will be strengthened. This will lead, in turn, to a significant improvement in feelings of self-worth.

However, to achieve this, therapy must restore mourning processes that had been long avoided. This development is somewhat similar to the building of Klein's depressive position, in which there is recognition of both bad and the good in the self-experience of the patient, the analyst and others as well.

However, the mourning involved in victimhood requires recognition of something else, namely, real losses in the person's life. In therapeutic self-examination, the patient will re-encounter good aspects of his past, which tragically will not return. People he has lost and time that has passed are gone forever. He encounters the need to renounce his victimhood way of life, which had worked for him until recently. He encounters the difficulties of adopting another attitude of mutual efforts and concern.

Recovery in such instances can be a complex and extremely difficult matter, involving sadness and joy, pain and relief. A significant accomplishment of therapy is the patient's ability to relate in a more satisfying way to his relatives and particularly to his children. These people can finally become freer of the burden of needing to always be there, on standby, for their relative or parent. The danger that they themselves will develop post-traumatic victimhood patterns will diminish. Finally, the passing of victimhood patterns from one generation to the next will cease, which is a worthwhile outcome.

I think that it is clear to all of us, as it has been clear to the analyst, that compassion and empathy is the "home" for psychotherapy. Therefore, it is important that whatever else is going to be said about mutual difficult moments between patient and analyst, empathy and compassion is both where we start and where we go back to.

Post-traumatic victimhood aggression is often presented by guilt-provoking behavior, including intensive complaints, accusations and demands often accompanied by nonverbal expression of suffering and dissatisfaction. People who are subjects of this behavior often feel that they are pushed (sometimes vigorously) to compliance and placating by the victim, trying to cope with his accusation by overdoing compensatory behavior. Many times, they are losing their vital balance between their own self-protecting functions and their concern for others.

BIBLIOGRAPHY

Aron, L. (2000). "Self-Reflexivity and the Therapeutic Action of Psychoanalysis." *Psychoanalitic Psychology* 17: 667-689.

Aron, L. (2003). "The Paradoxical Place of Enactment in Psychoanalysis: Introduction." *Psychoanalitic Dialogues* 13(623-631).

Balint, M. (1969). *The Basic Fault*. London, Tavistock Publications Ltd.

Benjamin, J. (1988). *The Bonds of Love: Psychoanalysis, Feminism, and the Problem of Domination.* New York, Pantheon Books.

Benjamin, J. (1991). "Father and Daughter: Identification with Difference." *Psychoanalitic Dialogues* 1: 277-299.

Berman, A. and H. Weinberg (1998). "The Advanced Stage in Therapy Group." *International Journal of Group Psychotherapy* 48: 499-518.

Bersani, L. and A. Phillips (2008). *Intimacies.* Chicago and London, The University of Chicago Press.

Bromberg, P. M. (1991). "On Knowing One's Patient Inside Out: The Aesthetics of Unconscious Communication." *Psychoanalitic Dialogues* 1: 399-422.

Bromberg, P. M. (1998). *Standing in the Spaces: Essays on Clinical Processes, trauma and Dissociation.* Hillside NJ & London, The Analytic press.

Bromberg, P. M. (2004). "More Than Meets the Eye: A Professional Autobiography." *Psychoanalytic Inquiry* 24: 558-575.

Davies, J. M. and M. G. Frauly (1994). *Treating the Adult Survivor of Childhood Sexual Abuse*. New York NJ, Basic books.

Fairbairn, W. R. D. (1940). *Psychoanalytic Studies of the Personality*. London, Routledge Press.

Felman, S. and D. Laud, Eds. (1992). *Testimony: Crises of witnessing in literature, psychoanalysis, and history*. New York & London, Routledge.

Ferenczi, S. (1933). Confusion of tongues between adults and the child. *Final Contributions to the Problems and Methods of Psycho-analysis.* M. Balint. London, Karnac Books: 156-167.

Fonagy, P. and M. Target (1995). "Understanding the Violent Patient: The Use of the Body and the Role of the Father." *Int. J. Psycho-Anal.* 76: 487-501.

Foulkes, H. S. (1964). *Therapeutic Group Analysis*. London, Allen and Unwin.

Foulkes, S. H. (1948). *Introduction to Group Analytic Psychotherapy*. London, Kamac Books

Freud, S. (1917). *Mourning and melancholia*. Standard Edition. 14.

Gabbard, G. O. (2003). "Miscarriages of psychoanalytic treatment with suicidal patients." *Int. J. Psycho-Anal.* 84: 249-261.

Gerson, S. (2004). "The Relational Unconscious: A Core Element of Intersubjectivity, Thirdness, and..." *Psychoanal Quarterly* 73: 63-98.

Grand, C. C. o. t. C. C. J. I. C. A. P., 1:143-145.

Grand, S. (2002). "Action in the Psychoanalytic Situation: Reflections on Its Relation to I..." *Psychoanalytic Psychology* 19: 254-280.

Klein, M. (1946). Notes on Some Schizoid Mechanism. *Envy and Gratitude*. London, Vintage.

Kohut, H. (1971). *The Analysis of the Self: A Systematic Approach to the Psychoanalytic Treatment of Narcissistic Personality Disorder.* Medison & Connecticut, International University Press.

Kohut, H. (1984). *How Does Analysis Cure?* A. Goldberg, University of Chicago Press.

Meissner, W. W. (1985). "A Case of Phallic-Narcissistic Personality." *Journal of American Psychoanalytic Association.* 33: 437-469.

Mendelson, E. (2002). "The Analyst's Bad-Enough Participation." *Psychoanalytic Dialogues* 12: 331-358.

Miller, A. (1990). *Banished Knowledge.* New York, Doubleday.

Mitchell, S. A. (1988). *Relational Concepts in Psychoanalysis: An Integration.* Cambridge, MA, Harvard University Press.

Mitchell, S. A. (1992). "Commentary on Trop and Stolorow's 'Defense Analysis in Self Psychology.'" *Psychoanalitic Dialogues* 2: 443-453.

Ogden, T. (1997b). "Reverie and Metaphor: Some Thoughts on How I Work As a Psychoanalyst." *Int. J. Psycho-Anal.* 78: 719-732.

Ogden, T. H. (1986). *The matrix of the mind.* New Jersey, Jason Aronson, Inc.

Ogden, T. H. (1991). "Some Theoretical Comments on Personal Isolation." *Psychoanal. Dial.* 1(377-390).

Ogden, T. H. (1997a). "Reverie And Interpretation." *Psychoanalytic Quarterly* 66: 567-595.

Orange, D. M. (2003). *"The Post-Cartesian witness and the Psychoanalytic Profession."* Unpublished Manuscript.

Poland, W. S. (2000). "The Analyst's Witnessing and Otherness." *Journal of the American Psychoanalytic Association* 48(1): 17-34.

Racker, H. (1957). "The Meanings and Uses of Countertransference." *Psychoanal Q* 26: 303-357.

Renik, O. (1993). Countertransference enactments and the psychoanalytic process. *Psychic Structure and Psychic Change.* M. Horowitz, O. Kernberg and E. Weinshel. New York, International Universities Press: 135-158.

Sander, L. W. (1995). "Identity and the Experience of Specificity in a Process of Recognition: Commentary on Seligman and Shanok." *Psychoanalitic Dialogues* 5: 579-593.

Searles, H. F. (1967). The "Dedicated Physician" in the Field of Psychotherapy and Psychoanalysis. *Crosscurrents in Psychiatry and Psychoanalysis.* R. W. Gibson. Philadelphia and Toronto, J. B. Lippincott.

Slavin, J. and L. Pollock (1997). "The Poisoning of Desire: the Destruction of Agency and the recovery of Psychic integrity in Sexual Abuse." *Contemporary Psychoanalysis* 3: 573-593.

Steiner *The recovery of Parts of the self lost through projective identification: the role of mourning.*

Stern, D. B. (2004). "The Eye Sees Itself: Dissociation, Enactment, and the Achievement of Conflict." *Contemporary Psychoanalysis* 40: 197-237.

Ullman, C. (2006). "Bearing witness: Across the barriers in society and in the clinic." *Psychoanalytic Dialogues* 16(2): 181-198.

Chapter 3

SOCIAL AND NATIONAL VICTIMHOOD: THE SOCIOPOLITICAL ASPECT

Avi Berman

At times, we may ask ourselves why and how evil begets more evil, suffering and even more suffering. Some of us might become aware of feelings of anger brought on by a wrong done to us and of resulting desires for vengeance through retaliation (which are usually not acted upon). For the most part, we perceive ourselves as passive victims of other people's wrongdoings. Our reactions to these wrongs oftentimes seem feeble protests compared to the strength of our nemeses, or—in some cases—as courageous and justified acts of self-defense. Usually, we are the few against many, the weak against the strong, good versus evil.

This chapter proposes that what we consider feeble protests or acts of self-defense might be, from a more systemic viewpoint, part of an aggressive dialogue, in which both sides provoke each other and concurrently feel justified in doing so. Both sides feel victimized by the other. The experience of victimhood (the complementary relations of doer and done to, according to Benjamin, (2004)) becomes so real and so vested as to disrupt the possibility of gaining essential insights into the circle of cause and effect in our lives.

The parallel processes between the individual and the group are thoroughly discussed by Bion (1961) and the collective mind of individuals is mentioned by Foulkes (Foulkes, 1948, 1964). The group, as an entity, responds to the basic needs of individuals to belong (Foulkes, 1948, 1964). Belonging to a group enhances each member's self-worth and, within a benign circle, the collective value of the group as a whole. In a group, the experience of entitlement grows stronger as well as the broad support and cooperation in threatening situations. When there is strong group coherence, individual wishes may join together and unify. Under these conditions, boundaries between subconscious fantasies, plans and acts might break and collective acting-out might be encouraged.

There are parallels between the victimhood self-state as it appears in individuals and as it appears in social groups. Societies and nations may be viewed as large groups. The psychoanalysis of the individual parallels that of the group and the society. Freud suggested that inter-identifications together with collective identification with the leader turn collective views into personal ones and vice versa; the leaders' intentions and attitudes are adopted by the group as a whole (Freud, 1921).

Regarding societies and nations, it seems to me that it is important to distinguish between national trauma and national post-trauma on the one hand and national victimhood on the other. At the height of national trauma, people are desperate to survive. They have experienced terror and helplessness and must struggle to simply live through each day. In post-traumatic situations, past horrors continue into the present and the threat to one's life is perceived as ongoing.

Victimhood bears some specific additional aspects when people belong to a group. The victimhood state includes an element of returning to life and signs of rehabilitation. These are responded to with acknowledgement, and sometimes even compensation, from a sympathetic environment. I would like to suggest that in the society, the victimhood state often appears at the crossroads between rehabilitation and reconciliation on the one hand, and the preservation of suffering and rage on the other.

In "national victimhood" situations, one byproduct of increased group cohesiveness and worth is the revival and re-experiencing of feelings humiliation, rage and vengefulness that were once suppressed under past oppression. Increased group cohesiveness and the revival of post-traumatic negative emotions bear also some important aspects that may empower national assertiveness.

It is important to acknowledge that despite the inherent positive value in rehabilitation and reconciliation, these processes exact a heavy price. Embarking on the route of rehabilitation and reconciliation implies going through a process of deep mourning, since it necessitates acknowledging losses that can never be recouped. Mourning is one of the most painful processes in the human experience, since it deals with the most important losses. Yet it gives way for forgiveness (Urlic, following chapters), renewal of capabilities, peaceful relations and better adaptations (Freud, 1917; Fogelman, 1998; Montville, 1989).

At the same time, any personal and social tendencies towards mourning and forgiveness may arouse emotional (and then national and political) objections. A collective legacy of loss remains in the group memory, enshrining particular standards and ideals. This route also requires a painful surrender of socially supported, aggressive solutions to many problems. The fact that the alternative to these socially valued, aggressive solutions is a detested one, namely, compromise with the Enemy, only adds salt to the wounds.

Consideration of this alternative incites differences between members of the group, between supporters and opponents. It thereby may jeopardize the society as a whole, stimulating as it does the creation of social conflicts and internal hostility. It threatens to undermine the experience of camaraderie and belonging, which so consolidates the social group and perhaps the whole nation.

Preserving the experience of grief and rage, on the other hand, leaves group solidarity intact. The dream of an ideal solution perpetuates, unchallenged. People are spared the painful experience of mourning and of reconciliation with an enemy. However, there is a price for this, too. Preserving grief and rage inhibits rehabilitation and postpones the social and economic prosperity that can be achieved through cooperation with neighbors, even if they are former enemies. Furthermore, preserving grief and rage may aggravate social hostility and sometimes lead to the next war.

Victimhood, when it is a component of a system of social values and identity, constitutes fixation at the crossroads I cited above. It reflects a partial rehabilitation only, while the enduring reminders of national suffering serve to ensure national solidarity. "Social victimhood" is represented in what I term "victimhood ideology." Such ideology is part of an overall national perspective, reflected and disseminated by leaders in public discourse. This phenomenon can be considered as "victimhood leadership."

I am suggesting here that what I refer to as "social victimhood" is not only a consequence of fear and loss (Montvile, 1989). Rather, it seems to me that victimhood is a collective attitude, partly unconscious, which is somehow chosen in order to ensure national solidarity, even when this is at the price of increased aggression and inhibits reconciliation and cooperation.

A social or national victimhood may reflect all four aspects of the victimhood syndrome as were described above. However, when thinking about victimhood phenomena in social groups (in contrast to victimhood in individuals), each of these aspects has particular characteristics. What they each have in common is their contribution to the consolidation of the group and the enhancement of collective identity.

Claiming a "Social and National Victimhood Identity"

Victimhood social identity is based on a collective experience of injustice. In this case, memories of injustice are a central factor in the nation's common history. People come to believe that they are still victims of an injustice done them by a relentless and permanent enemy. For example, the Jewish archetypal enemy, "Amalek" is mentioned in prayers instructing the Jews that they should remember it forever.

Owing to processes of identification within the group, national perception of injustice is experienced as personal, even if the individual him/herself was not personally involved or if the incident of injustice took place long before he was born. Evidence of the injustice is put before the group, assuring that the trauma that took place in the past influences the lives of group members in the present.

One of the most significant elements of claiming national victimhood identity is focusing on a chosen trauma (Volkan, 1997; Volkan, 2004). A chosen trauma is the shared mental representation of an event in a large group's history in which the group suffered a catastrophic loss, humiliation, and helplessness at the hands of enemies. [...]As decades pass, the mental representation of such an event links all the individuals in the large group. Thus, such a mental representation of a historical event emerges as a significant large-group identity marker. A chosen trauma reflects the "infection" of a large-group's mourning process. A reactivation of a chosen trauma serves to link the members of a large group. Such reactivation can be used by the political leadership to promote new massive societal movements, some of them deadly and malignant.

The Israeli and Palestinian cultures, for instance, seem to be based on chosen trauma, such as the fall of Masada or the Holocaust for Israelis and the 1948 expulsion of the Palestinian civilians from their homes (The Nacba) for the Palestinians. I suggest that for both nations, claiming a national victim identity is based on these chosen traumas.

Victimhood Displacement of Aggression

Two typical forms of displacement can be identified in social and national victimhood. In both forms, rage that originated with some past injustice is now displaced onto others. In one case, the rage following a trauma in the past is directed towards a group or a nation in the present. Usually, the new enemy is a neighbor that the victimized group believes it can vanquish. (This is in contrast to a past enemy who has caused suffering, loss and terror but was then or is presently seen as unbeatable.) In such cases, the group or the nation is charged with hostility and defined as an enemy. For example, many Palestinians, referring to Israeli hostility towards them, claim that Jews who became Israelis have displaced their rage and vengefulness from the Nazis to their present neighbors. This may be a case of displacement that deserves attention.

There is another form of displacement, with crueler implications. It permits "the blood of the innocent" to be shed. People within the group that is defined as the enemy become targets, and their deaths become permissible elements in the war against the enemy. In some war-time declarations, no distinction is made between attacking soldiers and attacking innocent civilians. One such example is that of Arab terrorist leaders declaring that killing Israeli children is permissible as they will grow up to become soldiers.

Like in individual victimhood situations, the possibility of displacement often remains outside the authentic experience of the members of the society. The existence of a real threatening enemy is a much more immediate experience for them. Differentiating between victimhood aggressive displacement and measures of self-defense becomes difficult.

Many Israelis still feel hurt when they encounter the Palestinian accusation that they have displaced vengeful feelings from the Nazi's to their Arab neighbors. Many of them see this as an aggressive devaluation of their suffering during the Holocaust. Acts of oppression towards Palestinian civilians may be justified or overlooked.

Displacement of aggression from a real perpetrator to innocent people might bear harsh consequences. The circle of violence increases as many of the attacked people might become vengeful and self-justify their retaliation. This kind of victimhood displacement of aggression might multiply, sometimes polarizing societies into mutual formation of enemies.

Turning Suffering into Over-Powering

The demand for compensation does not necessarily hinder the process of atonement and reconciliation. Compensation carries the opportunity of correcting injustice and returning normalization to relationships. This process may be further validated by an acknowledgement of past crimes committed against the people.

When a society is not united around victimhood ideology, combined acknowledgment and compensation can generate an experience of renewed equality, enabling the establishment of cooperation between the two sides. It brings with it the possibility of terminating the generational transmission of hostility typical of victimhood and the possibility that hostility will be forgotten in a generation or two.

In contrast, national victimhood might encourage the transformation of victim identity into domination and aggressive use of power. In such cases, it is defined in absolute and ideological terms, making it impossible to achieve reconciliation. The demand for compensation may become fixated and inspire belligerent acts.

Victimhood serves to eradicate doubts. It sharply defines a deprived nation on one side and its enemy on the other (Volkan, 1988). This definition might become a component in paranoid patterns of thinking. Within the experience of certainty, the group clarifies and solidifies its concept of the enemy and the enemy's hostile behavior. The concomitant increase in belligerency and the claim of "self-defense" becomes more and more convincing to the group. Freud (1921) referred to this in his essay, *The Psychology of the Masses and the Analysis of the Ego*" when describing the masses' intensifying feeling of hatred and paranoid behavior:

> The feelings of a group are always very simple and very exaggerated. So that a group knows neither doubt nor uncertainty. It goes directly to extremes; if a suspicion is expressed, it is instantly changed into an incontrovertible certainty; a trace of antipathy is turned into furious hatred (pp. 77).

National victim identity might be abused to the point of national self-justification of aggressive attack on others. For example, during the war in the former Yugoslavia, the Serbs published a national slogan saying "Where there is a Serbian grave there is Serbia." There is a hint that the graves belong to Serbian victims. In other words, the dead give the right to conquer other's territories.

The most clear-cut and cruel expression of transformation of victim identity into ideology and then into aggression that I found is the following:

> A nation denied its rights may use any weapon even bacterial warfare. I have no scruples, and I will use whatever weapon I require.

This is a quote from Adolf Hitler's declaration (cited in Herman's Rauschning documentation) (1940). Hitler adds:

> The new poison gases are horrible. But there is no difference between a slow death in barbed-wire entanglement and the agonized death of a gassed man or one poisoned by bacteria. In the future, whole nations will stand against each other, not merely hostile armies. We shall undermine the physical health of our enemies as we shall break down their moral resistance. I can well imagine that there is a future for bacterial warfare. We have not quite perfected it yet but experiments are being made. I hear that they are very promising. But the use of this weapon is limited. Its significance lies in wearing down the enemy before the war. Our real war will in fact all be fought before military operations begin. I can quite imagine that we might control Britain in this way or America (pp 13-14).

I suggest that the concept of victimhood ideology may offer an explanation of how the most aggressive national behavior may be represented as acts of self-defense and by that gain a wide national enthusiastic support. In this quotation of Hitler, he justifies taking measures of mass killing by gas and bacteria drawing on the denied national rights of the German people. I suggest that analyzing the victimhood ideology and leadership does not diminish the importance of self-defense but rather refines it and makes it more relevant and allows for a better differentiation between actual enemies and innocent bystanders or even potential allies.

Exemption from Concern

I claim that the most harmful process within a victimhood society happens when suspension of concern turns into exemption from concern. The exemption from concern for the opposing group might legitimize aggression and can bring about a self-justified takeover of another people's rights as a part of the secondary gain of the victimhood ideology.

As members of a society, we all expend some personal effort to overcome personal needs and instinctual urges and give space for other people's needs. We make an effort to bring about relief for others and to avoid causing them undue distress. We stand in line, pay our debts, give right of way and supply helpful information to other people. We try to avoid acting out on egocentric desires at the expense of others. We could be considered as fulfilling a basic social contract. This behavior can also be considered a sort of developmental moral achievement and successful socialization process, engendered by an innate empathic source that we forge throughout our lives. Moreover, many people find this effort to be highly rewarding and a basis for mutuality in relations. If we become aware of this effort, we will find that such efforts are abundant in every aspect of our lives and are often aimed not just at the people closest to us but also at complete strangers.

If every behavioral pattern can be said to accrue profit and loss, we can acknowledge the existence of a short-term economic aspect of victimhood, with its own scale of profits and losses. Exemption from concern may excuse the person from having to meet interpersonal obligations. On the other hand, it might arrest personal development, partnership and mutual exchange.

The early Zionist movement (years before the contemporary concept of two-state solution) had adopted Lord Balfour's proclamation in Jerusalem (1918) supporting the relocation of Jews to Palestine "A land without a people to people without a land." In saying so, any concern for Palestinian people who did live in Palestine was excused.

The most brutal exemption from concern is made possible during wars. Beevor (2002) describes the behavior of the Russian soldiers during the conquest of Nazi Germany in WWII. Killing, pillaging and rape were common. German civilians' property was appropriated and sent back to the soldiers' homes in Russia by military trains. Two million German women were raped.

Under exemption from concern, anger and vengefulness have no counter-point and go out of balance. Aggressive behavior patterns are met with empathy and understanding, or, at best, denial.

Victimhood Ideology and Victimhood Leadership

Victimhood in groups and nations tends to lead to the formation of ideology in addition to self-justification. Victimhood then becomes supported, in some cases, through Holy Scripture and contemporary philosophy and literature. The wrongs done to the group or nation become an integral part of formal education, and the sense of entitlement for compensation is perpetuated. By that, victimhood may become a part of social internalization process (Horney, 1939).

Victimhood ideology reinforces the distinction between "us" and "them" (Freud, 1921; Elias and Stockson, 1994; Volkan, 1988; Berman, Berger and Gutman, 2000), and fortifies the "us" experience around typical concepts such as: "They have harmed our ancestors;" "We, today, share the suffering wreaked on our forefathers;" "We have been wronged;" "It is our duty to correct this wrong;" "It is our rightful duty to correct the historical wrong and reclaim our right." The victimhood ideology is a powerful unifying force, creating a sense of unity based on experiences of suffering and pain but also based on paranoid fantasies and aggressive rectification wishes.

Freud (1921):

> Of two neighboring towns, each is the other's most jealous rival; every little canton looks down upon the others with contempt [....] We are no longer astonished that greater differences should lead to an almost insuperable repugnance, such as the Gallic people feel for the German, the Aryan for the Semite, and the white races for the colored (pp. 100).

As mentioned before, a society might contain many individuals (sometimes the majority) who have never experienced the founding trauma of the national myth, and yet these people, consciously or unconsciously, share the national victimhood ideology.

The victimhood leader constantly brings up past transgressions and seeks to invoke feelings of injustice, anger and vengefulness. These feelings may form a national unifying force. Moreover, victimhood ideology supplies the leader with means of seduction. He may compliment his followers by defining them as underprivileged yet specially chosen. He may suggest they are exempt from concern for others because of the suffering they have endured or from having to go through painful mourning and forgiving processes including unfair losses. He might promise them restoration of their former rights and a full compensation for the suffering they endured. Building reliance on the leader by his supporters creates a collective victimhood illusion that might prevent realistic solutions.

The Dead Ancestors

In many cases, dead ancestors may come to represent mythical victims in the social ideology. The mythical victim is created in order to serve as a collective archetype for a particular group or nation. Belonging to him and his belonging to the group help define the boundaries of the "us" group (Berman, Berger & Gutmann, 2000). The partners in mourning are "our own." Identifying with the dead victim turns all members of the group into victims. His suffering may create collective rage and induce plans for joint action. The latter may contain an aspect of vengeance, which solidifies a collective intention to correct the injustice, along with revenge, which itself is a form of correction.

Slobodan Milošević, the Serb leader who was brought to trial by The Hague international tribunal, had made intensive use of victimhood ideology. In his political declaration, he demanded national honor for the murdered Serbian ancestor, Prince Lazar. In 1989, Milošević had Prince Lazar's coffin exhumed on the 600th anniversary of his fall in the Battle of Kosovo in 1389, and proceeded to parade it around Serbia for a year in order to stir up public sentiments of having been wronged and seeking vengeance. He did, in fact, manage to imbue his people with motivation for war and caused the massacre of many innocent citizens. Milošević was the leader of the Serbian communist party, but this didn't stop him from using the prince and the church in order to accomplish the task of reuniting Serbia. Many ethnic groups in former Yugoslavia rebelled by war against the Serbian domination.

There are leaders who died fighting for the cause they believed in. There is no doubt that their deaths constitute a group and society-unifying factor. However, the fact that they sacrificed their lives for a social cause does not necessarily make them victims, and they are not necessarily integrated into an ideology of victimhood. These are leaders whose life-cause was reconciliation and dialogue, and a victimhood ideology is not produced after their death. Abraham Lincoln, Anwar Sadat, and Itzhak Rabin are examples of leaders who did not leave a legacy of victimhood and vengeance.

In contrast, in national victimhood situations, the death of a leader may be integrated into ideology and enhance it. I contend that a deceased ancestor might be exploited to prevent processes of forgiveness. A dead leader cannot forgive. No one can forgive on his behalf. All who try to do so are viewed as traitors to his memory. The impossibility to forgive may arrest processes of mourning and reconciliation.

The following is, in my view, an example of a victimhood political ideology that summarizes all of the above. It is taken from a speech by Iranian President Mahmud Ahmadinejad, in a conference called "A World without Zionism," held in Tehran in October 2005 (Quoted from the official Iranian government web publications):

> I am grateful to God for giving me the great pleasure of speaking at this very important gathering. I thank God for seeing the pious faces of you, the valiant, aware, God-fearing and selfless children of the revolution, who understand with vigilance and intelligence the most important issues of our times and are active with great zest and in a decisive way in the most central issues of the Islamic world. I thank God for the presence of you dear young people.
>
> The creation of the regime occupying Al-Qods (Jerusalem) was a heavy move by the globally dominant system and Global Arrogance against the Islamic world. There is a historic battle going on between the Oppressor World and the Islamic world, and the roots of this conflict goes back hundreds of years.
>
> Unfortunately, in the past three hundred years, the Islamic world has been on retreat in the face of the Oppressor World.
>
> The occupying state (Israel) is the bridgehead of the Oppressor World in the heart of the Islamic world. They have built a base to expand their domination to the entire Islamic world. There is no other raison d'être for this entity without this objective.
>
> But when the dear Imam [Ruhollah Khomeini] said this regime must be destroyed, and we want a world without a client state, many of those who claim to be political gurus and other things said it's not possible. [....] The Imam said the domination of the East and the West must be destroyed, but weak-minded persons, who only see the little world around them, didn't believe him...
>
> Our dear Imam ordered that the occupying regime in Al-Qods be wiped off the face of the earth. This was a very wise statement. The issue of Palestine is not one on which we

> could make a piecemeal compromise... This would mean our defeat. Anyone who would recognize this state [Israel] has put his signature under the defeat of the Islamic world. Today, the unity of the front in Palestine on its goals is a pressing necessity. The issue of Palestine is by no means finished. The issue of Palestine will only be resolved when all of Palestine comes under Palestinian rule, when all the refugees return to their homes, and when a popular government chosen by this nation takes the affairs in its hands. Of course, those who have come to this land from far away to plunder this land have no right to participate in the decision-making process for this nation.
>
> I warn all the leaders in the Islamic world to beware of this conspiracy. If any of them takes a step towards the recognition of this regime [Israel], then he will burn in the fire of the Islamic umma (nation) and will have eternal shame stamped on his forehead, regardless of whether he did this under pressure by the dominant powers, or lack of understanding or naiveté or selfishness or worldly incentives.

In his speech, Mahmud Ahmadinejad refers, first of all, to his “Us” group and compliments them as “pious,” “valiant” and “children of the revolution.” Then, he describes the Western world as the “Oppressors,” defining the “Them” group. The Islamic people are defined as victims of the oppressors. The dead ancestor, Imam Khomeini, ordered that the evil regime must be destroyed without compromise or reconciliation. His word must be kept as a respect for his sacred memory. Use of force is permitted in order to wipe out that regime from the face of earth. Exemption from concern takes the form of denying the rights of people who came to Palestine from other counties (in this case, millions of Jews whose parents immigrated, most of them as war refugees).

THE ENCOUNTER BETWEEN VICTIMHOOD GROUPS

It seems to me that the first phase of the encounter between victimhood groups is characterized by a manifestation of victimhood agenda within each group. I have found that one of the most disheartening facts relating to victimhood relationships is that they intensify each other. It is my experience that in many cases, one side's victimhood complaint is responded to by a victimhood complaint by the other side. “You hurt me and I am suffering.” produces the statement, “You hurt me first.” In many quarrels, each side is quick to point out the suffering the other has caused him. More so, people get caught up in building a balance sheet of damages and mutual injury. They blame each other; and each yearns to be heard by a fair judge, who will recognize prioritize his/her suffering.

Unfortunately, though, the statement “You hurt me” is usually experienced by the complainant as an empathic failure and not as an equivalent expression of distress. Not only has the defendant not recognized that he himself is the source of the complainant’s suffering, he even shuts the complainant up with his own complaints and, by that, inhibits all possibility of tolerant listening. In this situation, people either shut down or go to the other, aggressive extreme. In this way, victimhood may make the impression of being a “contagious disease.”

Yet, exchange of victimhood expressions of suffering may be understood also as a wish for acknowledgement. Whenever people succeed in breaking free from national victimhood ideologies and leadership, mutual acknowledgement of both side's suffering may lead to change. Moreover, it appears to me that responding to a complaint with a counter-complaint may be also an unconscious authentic attempt to disarm the victimhood syndrome of its major weapon. “You hurt me, too” is a statement designed to transmit the message that suffering is not the sole property of one side only. It may be a demand for mutual recognition. Since one of the victimhood, characteristic is exemption from recognizing the needs of the other, this demand for recognition is understandable. If accepted, the victimhood system can give way to a dialogue in which both sides acknowledge being a contributor to the situation as well as a victim.

Unfortunately, as I stated above, this strategy usually fails. The victimhood system is more powerful. The statement “you hurt me, too” may not disable the victimhood system but rather more often reinforces it. It seems to me that in these situations, it is expected that the side that recognizes its contribution to the other side’s suffering will lose its patience while waiting in vain for the desired mutuality. Frustration and losing patience may once again produce the counter-blame of “You hurt me, too,” bringing us back to square one.

Victimhood Aspects within the Israeli-Palestinian Conflict

Apparently, the Israeli and the Palestinian nations demonstrate a clash between two victimhood societies. Some authors have referred to the subject of the Israeli-Palestinian conflict as a clash between two victimhood national attitudes. (Montville, 1986, 1989; Akhtar, 2002; Govrin, 2006).

There exists a debate regarding the return of the Arab refugees from 1948, to reside within the borders of Israel. The Palestinians claim this as their absolute right. The Israelis claim that the Palestinian demand to give millions of refugees the option to return to Israel is simply impossible to carry out and annihilate the right and the very existence of Israel as a Jewish state.

It is possible that the Palestinian demand for complete relocation of the refugees contains a victimhood component by insisting on absolute compensation at the expanse of mutuality and concern. At the same time, Israeli nationality may bear some victimhood components, too. The suffering of the Jewish people could be used to form an Israeli victimhood ideology. This ideology, combined with victimhood leadership, could create a repeating cycle of provocation—aggression—secondary gain— war—suffering and reinforcing victimhood ideology.

The choice of trauma for the Israeli and Palestinian sides might justify using military oppression and abandoning the path of negotiation on Israel's part and the equivalent use of terrorism on part of the Palestinians. It enables each side to further cleave to its own rigid, uncompromising position and to justify the destructive acts it chooses to inflict upon the people of the “other” collective.

The victimhood positions often sound “moralistic,” as the Jewish side establishes a war-time moral viewpoint that permits it to harm Palestinians, while the Palestinian side justifies violence on the basis of desperation and hopelessness in the face of Israel’s unyielding military strength. What else can a conquered people do to regain its lands, dignity and freedom?

Each side of the Israeli-Palestinian dialogue reinforces its victimhood collective identity by using emotional and ideological lessons drawn from its traumatic history, lessons that it seeks to pass on. On the Jewish side, such claims can be heard as: "the Arabs want to destroy us." "They do not accept us a neighboring nation." "They do not accept our equivalent right for Jewish national state." "They use terror against innocent civilians." The Palestinian side also makes known its justifications for using terror as an instrument to promote national interests: "The Jews have taken away our dignity, our land, our freedom." "Only terrorism will make them leave." "They must return to whence they came from; they must understand that this is not their place. We should not be the ones left to pay the price of their Holocaust, the massacre leveled by the Germans, they have harmed us, driven us away, and to that we can never agree." Both sides seem to believe reciprocally that "strength is the only thing the other side understands."

I have personally encountered two ideological representatives of victimhood, the Israeli and the Palestinian, and specifically their aggressive elements. The following report comes from my personal experience.

In 2008, at the peak of tension between the two national groups, an Israeli/Palestinian meeting took place at the initiative of Jessica Benjamin[1]. The purpose of the meeting was to facilitate mutual acknowledgement between the two national groups. Representatives of both sides were invited, as were representatives of the international community. The common denominator among participants was their social activism and connection to the field of behavioral science.

The meeting took place in Aqaba, Jordan, and lasted three days. At the gathering, there were intense encounters: in plenary sessions, in small, nationally-mixed groups and in small, single-nationality groups. As expected, there were many moments of tension, since the forum was specifically designed to facilitate direct dialogue between the participants.

In contrast, during the breaks between formal activities, a process of people becoming acquainted with each other developed that was very heartwarming and uplifting. In these informal meetings, more personal, person-to-person conversations took place, which sharply contrasted what happens in the outer world of nationalism. In the evenings, there was much singing and dancing, as people from all groups truly let their hair down. Hotels guests who came from different Arab countries and from the rest of the world were flabbergasted. Here was clear evidence that the development of warm and direct human contact between Israelis and Palestinians is really possible. At the end of the three days, everyone returned to their homes.

I couldn't hold back and angrily challenged my Palestinian counterparts for their disregard of the pain caused by suicide bombers. I recalled the shock I felt when buses exploded in the neighborhood in which I grew up. I could not believe that people could be so cruel. When I talked about all this, I was totally immersed in my own experience of injustice and horror. The Palestinian partners responded that I was making myself into a victim and told me that I was "shooting and whining," i.e., exhibiting violence and then complaining. When they confronted me, I felt rage, humiliation, despair and the impossibility of any further dialogue. All I wanted was to walk away and never see them again. I stayed. As an Israeli, I found myself personally accused of ruining the lives of the Palestinian refugees, who were expelled from their lands in 1948.

---

[1] Together with Prof. Uri Hadar, and a group of Israeli social activists.

The resentment of the Palestinians had a parallel on the Israeli side. The expectation of some of the participants in the meeting that the trauma of terror victims would be acknowledged by the Palestinians, as would the existential fear experienced by Israelis, was met with disappointment time and time again. The clearest expression of this was by one of the Palestinian participants, who, responding to the Israelis' request that the Palestinians empathize with the Israeli suffering of terrorist attacks, had said “I will never criminalize the Palestinian resistance.” The other Palestinian participants supported her, through their words or their approving silence.

The portrayal of terrorism as legitimate resistance to oppression defines terrorism as an act of self-defense and turns the “resistor” into a victim. The Palestinians’ lack of willingness to distinguish between ordinary, innocent people and active oppressors, in this case, reciprocated the Israeli victimhood. The lack of concern for the suffering of the other is clear and troubling. Victimhood blaming and counter-blaming prevented acknowledgement and empathy for mutual suffering and arrested any possibility of reconciliation at those moments.

Nevertheless, the non-formal and friendly dialogue between members have reestablished a certain amount of concern. Personally, I felt, as an Israeli, that I could observe victimhood aspects in my "Us group" from a more comprehensive point of view. The event I would like to focus on began on the journey back from Aqaba to Israel. Upon leaving, the mood of the whole group grew very sad and somewhat anxious. It was clear that the Palestinian participants would have to go through very rigorous security checks, while the Israelis would simply cross over the international border and go directly home.

The group included three Arab-Israelis, all young female psychologists. They went through the security check at the Israeli border with relative ease. Certainly none were treated with suspicion, and we began to look forward to traveling north, to the center of the country. But, when we arrived at the airport in Eilat (Aqaba’s Israeli twin-city), our Arab-Israeli companions—the three female psychologists—were immediately separated from the Jewish-Israelis. They were taken to a separate part of the airport for interrogation.

All Israelis, Jews and Arabs alike are used to the hassle of security checks and have learned to maintain a certain tolerance for them. Arab passengers, in particular, must undergo extremely exacting security checks. However, the security checks given to the three Israeli women were far more difficult and discriminative than anyone had anticipated. They were taken to a side room, where for two hours they underwent a humiliating interrogation: their suitcases were taken apart, they were forced to stand up during the whole check-up, to take off most of their clothes and to have strangers poke around their body and through their hair. The Jewish Israelis among us who tried to intervene and help out, testifying that our colleagues were indeed part of our group and perfectly good citizens, were rudely told to stay away. The women being investigated were crying by now, but this didn’t stop or even seem to move any of the security personnel.

We were shocked by the interrogators’ lack of compassion. These women were part of us, the very people with whom we had spent such moments of warmth and intimacy during the breaks at the conference. The injustice and lack of concern were brutally painful.

Later, together with some of my Israeli colleagues, I responded to these events by going to the press and sending letters to the Minister of Internal Affairs and to the Director General of the Airports Authority. The written responses we received were cold and indifferent.

Of the several newspaper articles describing the event, one was published in an online, Internet newspaper, along with readers' responses, of which there were many. Ninety-five percent of them were hostile, justifying the abusive security check. Here are some examples:

> "I can tell you that if those passengers were put through such a search, then there must have been good reason for thinking they might be sympathetic to the enemy and even involved with terror organizations. Believe me when I say that airport supervisors and security personal have no extra time to waste on two women who innocently came to Israel. Surely they weren't examined for amusement or racial discrimination but because of real and sincere fear. It is true that foreigners and Arabs are checked more carefully than Jewish Israelis, who have no nationalistic motive to carry out a terrorist action. This, however, is the reality in which we live."

> "Arab Israelis help Palestinian terror, and it is clear that blowing up a plane is a "quality" terrorist attack. Is it any wonder? Our lives and security take precedent over "respect" for passengers. Not nice? Don't mix up these two things. "Hats off" to the security service."

> "Don't be ridiculous! Stop complaining, trying to get attention. It always feels good to be members of the "weak and oppressed." This is life and there's a good reason for all these unpleasant security examinations. If flying were as safe as a stroll through the park, we could all board planes without hassle. But this is not the case! Wake up! Nowadays, terrorist attacks on airports are one of the biggest threats. And instead of showing your gratitude and saying "thanks" to the people protecting us all, who enable us to reach our destination, you bad-mouth them as if they do these security checks for their personal pleasure. I, too, am a Jew, and, "yes," I take off my shoes when I am aboard! I, too, went through a body search and to tell you the truth, I didn't care. I know that if I am checked, then others were checked as well. And it is not because the security guys wanted to "feel me up." So, that's enough!"

It would only be fair to report that there were a few different responses that emphasized support and understanding for the three Arab women and rage at the injustice done to them.

It was clear that the Israeli Arabs were indeed victims of prejudice and hatred. But, it was also clear that the writers saw themselves—the Jewish Israelis—as victims as well: of terrorist attacks and the total rejection of their national feelings and rights. For them, the right to self-defense justified all aggressive measures. In this event, as in so many others, hatred and aggression were displaced from real terrorists to innocent people who happen to belong to the same national group as the terrorists. Suspicion did not require proof. There was no regard for human suffering. The exemption from concern was clear, and no second thoughts were necessary.

While writing these chapters, I realized that my extensive efforts to understand the victimhood phenomenon have not helped me stop being part of it. Yet, it seems that face–to-face meetings between people may moderate victimhood's expressions. During the three-day dialogue, relations among members had become personal when people from all national groups had become cut off from their social roles and stereotyped views. The victimhood mechanisms were declining. Aggression gave way to compassion, and the concern that belongs to "our" group began to spread towards other people from "their" group.

MUTUAL RECOGNITION AND COMPENSATION

It seems to me that combining mutual recognition and compensation may be helpful in finding a way out of victimhood fixations. Acknowledging responsibility for causing others to suffer and replacing victimhood accusations with self-responsibility may help to build dialogue between enemies. It may facilitate processes of forgiveness and reconciliation.

Without real efforts towards material compensation, recognition might be received as "taking away everything and giving words in return." Compensation means more than money and economic redress. It is a part of the regressed language of victimhood that validates recognition and demands the other side be willing to make visible sacrifice in order to meet the victim's needs. Many times, enemies may produce mutual compensation just by cooperation. Yet the other side's efforts are still presented in positive terms by making visible reparation efforts.

Compensation by itself, without accompanying recognition, might fail. It might be suspected as a bribe offering and add to feelings of humiliation. From the point of view of victimhood self-state, those who accept it may be viewed as traitors. Recognition may present "taking responsibility." Compensation may represent "the willing to pay." Therefore, only combined compensation and recognition have a chance to make a difference. The symbolic meaning of the conjunction of the two may change people's metallization of their raw and archaic victimhood's perceptions. Combined compensation and recognition may be experienced as atonement. Atonement may be experienced as a plea for forgiveness.

The spirit of atonement may change victimhood social internalization in both sides. Those who offer it crack their society's victimhood ideology and present concern for the other side's pain and injury instead. Those who accept it crack their own victimhood ideology in an equivalent manner. They present forgiveness instead.

A degree of tolerance of disobedience within the society is crucial for change. An individual will have a better chance of breaking out of the victimhood consensus in societies that tolerate a certain degree of disobedience. Not all societies will permit it. In such situations, people may lose their freedom, or even their lives, if they break the hard and fast codes of social and group belonging. Breaking out of the victimhood ideology, or any other ideology, may be totally impossible. A particular society's openness towards disobedience can be considered an index of its ability to consider alternatives to the victimhood ideology. When there is no such openness, there is no leeway for individuals who become agents of change.

During my childhood in Israel, I was exposed, as were so many others at that time, to the political/social storm created by Israeli government's decision to accept compensation from Germany. German compensation was to be given to the State and to individuals who had been persecuted by the Nazis. The leaders of both countries, David Ben Gurion of Israel and Konrad Adenhaur of Germany, had met and reached an understanding regarding German responsibility for severe damages to the Jewish people. The decision to accept compensation from Germany received approval from the Knesset (Israel's parliament), despite protests of rage and pain in the parliamentary chamber and on the street. For many people, the German money was "tainted" and desecrated the memory of those killed in the Holocaust. The entire Israeli young national unity had been jeopardized by threat of this agreement displaying an unbecoming forgiveness towards the German murderers.

However, there was a parliamentary decision to take the compensation money, and funding began to arrive. The Israeli streets became populated with people who had received German money. German cars began to appear. People could afford to upgrade and change their homes, and a general economic improvement was evident.

The people who received this money were Nazi victims. It was clear that Adenhaur's recognition of their suffering and of Germany's responsibility (as well as the fact that he had not been part of the Nazi government and was actually arrested by the Nazis) had made this move possible. Compensation without the accompanying recognition of the suffering the Jewish people had experienced would not have been enough. In any case, despite the German gesture, many people had strong reactions. Many of them took the money, swearing to maintain their hatred of the Germans. But many others took the money and after a while even began visiting Germany. People were talking now about "new Germany."

The most significant agents of change, the turmoil within Israeli society, were the Nazi victims who decided to move out of their state of victimhood and non-forgiveness by accepting recognition and compensation. Others who did not agree with the government's decision could nonetheless accept those who took the "tainted" money because, in the end, they were part of the "us" group and had truly suffered at the hand of the Nazis. These Nazi's victims became, unconsciously, agents of change.

The need for mutual recognition seems to be universal. Victimhood societies and people want it to be acknowledged that they committed their aggressive actions out of self-defense and fear. Benjamin refers to the issue of mutual recognition: ".... the only alternative to the doer-done to relation is recognition of the other as an equivalent center of being with equal value, common humanity, with legitimate feelings, with an independent perspective and likewise reciprocally capable of being a subject who is responsible for recognition of her Other" (Benjamin, 2004).

Mutual recognition is apparently a key factor in the reconciliation processes (Benjamin, 1990). Each side aspires to be recognized by the other. Mutual recognition requires reciprocity. Waiting patiently for reciprocity is possible for a limited period. It seems to me that this waiting period is characterized by a dynamic similar "frustration tolerance," as described by Winnicott (1967). According to Winnicott, there is *X* amount of time during which the baby is with the mother and feels secure and satisfied. In her absence, the baby is able to organize himself for *Y* amount of time, during which, owing to his/her basic belief that she will come back soon, he still feels a certain amount of safety and satisfaction. But, after a certain amount of time has gone by, in a *Z* point in time, the experience of security, hope and trust is lost.

So it may be in the wait for mutual recognition. There is a *Z* point in time at which the wait for mutuality reaches its limit. At this point, when recognition remains one-sided, there will be feelings of disappointment and grievance. The side that does not return recognition comes to be viewed as aggressive and a source of humiliation. It has now been re-confirmed as the Enemy.

I would like to end this chapter by suggesting a necessary ethical counterpoint to victimhood. Itzhak Mendelson, one of the members in the mutual acknowledgement project and a contributor to the ideas of victimhood in society, has suggested an ethical principle to replace victimhood. According to this principle, suffering can never justify causing the suffering of someone else. The application of this principle is complicated, especially because of the widespread practice (justified at times) of people rationalizing violent actions in terms of self-defense. Nevertheless, it may help us to reconsider the difference between self-defense and aggression and between active enemies and innocent people.

A Remark on Consultancy

It seems to me that aside from situations in which either of the sides manages to get out of the victimhood system on his own, the only way to salvation is through a third party. If indeed both sides yearn for an impartial judge, a third party is welcomed. Based on understanding victimhood's processes, the third party's assistance must be based on two principles: 1. His ability to move from side to side while switching empathic attunements and alternating recognition of each side. By switching empathic attunement,[2] the consultant is able to hold both sides in his mind, identifying himself with the opposite side's point of view while working with each of them. 2. His determination to interpret the behavior of both sides according to the four aspects of victimhood as mentioned above. The third party is experienced equally as both encouraging and frustrating. He expresses both empathy and failure of empathy. He gains at the same time responses both of neediness and of anger.

The role of the consultant as a witness to both sides may be insufficient for contradictory reasons. When the consultant/witness does not express his concern for the suffering and desire for recognition and compensation of one of the sides, he may be perceived as too neutral and distant and eventually irrelevant and even hostile. On the other hand, when he expresses his exclusive identification with one of the sides, he may be considered as a supporter of the victimhood perception of that society. Then, too, he may lose his effectiveness.

It appears to me that switching empathic attunements from one side to the other and back again has higher potential to contribute than taking on the role of impartial witness. Switching empathic attunements enables each side to feel understood and totally supported in its suffering and aspirations, even though those on one side know that the other side, whom he views as an enemy, is also about to meet with understanding and attentiveness from the consultant. This position, when kept, turns the consultant into a figure who cannot be controlled by victimhood patterns. His complexity, as someone who speaks with the enemy and understands him as well, may be frustrating and infuriating, but it does contain the power to crack victimhood rigidity.

The third party should aim at achieving mutual recognition. Switching of empathic attunements may represent this attitude. By switching empathic attunement, the consultant declares that he recognizes each side's suffering and its need for concern. If the third party involved is viewed as not having worked hard enough to achieve mutuality, he may lose its status as an "honest mediator."

Some Personal Conclusive Comments

While writing this, encountering many historical evidences of violence, I found myself thinking that the world can be a better place if victimhood ideologies and leadership should

[2] This term is elaborated in Chapter 2.

be detected, diagnosed and outlawed. By suggesting victimhood social and national concept, I am trying to contribute something to our sobriety within overwhelming social forces that may engulf us to emotional experiences of "us" and "them" (Berman, Berger, and Gutmann, 2000), victims and perpetrators.

I found how difficult it may be to step out of the social emotional system and to gain sufficient estrangement that makes other points of view possible. Yet, it was encouraging to me to realize switching empathic attunement is possible even under the most emotional over-involved national situations. There is always someone on the other side who is looking for an alternative way, as I am right now.

BIBLIOGRAPHY

Akhtar, S. (2002). *The psychodynamic dimension of terrorism. Terrorism and war: Unconscious dynamics of political violence*. C. Covington, P. Williams, J. Arundale and J. Knox. London, Karnac: 87-96.

Beevor, A. (2002). *The Fall of Berlin* 1945. New York, Penguin Books.

Benjamin, J. (1990). Recognition and Destruction: An Outline of Intersubjectivity. *Relational Psychoanalysis: the Emergence of a Tradition*. S. A. Mitchell and L. Aron. London, The Analytic Press.

Benjamin, J. (2004). "Beyond Doer and Done to: An Intersubjective View of Thirdness." *Psychoanalytic Quarterly* 73: (1): 5-46.

Berman, A., M. Berger, et al. (2000). "The Division into Us and Them as a Universal Social Structure." *Mind and Human Interaction* 11: 53-72.

Bion, W. R. (1961). *Experiences un Group and Other Papers*, Tavistock Publications.

Elias, N. and J. Stocson (1994). *The Established and the Outsiders*. London, Sage.

Fogelman, E. (1998). "Group Belonging and Mourning as Factors in Resilience in Second Generation..." *Psychoanal. Rev*. 85: 537-549.

Foulkes, S. H. (1964). *Therapeutic Group Analysis*. London, Allen and Unwin.

Foulkes, S. H. and E. J. Anthony (1984). Group Psychotherapy: *The Psychoanalytical Approach*. London, Karnac.

Freud, S. (1917). *Mourning and melancholia*. Standard Edition. 14.

Freud, S. (1920-1922). "Group Psychology and the Analysis of the Ego." *The Standard Edition of the Complete Psychological Works of Sigmund Freud* 18: 65-144.

Govrin, A. (2006). "When the Underdog Schema Dominates the We-Ness Schema: The Case of Radical..." *Psychoanal. Rev*. 93: 623-654.

Horney, K. (1939). *New Ways in Psychoanalysis*. New York, Horton.

Montville, J. V. (1986). " A Diplomat among Psychoanalysts." *Psychoanal. Inq*. 6: 247-250.

Montville, J. V. (1989). "Psychoanalytic Enlightenment and the Greening of Diplomacy." *J. Amer. Psychoanal. Assn*. 37: 297-318.

Ruaschning, H. (1941). *Hitler Speaks: A Series of Political Conversation with Adolf Hitler on His Aims,* Kessinger Publishing.

Volkan, V. D. (1988). *Us and Them: The Psychology of Ethnocentrism*. New York, Brunner/Mazel.

Volkan, V. D. (1997). *Bloodliness: from Ethnic Pride to Ethnic Terrorism*. New York, Farrar Straus and Giroux.

Volkan, V. D. (2004). *Blind trust: Large Groups and Their Leaders in Times of Crisis and Terror*. Charlottesville, VA, Pitchstone Publishing.

Winnicot, D. W. (1967). "The Location of Cultural Experience." *International Journal of Psycho-Analysis* 48: 368-372.

PART TWO

Chapter 4

VENGEFULNESS AS A DISCREDITED EMOTION

Miriam Berger

If there is justice, let it appear at once!
But should it wait to appear until I am wiped out from under the sky,
Let its seat be overthrown forever!
(Hayim Nahman Bialik, "On the Slaughter")

I was about four years old, standing in a street in Kraków, my hand tightly held by my uncle. We were in the midst of a crowd of people, listening tensely to announcements coming through loudspeakers. I could not understand what was happening, what the announcements meant, or why people around me were shouting. It was as though the crowd had been electrified and its electrical current was going through me.

Years later, I learned that that day was September 13, 1946; the day of Amon Göth's hanging in Krakow.[1] The Supreme Polish Tribunal at Kraków had found him guilty of the murder of thousands of Jews and sentenced him to death. I also learned that my father had testified in his trial as one of the inmates of Płaszów, the labor camp Göth constructed and commanded, to which my father had been sent along with others who had survived the liquidation of the Kraków ghetto in March 1943. The execution took place at a site near Płaszów.

---

[1] In February 1943, Amon Göth, an SS officer, was assigned to construct and command a forced labor camp at Płaszów. The camp took one month to construct using slave labor. Then, on March 13, 1943, the Jewish ghetto of Kraków was closed down, with the surviving inhabitants imprisoned in the new labor camp. Approximately 2,000 people died during the evacuation. At his war crimes trial, Göth was accused of having personally shot many people during the evacuation. On September 3, 1943, Göth was further tasked to close down the ghetto at Tarnów, where an unknown number of people were killed on the spot. On February 3, 1944, Göth shut down the concentration camp at Szebnie by ordering the inmates to be murdered on the spot or deported to other camps, again killing several thousand people. He was also appointed a regular officer of the Waffen-SS. It was Göth's firm belief that the Jews themselves should pay for their own executions; it was in this spirit that, on May 11, 1942, the Gestapo ordered the Jewish council of the small town of Szczebrzeszyn to pay 2,000 zloty and 3 kilos of coffee to cover the expenses for the ammunition used to kill the town's Jews. In Płaszów, Göth tortured and murdered prisoners on a daily basis. During his time there, Göth allegedly shot over 500 Jews himself. Poldek Pfefferberg, one of the Schindler Jews, famously said, "When you saw Göth, you saw death."

Amon Göth was the epitome of evil. Justice was done.

The echo of those loudspeakers stayed with me for many years. As a small child, I unknowingly became a living witness to one of the worst manmade catastrophes in history, to its atrocities as well as to its heroic acts of dignity and courage. The utter destruction that accompanied my early life was also strewn with the noblest manifestations of humane concern.

I was born in January 1943, in the Krakow ghetto, a few weeks before its final liquidation. My father managed to smuggle me out of the ghetto, hidden in a bag he carried with him while marching to his daily labor site. After passing through the hands of several non-Jews, who were risking their lives by engaging in such forbidden actions, I found refuge with a Polish woman, a devout Catholic whose faith in Christian values motivated her to save my life; she raised me for almost three years, presenting me as her niece who had lost her parents in the war. It took me long years to realize that she lived with chronic fear for herself, for her family and for the baby she took upon herself to protect. Her neighbors were hunting Jews, and those who attempted to hide them risked the same lot: deportation and death.

My parents survived against all odds. My father was a "Schindler Jew"; my mother managed to escape the ghetto with forged "Aryan papers." She fled from one hiding place to another with some help from Polish friends. I think it is accurate to state that there is no such thing as a Holocaust survivor without a savior who risked his life to help.

My mother reappeared unexpectedly at the doorstep of my benefactor after the war to claim me back. From what I could gather later, it was a devastating event in the lives of everyone involved. As for myself, I must have been a vengeful child all set to protest and revolt — mostly against my mother, a "stranger" who showed up from nowhere to disrupt my life, to take me away from where I belonged.

When I finally settled with my family in Israel at the age of eight, I was a Jew baptized into Christianity, possessed seven names, spoke five different languages and had at least two passports. Acknowledging that what happened indeed did happen, struggling to incorporate these experiences into my personal life, to understand that they were "for real," becoming increasingly aware of their impact on my life, my work and on the society of which I am part — all these are ongoing processes that are represented in this work.

I suppose that my preoccupation with issues of revenge, evil, justice, accountability, acknowledgment along with the quest for human concern is rooted somewhere there in Krakow, between the executioners, the rescuers and the survivors. Since the time I started to *know*—in the real, experiential sense of the word—my history along with the emotional/cognitive issues it evoked (namely, mutuality, legitimacy, belonging and the capacity to feel a subject in one's own right) have been very much part of my involvement with those vital human concerns, personally and professionally.

This book is part of an ongoing, lifelong struggle with the aftermath of trauma, individually and socially. Working out a conceptual framework that enhances the capacity for mutual concern is (among other things) also an attempt to resist wrongdoing and injustice. Regrettably, I do not have any other effective ways to contribute directly to prevent the destructive processes engineered by society.

VENGEFULNESS: "A DISPOSITION TO RETURN EVIL FOR EVIL"

Vengefulness and its various ramifications stir up uneasiness.

Jean Améry (1980), to whose work about feeling vengeful I will refer throughout these chapters, concludes his poignant essay *Resentment* with a plea to bear with him and with those for whom he speaks: "We victims must finish with our retroactive rancor (in the sense the KZ argot once gave to the word 'finish'; it meant as much as 'to kill'). Soon we must and shall be finished. Until that time has come, we request of those whose *peace is disturbed by our grudge that they be patient*" (p. 81, my emphasis).

Whereas Améry describes his desire for vengeance as "grudge-holding" or "resentment," the Webster dictionary defines "revenge" as the desire "to see another suffer ... a disposition to return evil for evil." A "vindictive" person is one who "will look for accusations of resentment" or has "a bitterly vengeful character."

Dictionary definitions are mostly neutral; their aim is to describe the use of words and to point to their etymology. Language, however, is a living relational entity; it carries multilayered meanings that are embedded in shared realities and depend on social, cultural, and historical contexts. From this perspective, the dictionary definition of vengefulness as "the desire to see another suffer" is not a neutral description; it has derogatory and prohibitive connotations. In view of this definition, it is understandable that Améry would feel he needs to be apologetic when he claims recognition for his wishes for revenge and when he presents his attitudes towards vengefulness which he knows as being unacceptable.

Vengefulness seems to be out of place as a feeling, as an experience to think about, to talk about and to share with others. At the same time, revenge is very much part of our personal, social, and political reality. This discrepancy between the prevalence of vengeful behaviors and the paucity of psychological discourse about them is one of the issues I wish to explore in this chapter.

Another issue touches upon the very essence of all my arguments: why do I find a need to question the seemingly obvious truth that ill-wishing towards others is detestable? Isn't it self-evident that people should shun this type of attitude? Isn't vengefulness a threatening, destructive disposition that deserves denouncing? Does Améry endorse revenge while he should really strive to let go of past injuries and adopt a stance of forgiveness and reconciliation? Certainly such a standing would be more in line with nowadays sensibilities.

In response to these questions, I'd like to put forth a preliminary thought that will have to await fuller elaboration: I suggest that accepting Améry's need to "disturb" his fellow men with unpopular retributive claims can have a redeeming quality, not only for the victim but for everyone involved. The perpetrator's readiness to suffer by, for, and with the victim may help the victim build a bridge back from his sense of alienation and exclusion, into a culture that has faith in the capacity for mutual concern. In other words, the perpetrator who is ready to respond to this "disturbing claim" (namely, to acknowledge the rightfulness of the wish for revenge), who is willing to take responsibility for making the other suffer, receives a precious opportunity to make amendments for his wrongdoing. His acknowledgment of accountability is an invaluable move towards the re-inclusion of perpetrator and victim alike in the human community. The victim's claim for recognition and the perpetrator's act of acknowledgement are both needed, I suggest, in order to restore the bonds inherent in human connectedness. Victim and perpetrator both take part in the process of repairing a vital link broken by acts of violence. (I will shortly discuss in this context the myth of Cain and Abel; it is worth noting at this point, however, that the biblical Cain is the one who has to recognize his crime in order to live, while God claims revenge for Abel's murder.)

Améry states that if such an emotional link were created (that is, if Germans as well the European community recognized openly and explicitly their responsibility for the Holocaust crimes and denounced them adamantly), he would be able to forego his “grudge”; such recognition would make his vengefulness unnecessary in a deep sense. Since people are excruciatingly interconnected, since one’s feelings and needs mirror, shape, and resonate with the feelings and needs of others, others’ emotional participation in acknowledging one’s suffering and in recognizing the culpability of those who caused it is transformative, just as the lack of it constitutes a traumatic experience.

A quote by Mahatma Gandhi conveys this idea in a concise manner: “We must become the change we want to see.” Change in this context would entail the acknowledgment that vengefulness is related to vulnerabilities that are uniquely human and is therefore part of regular emotional exchanges between people. Acknowledging hard feelings and including them in our struggle to connect and to understand each other may help to humanize conflicts and to open up alternatives for a more peaceful coexistence than the last century has produced.

With this in mind, I go back to the task of exploring the issues at stake. Attempts to discuss vengefulness tend to become hostile, personally, socially, and professionally. Apparently, they “disturb peace” too much.

Vengefulness is considered low and primitive, inappropriate in the civilized, liberal Western culture in which we live. The disposition to express a desire “to return evil for evil” is excluded from legitimate social interactions and relegated to its backyards. Cultures that encourage personal “score-settling,” in which blood feuds and vendettas are “familial obligations,” are considered backwards, undeveloped and barbaric in the eyes of Western democratic society.

It appears that vengefulness goes against the grain of social sensitivity; modern discourse emphasizes connectedness, understanding, dialogue, and reconciliation. We tend to identify Western culture with constructiveness, hope and progress, whereas vengefulness is associated with destruction and regression. Thinking in terms of revenge, of “getting even,” is perceived as an “obstinate” stance that insists on looking backwards, on clinging to some dark, sinister past. Vengefulness is associated with unsettled scores that threaten to drag us down into an abyss of uncontrollable deeds.

These social attitudes towards vengefulness resonate in the professional community as well. To begin with, psychoanalysis deals with vengefulness very marginally (Stuckless, N. & Goranson, R., 1994). The few papers that care to address “revenge” as a distinct issue tend to see it as derivative of primitive emotional states or as a mental disorder in its own right. Vengeful fantasies, wishes, affects and behaviors are bound into one “bundle,” which is treated in a derogatory way. Since the *wish* for revenge is mostly identified with vengeful *acts*, it is met with condemnation. This condemning attitude is inherent in many of the dynamic understandings embedded in drive theories.

Much of the psychoanalytical discourse that adopts this line of thinking perceives vengefulness as a byproduct of raw aggressiveness, crude rage or pathological narcissism. It is rarely explored as an issue in its own right.

VENGEFULNESS, LITERATURE, DRAMA

As mentioned above, psychoanalysis largely avoids the subject of vengefulness. However, works of drama, literature, and popular entertainment have apparently known all along that there is something vitally inherent in the subject of revenge; its tremendous presence in such works is second only to the presence of religious subjects. From *Medea* to *Othello,* from *Spiderman* to *The Godfather*, vengefulness has been one of the most popular themes to hold our attention. The protagonists' suffering, their struggle against wrongdoing and evil, and the vengeful feelings they harbor, all form a perpetual focus of emotional involvement.

Literature and drama accord vengefulness a highly respectable position. It is central among the most meaningful subjects that have occupied authors of different periods. From Greek drama through Shakespeare to the latest action and suspense movies, vengefulness fuels the motivations of dramatic protagonists and sets innumerable plots in motion. It provides the organizing principle around which much dramatic action revolves; its dynamics shape the relationships between characters and provides a rationale for their actions.

The tapestry of narratives dealing with vengefulness is broad and deserves a separate discussion: such narratives are frequently excessive and bloody, ending up in the death of all parties involved. Plays that deal with vengefulness usually end up with a body-strewn stage of perpetrators and victims alike.[2]

CAIN AND ABEL: "AM I MY BROTHER'S KEEPER?"

The Bible introduces vengefulness early on, at the very beginning of human history: Cain kills his brother Abel, because God did not acknowledge ("*had not respect for*") his offering. Here is the biblical account of Cain and Able fully quoted:

> And Adam knew Eve his wife; and she conceived, and bare Cain, and said, I have gotten a man from the Lord. And she again bares his brother Abel. And Abel was a keeper of sheep, but Cain was a tiller of the ground. And in process of time it came to pass, that Cain brought of the fruit of the ground an offering unto the Lord. And Abel, he also brought of the firstlings of his flock and of the fat thereof. And the Lord had respect unto Abel and to his offering: *But unto Cain and to his offering he had not respect. And Cain was very wroth, and his countenance fell.* And the Lord said unto Cain, Why art thou wroth? And why is thy countenance fallen? If thou doest well, shall it not be lifted up? And if thou doest not well, sin coucheth at the door, and unto thee is its desire, but thou

[2] To mention just a few works of art that are engraved in our collective consciousness:

In *The Count of Monte Cristo* (Alexander Dumas, 1998), the eponymous protagonist returns to settle the score with a band of friends who destroyed his life and caused him to be imprisoned in a terrible isolated fortress for many years. A professional article (Castelnuovo-Tedesco, P., 1974) even coins a "Monte Cristo Syndrome" after the novel.

Moby Dick (Herman Melville, 2003) tells the saga of Captain Ahab, who seeks to avenge himself of the "Killer Whale" and sacrifices his life, his ship and all of its sailors in pursuit of the big "monster" who had taken his leg.

The protagonist of *Michael Kolhaas* (Von Kleist, 1997) burns down an entire town in response to the insult of having arbitrarily and unjustly been forced to pay border passage for his pair of horses.

mayest rule over him. And Cain spoke unto Abel his brother. And it came to pass, when they were in the field, that Cain rose up against Abel his brother, and slew him.

And the Lord said unto Cain, Where is Abel thy brother? And he said I know not: *Am I my brother's keeper?* And he said, What hast thou done? The voice of thy brother's blood crieth unto me from the ground. And now cursed art thou from the ground, which hath opened her mouth to receive thy brother's blood from thy hand; when thou tillest the ground, it shall not henceforth yield unto thee her strength; a fugitive and a wanderer shalt thou be in the earth. And Cain said unto the Lord, My punishment is greater than I can bear.[3] Behold, thou hast driven me out this day from the face of the earth; and from thy face shall I be hid; and I shall be a fugitive and a wanderer in the earth; and it shall come to pass, that whosoever findeth me will slay me. And the Lord said unto him, therefore whosoever slayeth Cain, vengeance shall be taken on him sevenfold. And the Lord set a sign upon Cain, lest any finding him should smite him. And Cain went out from the presence of the Lord, and dwelt in the land of Nod, on the east of Eden.
(*Genesis*, 4:1-16)

The biblical tale is somewhat cryptic and leaves room for our imaginative interpretations. As I see it, Cain's envious killing of his brother and his redemptive act of accepting guilt is a formative myth. God did not recognize Cain's offering and favored Abel's instead; we may say, then, that Cain avenges God's disregard by slaying his beloved "son" Abel. Upon God's intervention, Cain admits to his crime and accepts personal responsibility for what he had done. This act of acknowledgement on Cain's part safeguards his life and prevents the cycle of vengeful attacks and counterattacks that would commence otherwise. Cain's move from denying responsibility for his horrible deed to owning it becomes constitutive: it represents a passage from a culture of indifference to a culture of accountability.

It may be meaningful to mention that Cain is credited as the founder of civilization: he is the builder of the first city and the inventor of agriculture. I suggest that this story conveys the values inherent in human beings' belonging to society. Being part of the human community means, among other things, being bound to a culture of reciprocity; it signifies the existence of an "emotional agreement" about rights and obligations between Cain and Abel, between man and his brother, between self and other (even in face of God's failure to treat both his sons with due respect).

The biblical story may also be a symbolic depiction of the personal flourishing and strength that can grow out of one's readiness to acknowledge one's deeds, horrible as they may be. God himself takes it upon himself to rectify his act of non-recognition by protecting Cain and affording him an honored position in creating society. Thus, Cain's final acceptance of his guilt grants him the right for human life in a shared social reality. I shall return to this idea later (in Chapter 3) and further elaborate what to me is implied in being one's "brother's keeper."

[3] Whereas most English translations of the Bible render the Hebrew *avon* as "punishment," in modern Hebrew, the word usually takes the meaning of "crime." Traditional Jewish interpreters of the biblical story disagree on the word's meaning, and thus on the meaning of Cain's response. (For more on this, see Chapter 6 in this volume, especially footnote 9.)

VENGEFULNESS: A TWO-FACETED MATTER

My basic hunch, as already noted, is that the prevalence of revenge in art and popular entertainment indicates that it is an issue touching on central human concerns, though its depictions tend to emphasize its demonic and destructive facets.

The abundance of bloody, violent revenge narratives may be due to certain duplicity in our common attitude towards vengefulness. Such narratives disclose at least two opposing states of minds:

1. Fear and hostility towards vengefulness.
2. Attraction to and fascination with vengefulness.

This combination of fear and attraction compounds the difficulty, experienced both in psychoanalysis and in social affairs, to distinguish reality from fantasy, vengeful deeds from vengeful wishes, and feelings from acts.

The sweeping, indiscriminate stance of "bundling" feelings, on the one hand, and deeds, on the other, into one unified over-inclusive entity accords vengefulness an automatic condemnation; it obstructs our ability to understand its personal, interpersonal, social and clinical meanings.

Is it possible that we are warned time and again against revenge, because it is so much part of everyday relationships and so common in one's emotional repertoire? Since I claim vengefulness is both threatening and attractive, my answer is obviously a positive one; I will further address these complexities in the following chapters.

PSYCHOANALYTIC ATTITUDES TOWARDS VENGEFULNESS: THE NEGATIVE STANCE

As already noted, there are only a few articles devoted specifically to vengefulness, its motivations and the dynamic processes it involves. Most of their discourse (Boris, 1986; Socarides, 1966; Steiner, 1996; Arlow, 1980; and others) is rooted in Freudian/Kleinian drive theories, which view vengefulness as a sign of emotional pathology. According to these theories, vengefulness characterizes the disturbed among us, those who have not worked through their raw emotions properly and whose level of developmental functioning is low.

Following are several representative statements that illustrate this rather hostile and critical approach.

Boris (1986) points out that revenge was one of the "plagues" that escaped from Pandora's Box along with envy, greed, contempt, and the like; these he classifies as the "curses of the soul," while rheumatism, gout and other various "poisons" are the "curses of the body" (p. 47). Boris claims that Pandora's myth faithfully depicts vengefulness as one of the destructive "plagues of the mind," whose aim is to deplete other individuals of any goodness they may possess. Following Klein (1975), he believes that the infant is boundlessly greedy and avaricious; it seeks to control the mother's abundance in order to overcome its survival anxiety and its dread of its own inborn aggression.

It is worth noting what Boris neglects to mention; namely, that at the very bottom of Pandora's Box lay hope.[4] It seems that ancient human wisdom acknowledged that letting vengefulness out of the closet bears some good news as well.

From Boris' perspective, however, vengefulness is a projection of an innate death instinct onto the vital object, upon which the infant is so dependent. In his view, the Kleinian infant attributes its own aggression to the nurturing mother, thus defeating her and gaining control over its own unbearable inner emptiness and helplessness. This defensive maneuver provides the infant with a sense of vengeful "victory" that maintains an illusion of safety and self-worth. The developmental move is towards a "depressive position" ; namely, a sad realization that one is aggressive, deficient and dependent on the mother's goodness; one can now humbly acknowledge one's own guilt for being so avaricious and one's gratitude for the mother's goodness and for her giving.

Socarides (1966) writes in a similar vein:

> The vengeful person is defective in his ability to love and to bear frustration. He attacks others around him because they represent the bad breast, the rejecting father, the lost penis... The person is grudgeful, unforgiving, remorseless, ruthless, heartless, implacable, and inflexible. He lives for revenge with a single-mindedness of purpose ... [A]bove all other desires is the one to "get even" ... He does not experience guilt. He shows no concern about the possible moral and social consequences of his act (p.357)

Steiner (1996) argues that although vengefulness may appear as a response to injustice and a desire for justice and reparation, it is in fact derivative of destructive envy stemming from innate destructive instincts.

The implications of these ideas are that vindictiveness is a shameful, mindless, infuriating and primitive emotion that is more indicative of the deficiencies of its carrier than of the object of the retributive wish.

Needless to say, this professional stance is rather far removed from the requirements of analytic "neutrality"; patients may be reluctant to share vengeful fantasies with their therapists, or even to be in touch with them, in order to protect themselves from criticism and shaming. This makes it even harder to explore the subject in an open, unbiased manner.

It should be mentioned that these psychoanalytical approaches view themselves as representing scientific objectivity. By contrast, I prefer to apply a postmodern perspective to the dynamics of vengeful wishes. I believe that our categories of knowledge are manmade, socially constructed, shaped, and organized, and subject to the power structures of knowledge, to its hierarchies and interests. Hence, definitions of pathology or normalcy are context dependent, determined by the norms prevalent in given social constellations; they reflect "the eyes of the beholder" rather than any objective "truth" that may be attributed to them. In light of this, the psychoanalytical approaches described above cannot be viewed as anything but biased.

---

[4] Pandora had been given a large jar, which Zeus instructed her to keep closed. But she had also been given the gift of curiosity, and so she ultimately opened the jar. All the evils, ills, diseases, and burdensome labors that had previously been unknown to mankind escaped from the jar; but at the very bottom of the jar lay hope.

VENGEFULNESS: A DISCREDITED FEELING

It seems to me that not all feelings are equal; since “the eyes of the beholder” determine their lot, some may be more legitimate than others, vengefulness being one of the more “banished” ones.

An example may illustrate this “banishing” attitude. In a recent paper about revenge and its dynamic meanings, Rosen (2007) talks about his own experience of avoiding feelings of revenge. Rosen was speaking to colleagues who had forced him to retire from an institute in which he had held a significant position:

> Speaking at the farewell dinner of the Topeka Institute, I said of the moment, “Feelings of pride, sadness, gratitude, anger, love, loss, and accomplishment shift rapidly within me, like the bits of glass in a turning kaleidoscopic lens”... *Revenge remained unacknowledged and unspoken* (p. 616, my emphasis)

His vengeful feelings towards the colleagues who had forced him to retire, to lose his cherished position at the institute and his identity as an honored member of their society, remained silent.

Understanding such attitudes towards vengeful feelings in the professional community and in society as a whole is no less important than understanding the feelings themselves. Vengefulness, the wish to retaliate, "to return evil for evil" is, I believe, a socially discredited feeling. My suggestion is that *socially discredited feelings* are transformed into *dissociated self-states*, and vice versa. In other words, an individual who harbors socially discredited feelings attempts to distance himself from them. The act of dissociation from vital parts of one’s personal experience (whether conscious or unconscious) may cause a sense of alienation from one's inner world as well as from his relationships with others. Dissociated self-states thus reinforce the social discrediting of the denigrated feelings, and vice versa; thus, inner and outer realities define each other and create continuous cycles that are difficult to discern.

One’s self-definition depends to a great extent on the social, historical, and cultural context in which one lives. The feelings one is in touch with and those one is detached from are not merely manifestations of one’s private world or personal history. They are part of a matrix woven out of one’s interconnectedness with one’s community; they are shaped by the context of one’s life and relationships in given situations (Dalal, 1998; Hooper, 2002).

Victims might thus feel twice discredited: once because of what had been done to them, and once again for having the “wrong” feelings about it. Thus, forgiveness, reconciliation and acceptance are the prescribed states of mind that accord social approval and legitimacy (Lansky, 2001, 2005); vengefulness, along with other ways of protesting one’s lot, is proscribed.

Excerpts from Jean Améry’s book (1980) can help illustrate what I have in mind. In a number of essays, Holocaust survivor Améry presents his thoughts about the vengeful anti-German feelings he has harbored in loneliness and growing isolation since the war.

Améry, a Jewish intellectual and a member of the Belgian underground, was arrested by the Gestapo in 1943. He was severely tortured and then sent to Auschwitz. After his liberation, he wrote a book of essays documenting his war experiences, including his thoughts and feelings about what had happened to him. He describes his very painful encounter with a post-war Europe that did not genuinely wish to acknowledge or to account for the atrocities of the Holocaust. Since the deeds to which he had been subjected were neither really acknowledged nor truly owned by the community responsible for them, he felt that he had become an inconvenient burden by his insistence in expressing explicitly what has been silenced,; his persistent "grudging" demands for accountability ostracized him from others who wished to "move on" and alienated him even from himself. He finally committed suicide in 1978, as did Primo Levi, Bruno Bethlehem and other noted Holocaust survivors with similar experiences.

Levi, who had suffered a similar lot and identifies with Améry's experiences, reveals his wishes for vengeance quite explicitly:

> If I were a judge, even though repressing what hatred I might feel, I would not hesitate to inflict severe punishment or even death on the many culprits who still today live undisturbed on German soil or in other countries of suspect hospitality (Levi 1988, pp. 184-185).

Levi's identification with Améry's stance toward his own discredited "resentment" against the perpetrators touches the core of the emotional reality the two authors share. As Levi writes on the back cover of Améry's reissued collection of essays, "these are pages that one reads with almost physical pain all the way to their stoic conclusion." Améry's pain speaks for itself and "bears witness" not only to the atrocities to which he was subjected but also to the humiliation and shame that vengeful wishes can evoke. Améry spells out bitterly the fear that his own "despicable nature," which he shares with other "spiteful ones," will be exposed and that once again he will be excluded and declared as the non-person he was turned into during the war. The vicious cycle of contempt, humiliation and rejection thus perpetuates itself, as one "joins forces" against oneself, justifying one's own exclusion.

The person who harbors vengeful wishes in his heart (whether a Holocaust survivor or "just" an ordinary person hurt within mundane interactions) may see himself as defective and unworthy; he may, therefore, hide the existence of such wishes even from himself, as a way to protect himself from the unbearable emotional pain that threatens to flood a person who comes close to touching upon unacceptable, and therefore shaming emotional states.

Victims of violence stand the danger of being perceived as "carriers of bad news." Their pitiful state may signify the existence of evil that manifests itself in practices of injustice, abuse, abandonment and isolation; those practices generate a sense of defeat, helplessness, humiliation, and indignity – unbearable emotional realities that orderly society prefers to keep silent about, evade and ignore (Howell, 2002; Herman, 1992).

The encounter with the loss of human dignity threatens to be overwhelming, not only for the victim of violence, but for those he is connected to as well. The aftermath of trauma, along with the people marked by it, is therefore expelled from the community's collective consciousness and wiped away from its memory. Victims and society alike join forces (consciously as well as unconsciously) to uphold pacts of silence about the willful infliction of injury and its catastrophic consequences; they collude in the dynamic process of removing the "bad news" from explicit discourse in order to maintain a sense of safe and orderly existence.

De-legitimized dissociated feelings, wishes, fantasies and needs do not simply disappear. Rather, they are more likely to go into hiding, to acquire a status of "illegal aliens" and to damage even further the self-esteem of those who are subjected to maltreatment and to the feelings it evokes. Améry expresses these thoughts poignantly:

> What matters to me is the description of the subjective state of the victim. What I can contribute is the analysis of resentments, gained from introspection. My personal task is to justify a psychic condition that has been condemned by moralists and psychologists alike: The former regard it as a taint and the latter as a kind of sickness. I must acknowledge it, bear the social taint and first accept the sickness as an integrating part of my personality [...] I must delimit our resentments on two sides, and shield them against two explications: that of Nietzsche, who morally condemned resentment, and that of modern psychology which is able to picture it only as a disturbing conflict (p. 64-68)

Vengefulness: Relational Emotional Communication

Améry's call to recognize his feelings as legitimate, even justified, is finally being heeded by some psychoanalysts and clinicians. Several psychoanalytic approaches that denounce the traditional hostility towards vengefulness (as towards other strongly felt hard feelings, like rage, hatred or envy) have emerged in recent years (Davies and Frawley, 1994; Feiner, 1995; Herman, 1992; Grand, 2000; Orenstein et al., 1983; Howell, 2002; Laub, 1985, 1989; and others). It is as if these newer approaches respond to Améry's poignant personal quest, in the name of all victims, that he be heard, that his "subjective state" be taken into account. They grant recognition of the reality of the brutal abuse he was subjected to, as well as of his vengeful feelings towards those who inflicted it. Some of these newer psychoanalytic works pertain specifically to Holocaust survivors, to victims of prolonged torture, violence, abuse and extreme degradations. Their authors deal with trauma, its aftermath and emotional consequences, basing much of their writings on clinical experience with post-traumatic patients. To set off the process of healing, they try to be attuned to the patients' specific needs without overly resorting to traditional explanations about the dynamics of inner destructive drives. In addition, they explore the emotional processes of disruption and repair in daily relationship on a much more mundane scale. It is evident from their conceptualization that "normal" difficulties, like abandonment, isolation and ("impingements" is Winnicott's definition for these relational wounds) can engender vengefulness, as well as other feelings like shame, rage, hatred submissiveness and self-loathing. These feeling states (or "self-states" as they have come to be defined by some relational writers) acquire a meaningful communicative function: they call one's own attention as well as the attention of others to relational ruptures that need to be addressed and acknowledged.

On the whole, psychoanalysts who have somewhat "softer" approaches towards vengefulness seem to be rooted in the relational tradition (Mitchell, 1998). They strive to create a more tolerant, accepting and emphatic therapeutic stance towards the vulnerabilities inherent in human interconnectedness. They emphasize the crucial significance of real relationships, of human ties (or the lack of them) and explore the feelings that are generated and shaped by relational exchanges. As for vengefulness, they tend to view vengeful wishes as normal, understandable, and even important emotional responses to manmade injuries.

From this perspective, a "defective symptom" (see Améry's quote) may turn out to be a meaningful communicative message about one's traumatic history; it may be understood as a coded personal biography pointing to experiences of rupture and emotional injuries waiting to be deciphered, witnessed, authenticated, and mourned properly with empathic others. Such an involved human presence can assist in the process of healing one's wounds and re-including one into shared reality.

Kohut (1972), one of the great advocates of the healing power of whole-hearted empathic acceptance by a significant other, says in this context:

> The uncompromising and unquenchable demand for justice is the response to a fatal personal narcissistic injury... The need for revenge, for righting a wrong, for undoing a hurt by whatever means, and a deeply anchored, unrelenting compulsion in the pursuit of all these aims, gives no rest to those who have suffered a narcissistic injury (p. 380, my emphasis)

As I understand it, this "fatal injury" occurs as a result of being dismissed, invalidated and disqualified as a person who counts. Not counting (whether in everyday interactions or in situations of extreme abuse) injures one's dignity; it consists of a failure to be recognized by others as a subject in one's own right; it entails discounting one's self-agency and dismissing one's authorship and sovereignty.

Reciprocity is a most meaningful dimension in relationships and in personal development. Disruptions in reciprocity are detrimental to one's growth in every sense. People are utterly connected and dependent on each other. These facts of excruciating interrelatedness, vulnerability, and mutual shaping generate utmost sensitivity to acknowledgment by others.

I think that vengefulness is one expression among many others of this unique human sensitivity. In this respect, it constitutes a "social feeling" (along with envy, love, hatred, and shame). It informs us that the relational matrix has been disrupted, that the waters in which we are swimming has become stormy. In other words, vengefulness tells us that something in the processes of reciprocity, mutual acknowledgment, and connectedness has been disrupted and needs repair. Vengefulness is thus related to the process of mutual recognition or rather to the lack of it.

Vindictive Wishes: A Quest for Mutual Acknowledgment

According to the intersubjective perspective in psychoanalysis (Benjamin, 1990; Mitchell, 1988), mutual recognition is a central factor in the development of a person's identity as a subject. One's ability to experience oneself as an equal, as a subject among other subjects is a function of acknowledgment and recognition by others. The capacity for mutuality and coexistence is an outcome of human interconnectedness, of recognition by others of the autonomy of each individual's unique subjectivity.

Mutual acknowledgment can be thought of as a separate developmental line (Benjamin, 1990). It forms a link between one's private life and one's social realities; it encompasses a relational space where the intrapersonal and the interpersonal, the inner world and the world of relationships with others, can meet.

Following these ideas, I would like to emphasize that the notion of mutual recognition is an emotional process suffused with personal and social meanings that are not easy to identify and take into account. Some of the feelings it is charged with are fear, hatred, rage, sorrow and loneliness; on the other hand, it can also generate pride, expansion, joy, a sense of growth in one's self-worth, connectedness and belonging. Mutual recognition involves passion; it is an emotional process of becoming *mindful* of others as separate, yet interconnected centers of initiative.

The nature of mutual recognition is paradoxical and cyclical: one's need for the other's recognition is an acknowledgment that this other is indeed a subject whose recognition is valuable; otherwise, it would be pointless to need his or her recognition.[5]

These reciprocal cycles expand one's emotional and cognitive range and deepen one's capacity to be an involved partner in the community he belongs to. Vengefulness, I believe, is very much part of these emotional processes; it may be perceived as a response to disruptions in the process of mutual recognition, a call for repair, an attempt at self-remedy in the face of troubles in the area of reciprocity.

Stated differently, the central role that mutual recognition plays in the creation and development of "subject relations" is closely related to the restorative-communicative functions of vindictiveness. Disruptions in mutual recognition and the vengeful wishes they evoke may thus be perceived as a common fact of mental life. They may be experienced in different subjective ways depending on the constellation and the context in which they occur, but I think they share a common ground: namely, they express various degrees of vulnerability regarding reciprocity; they denote sensitivity about self-esteem, connectedness and belonging.

Mutual Recognition and Vengefulness: Neither an Overarching Formula nor a Panacea to All Relational Injuries

The idea that vengefulness is interconnected with mutual recognition is by no means to be understood as a sweeping generalization that all manifestations of vengefulness are due to disruptions in mutual recognition or that each and every instance of non-recognition breeds vengefulness. I do not suggest that mutual recognition is a panacea for all the ills that vengefulness can generate nor that lack of recognition is the only reason for vengefulness. The compounds of emotional processes that comprise mutual recognition and vengefulness cannot be reduced to any simple equation. Human violence, evil deeds, and lack of concern for others are interwoven in complex ways with the capacity for concern, coexistence, and cooperation. The nature of this tapestry evades simple, clear-cut explications.

My aim in this chapter and in the ones that follow is to explore the relations of interdependence between vengefulness and mutual recognition. I suggest that a focused look into the interface between them may contribute to our understanding of certain relational

---

[5] Elster (1990) claims that recognition is worthless unless reciprocated by an equal other: "to ask for esteem from a slave is like a nation asking diplomatic recognition from one of its colonies" (p. 884). This idea has its source in Hegel's so-called "master-slave dialectic," in the "Mastery and Slavery" section of the *Phenomenology of Spirit* (1977, pp. 111-119).

processes, especially as they manifest themselves in our clinical work. I think that exploring the links between mutual acknowledgment and vengefulness lends us an additional lens through which to examine therapeutic relationships. This link can be especially productive when one strives to open up stalemates in therapy; it has clinical value in enhancing developmental processes.

With these restrictions in mind, I return to my arguments with the hope that I will be able to show their usefulness in the clinical setting as well as outside of it. The idea that vengefulness is as much a normal part of our emotional repertoire as the need for mutual recognition is relevant to most of the thoughts put forward in what follows.

Lack of Recognition: The Ultimate Injury

Lack of recognition may constitute the ultimate injury. In its extreme forms, it is a threat to one's ability to trust the authenticity of his actual lived experience and to feel he is entitled to struggle with his conflicts, make his decisions and be an independent agent of his actions. Discrediting weakens one's hold on personal reality and replaces it by the will of powerful others one submits to as a survival strategy. It can be felt as a negation of one's unique subjectivity and of one's right to a life of one's own; it generates shame, humiliation and fear, which in turn give rise to vengeful wishes and sometimes even to violent actions against self and others.

As I see it, to be recognized is to be granted a legitimate existence in the other's mind, and hence to have a mind of one's own. Subjectivity is a function of intersubjectivity (Benjamin 1990, Mitchell 1988). Recognition validates one's right to have a personal history, a personal name, a unique identity. It constitutes a sense of belonging, of being counted as a member in one's community. Recognition provides the regard by others–"the holding in mind"–that one needs in order to feel as a subject in one's own right.

Lack of recognition is not necessarily a single identifiable and discrete traumatic event; it can be perceived as an ongoing process that is actually part of the common flow of life, somewhere on a continuum between daily incidents of oversight in the course of normal relations and a deadly injury that can destroy the self and obliterate its existence.[6] Its manifestations may take various forms: domination and subjugation, prejudice in daily affairs, arbitrary demands for obedience, "educational" corporeal punishment, disregard, contempt, mockery, or plain indifference. Each of these moves can make people feel irrelevant, dismissed, frightened and worthless; it shatters their belief that they count.

Being hurt by others and wishing to "get even" is common enough. We do not need to consider extreme cases of victimization in order to learn that relationships are fraught with clashes of wills and conflicting motivations on a daily basis. Reciprocity entails continuous negotiations between competing needs, desires, interests and goals. One's personal choices, preferences or priorities may be experienced by an other as an intentional abandonment, as a relinquishing of commitments or disregard to personal urgent needs. Thus, mutual

[6] My four-year-old granddaughter declares, "*I* decide about me! I make up my own mind myself!" The bone of contention is the ice cream she wants, instead of the healthy salad I urge her to eat. It takes me a while to understand that the issue is not the nutritional value of the salad as compared to ice cream, but a meaningful declaration about her claim to autonomy and self-determination.

dismissiveness is as much part of relationships as mutual understanding and concern can be; it is very much part of the ongoing processes that make the fabric of relationships. Slights that are acknowledged have a chance to be redeemed. Accepting vindictive wishes (hatred towards the offender, the desire to punish him and “get even”) as common and legitimate enables us to abandon vengeful acts and make an effort to reach an understanding.

Viewing vengefulness as a normal part of relationships, as an emotional signal that indicates a disruption in reciprocity that needs repairing, can promote growth. Placing vengefulness as a quest for mutual acknowledgment and accountability, as one state of mind among others releases, our thinking from the grip of the bloody narratives in which it is trapped. It contributes to the capacity to tolerate difference and helps open up channels of understanding and cooperation that may otherwise be blocked.

VENGEFULNESS: THERAPEUTIC ASPECTS

I believe that viewing vindictive wishes as a response to disruptions in mutual recognition has clinical value. Such a therapeutic stance aids the therapist in joining the patient “from within”; it enables the therapist to “get into the patient’s shoes,” to identify with his pain and acknowledge his experiences. This acknowledgment provides the connectedness that non-recognition had ruptured.

If we urge the (so-called) victim “to get on with his life,” he may feel we are inviting him back into the same shaming experience to which he was subjected in the past. For those who had been disregarded and made humanly irrelevant, the pressure to be reconciled with the offender may be experienced as a request to release the offender from responsibility for his actions; it may be perceived as an abandonment that enables the offender to evade accountability and retribution; it leaves the injured person as lonely as ever, if not more so.

R., a Holocaust survivor, suspects that her therapist "urges her" unjustly to "move on"; to be more tolerant and less judgmental towards her brother’s rigidity, his raging outbursts and controlling manners; when she senses that her therapists does not accept wholeheartedly her resentment and bitter complains about her brother ("the big, conceited bully"), she becomes angry and desperate; she feels humiliated and abandoned by both of them and left completely alone in the world. R. and her older brother are the only survivors of their large family who lived in Warsaw. He somehow managed to save both of them as a boy of twelve. Nowadays, his mental condition is deteriorating, after a number of suicidal attempts that were culminated by prolonged psychiatric hospitalizations. R. perceives him as her main tormentor and demands the therapist's acknowledgment of her "just" need for retribution, even though it is evident that the target of her "resentment" is misplaced in this given situation *("First, he left me alone in the convent ;after I finally got used to those nuns, to the cruelty of the life in that place, he suddenly came back and took me out by force");* she can become quite relentless in her anguished need for the therapist’s unquestioning identification with her pain; her “stubborn resentment" and refusal to “forgive and forget” is a bitter reminder of the psychological truth embedded in the desire for revenge; R.'s distorted perceptions and her difficulties in her relationship with her brother are part of the traumatic wounds she carries from the war; they constitute central issues in the arduous, painful therapeutic process she undergoes.

The words of another patient, N., may illustrate this point in more mundane terms without resorting to the extreme evil of the Holocaust:

> I went to my mother in tears and told her what my husband had done to me. She said, "It always takes two to tango." I became a suspect right away; she urged me to go back home and make up with him. "You have to maintain the peace in your family. This is the most important thing." She told me she, too, had suffered all of her life from my father's violent outbursts, but had stayed with him nevertheless "for the children's sake."
> I could do nothing. I returned to my husband; I didn't have anywhere else to go.

Another patient, L., talks about an interaction she had with her mother; her description can illustrate some of the points I've made about the links between vengefulness, impingement, lack of mutual recognition, and injuries to self-esteem.

> L. meets her mother on her way out of the house. The mother interrogates her daughter, as she always does: Where is she going "out-of-the-blue," at this time of day? L. is upset. She lives next door to her mother and feels she was caught again, as usual. Then, all of a sudden, a feeling of revolt and protest surges in her: she turns to her mother and declares forcefully: "I'm going to the mental health clinic for therapy. It's your entire fault. I've been going there for years, but it's useless; I am no good. You have done me in."
>
> She continues:
>
> At first, I didn't want to answer her. She's always got her eye on me, following me everywhere. She always has her questions: what am I doing, what for, why now? I always give in and say something just to get by. She doesn't know about the therapy. I was about to go through the same routine again, but something stopped me; I wanted to punish her; to throw it in her face that she's the guilty one. I wanted her to know that I cannot cope with anything, that I am nobody. I really wanted her to finally know what she has done to me.
> Therapist: You're angry with your mother.
> L.: Not angry. I want to scream, so she'll see for herself what it feels like to be under her foot, to be afraid, dominated and helpless.
> She never let me do anything without prying; only when I went into the army, I could get away from her; I lied and pretended that staying overnight was demanded by the job I was assigned to do. It felt good then to sneak away from her watching.

L. feels worthless, helpless and angry. She needs her mother's acceptance and understanding, which are not granted; her response is to "get even," to punish her mother, to make her accountable for her wrongdoing. As far as L. is concerned, she has "succeeded" in rendering her mother as defeated and helpless as she herself feels; by finally "telling" her what she has done to her, she has initiated (albeit rather unconsciously) a move back towards a reciprocal relational state. Now, her mother "knows" that she has failed as a mother, just as L. "knows" she is "no good." Thwarted as this equation may be, L. feels that she has regained a state of mutuality; now, they are finally equals.

If she manages to make her mother suffer, she "counts"; now her mother will be able to identify with her, to feel with her and for her. From L.'s point of view, the broken connection between them has a chance to mend.

On this understanding, the meeting described above can be perceived as a turning point in L.'s therapy; an active move towards reconnecting, towards regaining self-esteem and personal dignity. It may well be part of a process of repair in L.'s relationship with her mother.

Non-recognition constitutes a double blow: Being brushed off is bad enough in itself, but in addition, it may cause self-abnegation. In other words, what has been done to one, one now does to oneself: one "erases oneself" and becomes a walking declaration of a negative self-definition. A patient in a therapy group thus responded to a critical comment directed at her by saying:

> I'm stupid. I don't have anything to contribute; everyone else here is so much cleverer than I. I will just stop talking and keep quiet.

Feiner (1966) defines this state as an "anti-self self-definition," while others speak of "no-self," "non-person" or "un-person."

Fairbairn (1943) is a foremost spokesman for the idea that an abusive environment settles into one's soul as an experience of personal "badness." Holding onto this "badness," thwarted and destructive as it may be, is still to be understood as an attempt to preserve hope and faith in basic "goodness." According to him, this is more of a default than a choice, as "it is better to be a sinner in a world ruled by God than to live in a world ruled by the devil" (p. 110). A person may thus sentence himself to "non-existence" as a protective shield against living in a godless world. This may well be one of the ways in which a pathological process of feeling victimized settles in and calcifies into a syndrome of "victimhood" (Berman in this volume).

M., a patient, talks about his growing up with parents that neglected his basic needs to be seen "held in mind" and taken care of adequately. He currently experiences great difficulties attending to the demands and needs of his old, ailing mother:

> My parents were busy fighting with each other, moving from one house to the next and having love affairs, each one in his or her turn. If I was around, they would both start with me: why don't I do better in school, why do I make myself such a nuisance; I used to walk the streets for hours, just to away from home as much as possible, to avoid their blaming and beatings. They "knew" I was "brilliant but lazy"; I was "trouble"; failing in school "just out of spite." Now, my mother is old, stay weak and ill, but I can't take care of her. I feel too bitter. I have an account with the world.

I think vengeful wishes are meant to keep precisely such *"an account with the world."* They communicate unbearable feelings; they provide a self-applied remedy meant to recover one's dignity and self-esteem; they fulfill meaningful socio-psychological functions, although they are often expressed in insidious, distorted ways that may be destructive to those who bear them.

As mentioned, the biased attitude towards vengefulness obstructs the ability to explore it openly, to understand its meanings and to facilitate a restorative process. I think that the ability to perceive vengeful wishes as normal responses to disruptions in mutual recognition can contribute to their humanization and ameliorate the demonic dimensions that make them so detestable for professionals and laypersons alike.

Clinical Vignette

Following is an example of disruptions in mutual recognition, as manifested in the life of Guy, a patient who sought therapy because he was depressed and anxious about the prospects of his relationship with his girlfriend. I will relate to his difficulties through a lens that explores the impact that denial of vengefulness may have on one's relations with himself and others.

From this point of view, Guy and his girlfriend hurt and punish each other unconsciously in various ways. The course of the process demonstrates that Guy's ability to get in touch with his injured feelings, to acknowledge his need for warmth and encouragement, is closely related with his growing awareness that he is being vengeful and punitive towards his girlfriend.

My aim in presenting this vignette in some detail is to illustrate, first, the workings of unacknowledged vengefulness and, second, the transformative value of owning up to a wish to punish the relevant other. It goes without saying that this therapeutic relationship is much more complex and contains multiple developmental and relational issues that exceed the scope of this work.

Guy: Growing into Accountability and Self-Agency

Guy, a thirty-five-year-old divorced man, father of a ten-year-old girl, who works in the security business is having a hard time defending his wish to buy himself a car:

> It's been years since I've owned a car. Consequently, my freedom and independence have been limited. I am constantly in need for favors and ask my mother to bring my kid back home from school. Now, with the new job, the first thing I want to buy is a car.

His girlfriend thinks that this is an unnecessary expenditure, another indication of "egoism" on his part: he is "putting his needs above hers." She wants him to invest his money in an apartment for the two of them. She sees in his plan a disregard for her need to build a home. As far as she's concerned, his priorities show lack of commitment to their relationship, another proof that he will not be able to become a responsible father for the children they will have in the future.

In the current state of their relationship, after a long period of angry arguments, his reaction to her complaints is to ignore her: "I don't hear her. It goes into one ear and out the other. Eventually, she'll get over this constant blaming, she'll get used to me."

At the beginning of their relationship, he used to make a special effort to explain himself; he was attentive, identified with her difficulties, was supportive of her desire to move up and improve their social standing. He invested a lot in proving he was worthy of her. However, it appeared as though his efforts had been in vain. His girlfriend was not convinced he really took her into account. The arguments continued, as did the increasing sense of distress to both of them. "I don't have the energy to keep fighting all the time," he says; "she is stronger than me." He becomes distant, evasive, shuts himself down and despairs.

It appears he'll buy the car he wants anyway, without telling her. She, for her part, feels that her need for a safe place with a responsible and accessible partner, someone she can truly rely on, is not acknowledged by him. After all, he promised her the world, but delivered nothing. So far he had not found his place in any job, left his studies halfway through, and never showed consistency in anything he took up. "It's all just talk," she says. He agrees shamefully: "She is right; I am no good."

The relationship is gradually in danger of disintegrating.

When Guy first came to treatment, he feared he was losing his girlfriend. He felt he was failing on all fronts. As mentioned, he thought that his girlfriend was right in her claims against him. Actually, he was "sent" to therapy by her. For his part, he came to please her. He was in despair and saw himself as hopelessly "weak," not deserving the trust he was given. He was scared by his uncontrolled rage attacks that lately had been growing stronger.

During therapy, he began to notice that while his girlfriend was urging him to study, to work, to "move up," she also saw him as an uneducated "barbarian" with no social standing. Only after a sustained period in treatment did he become aware that the way she used to encourage him turned out to be another factor in his downfall. Guy started to realize how embarrassed and humiliated he felt both by his lack of achievements and by her emphasis on his deficiencies. He could not bring himself to stand up to her, nor could he cope with the difficulties he encountered in his work. He felt stuck within but had a growing sense that her encouragements had a hidden "muscle" of criticism attached to them; they were demeaning and humiliating.

He started to realize that the prevailing feeling he had towards his girlfriend was fear rather than love. He tended to protect himself from shame and humiliation in ways that have become an issue unto itself. His defensive attempts to "save face" were manifested in distancing, avoidance and lying; he would tell her "stories" and become caught in a web of inaccuracies, feeling he was tying a rope around his own neck just to survive another turn of shaming arguments.

These interactions escalated gradually, undermining what little trust still existed between them.

However, as I saw it, his defensive strategies were not merely reactive. They included an active side of punishment and vindictiveness as well. They constituted an element of "fighting back"; a hidden desire to protest his girlfriend's domination and defeat her purposes was at work, although in a very indirect evasive manner. Unknowingly, he felt that each time he failed, she was going down with him; he sabotaged "her" goals for him to spite her, to "show her" what being it feels like to be a failure, albeit he did it unconsciously without owning up to any "doing" on his part. He was used to being in touch with *what was done to him*; much less so with *what he was doing*.

My suggestion that there was a vengeful side to his behavior, that he was actually "doing" something while perceiving himself as reactive only, started finally to catch his interest and to sink in. He became aware that he was "getting back" at his girlfriend and punishing her for her attempts to gain control over him and for ignoring both his difficulties and his contributions, although he himself was not able to be direct or explicit about what he felt or what he needed. It was very difficult for him to realize that he actually did have some sort of a personal presence, that he did have an impact, that he exerted power on others whether he acknowledged it or not.

Embarrassing and shaming as it was, and at times too foreign to his self-image, it turned out that he could hurt his girlfriend just as she was hurting him. He was not only afraid of her but also frightening and threatening to her in his own right. The idea that there is no such thing as "non-behavior" and that he was a willful (even if unintentional) participant in reciprocal interactions was a growing issue in the therapeutic process.

Guy's (unconscious) attempts at "self-cure"—failing, distancing, "turning a deaf ear" to his girlfriend's pleas—seemed to create further problems, as he really did feel incapacitated and helpless. He realized painfully that the price he was paying for this "self-remedy" was quite high; it threatened to become too destructive to him and his loved ones.

This growing awareness supported a long process of retrieving a sense of self-agency, of owning up to feelings, wishes, decisions, and behaviors, whether good or bad, intentional or "just happening" as if by accident.

Guy was used to being an object of pressures that were put upon him by his caretakers. His self-state as an initiator of feelings or actions was not part of the perception he had about who he was; he had great difficulties in understanding that he did have some say in his life, despite the fact that he felt he was totally powerless. In his words:

> I was always attracted to powerful women. They were the ones who had the ambitions, the ones who decided things... They always knew what I should want, do or feel. I was frightened and promised to deliver whatever they asked me to. I never managed to stand behind what I said, couldn't really do it when it came to it....

The vignette, as told so far, represents only one part of a complex therapeutic process. Since my aim here is to emphasize the dimension of vengefulness in that process, I would like to add a look at the vengefulness-related transference effects that played themselves out in our relationship. It was very important for me to feel with Guy to be in touch with his difficulties, his emotional pain and his needs. But it was no less important to confront him and recognize in him the active ***doer*** who punishes and hurts others, albeit unknowingly. The struggle concerning the ability to hold onto these two opposing poles without dissociation was an ongoing challenge for both of us. Guy needed me to be on his side; however, I believed, he also needed my "outside" perspective about the impact he had on others. My confronting him was an act of acknowledgment of his emotional strength and resilience, despite the distorted ways he expressed them; he could feel I respected him as a person with a voice of his own. Gradually, he became more of a professed, conscious "doer," and his unacknowledged vengefulness subsided. It was slowly replaced by attempts to be directly assertive and to struggle for what he needed in a more straightforward manner. He initiated some moves to advance his position in the company he worked for. His actions proved effective: he was promoted and got a raise. The frustrating and helpless bond he had maintained with his girlfriend reached a crossroads; he was able to confront her and told her explicitly that he may leave if their relationship did not change for the better. Guy's struggle to acknowledge his vengeful wishes was fruitful in terms of his personal growth; I felt there was "more of him" over time; so did he.

The process of strengthening Guy's ability to be in touch with his "wants" demanded, at times, all of the authentic presence I could muster in the therapeutic relationship. The pressure to "go easy" on him because "it was too difficult" or because "he couldn't bear it" was great. I often felt that I was forcing him into achievements, much in the same ways that those controlling "powerful women" did. Guy was a "pleaser"; despite the fact that he didn't keep appointments, procrastinated payments, disappeared for weeks without notice, he still would come to sessions with excuses, "stories" and explanations that "proved" his utter innocence and good will; things were really not up to him. The enactments of the abuser/avenger/victim cycles were played out on the stage of our relationship quite often. The way he dismissed me altogether, disrupted my schedule, or plainly just lied, often made me feel frustrated, angry, helpless and vengeful. My struggle to stay in touch with those hard feelings was significant, however, in the process of getting to know him more intimately as a *"dissociated doer"*; over time, it contributed its share to transform some of the tensions between into explicit therapeutic communications.

The implicit narrative that accompanied Guy's life like background music sounded like this: "You are ignoring what is really important and painful to me; it humiliates and hurts me. So I will ignore and hurt you in return. I'll show you. I do have an impact." Gradually, it became a more familiar tune to him.

Our growing ability to talk about this "tune" opened the space for sharing more biographical material and painful experiences that were not previously available in therapy. I learned from Guy that he was a neglected child in many ways: he had a severe ADD that was never diagnosed or properly treated, consequently he kept failing in school and getting into trouble; he was often beaten by his father, who suffered from a severe disability. He married young and was left as a single parent to his daughter after his wife deserted them both. Gradually, I got to know him more closely, as he allowed himself to "confess" to deeds he was initially ashamed of (such as lying, neglecting his daughter, overusing his mother's resources and goodwill, or hurting his girlfriend's feelings by lashing out at her in raging outbursts of jealousy, or spying on her secretly).

At this point, I could say that the process of his personal growth was slow and painful but productive: Guy eventually became a more concerned father, more hopeful about the possibility of establishing a warmer relationship with a woman and about finding a decent job he could be proud of.

Looking at the course of therapy from the perspective of awareness to vengefulness, Guy's ability to perceive himself as an active agent was empowering: it became a developmental asset. Guy no longer defined himself as a helpless victim in such a pervasive way. He was proud of his ability to give more to his daughter and was strengthened by her own progress. By contrast, his relationship with his girlfriend did not survive the difficulties that had accumulated between them: he decided he was ready to part with her. It may be that the timing of their meeting was too great an obstacle for them to be able to sustain this relationship. They were not ripe for it, not mature enough at that point to transcend the difficulties it presented. Apparently, their motivation to grow together and fight for intimacy was beyond their strength or motivation.

Some Afterthoughts

Broken up relationships may be one of the outcomes of disruptions in mutual acknowledgement. Unacknowledged slights are turned into mutual punishing, raising walls of distance, resentment and alienation. Unconscious vengefulness may accelerate and gradually obstruct the capacity for warmth, intimacy, friendship and cooperation.

I suggest that relationships controlled by passive-aggressive dynamics include some degree of the desire to punish and to exact revenge. Vengefulness tends to be a disowned desire, more readily perceived as "avoidance" and defined as "non-behavior" rather than seen as "behavior" (namely, action rather than re-action) in its own right. Since partners in conflict may not see themselves as "doers," they hurt each other without accountability; hence, their ability to contribute and to create a shared reality is damaged.

Feelings and actions for which no one claims responsibility may be described as *"deeds without a doer"* (much like Bion's "thoughts without a thinker"). Each participant in such exchanges is *"done to"* rather than a professed *"doer"* (Benjamin, 2004). This configuration hampers the potential for productive cooperation in personal and in social life. Relationships might thus become boxing rings in which each person claims from the other whatever he or she has been robbed of, until they finally crumble.

Since mutual recognition is an essential constituent in connectedness and belonging, its disruptions may create estrangement and set off cycles of destructive vengefulness. Owning up to one's actions, good or bad, is a leap of faith; it draws on one's inner resources, while at the same time nourishing and strengthening them.

Identifying these processes in the safety of a therapeutic intersubjective space may enable the injured person to reconnect to the sense that he does have *"feelings and actions of his own,"* even if they manifest themselves as vengefulness; it indicates that he does have a reflective mind through which he can manage these processes with more freedom. Acknowledging vengefulness may be the first contact one has with one's ability to be an agent, the initiator of one's own actions. Through this contact, one becomes aware that one is able to affect change, not only through revenge but also by direct, explicit communication and negotiations towards creating a shared reality.

These repeated experiences in therapy may enhance the reintegration of dissociated self-states and strengthen a process of personal and relational growth.

The ability to recognize vengefulness as normal and legitimate contributes to the process of differentiating between one's inner world and the world of others outside it. This distinction is a meaningful developmental asset: one's ability to feel that one owns an inner world lessens one's vulnerability while strengthening one's emotional resilience and capacity for coexistence. The ability to perceive difference, to feel connected yet separate, is of utmost value in personal and social development. The acceptance of vengefulness is in this respect a developmental asset: it contributes to one's ability to exist as a subject among other subjects.

REFERENCES

Améry, J. (1980). *At the Mind's Limit. Contemplations by a Survivor on Auschwitz and Its Realities*. Indiana University Press.

Arlow, J. A. (1980). "The Revenge Motive in the Primal Scene." *Journal of the American Psychoanalytic Association*. 28: 519-541.

Beattie, H. J. (2005). "Panel Report: Revenge." *Journal of the American Psychoanalytic Association*. 53: 513-524.

Benjamin, J. (1990). "An Outline of Intersubjectivity: The Development of Recognition." *Psychoanalytic Psychology*. 7S (Supplement): 33-46.

Benjamin J. (2004). "Beyond Doer and Done to: An Intersubjective View of Thirdness." *Psychoanalytic Quarterly*. 73 (1): 5-46.

Boris Harold N. (1986). "The 'Other' Breast: Greed, Envy, Spite and Revenge." *Contemporary Psychoanalysis*, 22: 45-59.

Castelnuovo, T., P. (1974). "Stealing, Revenge and the Monte Cristo Complex." *International journal of Psychoanalysis.* 55: 69 -177[À].

Dalal, F. (1998). *Taking the Group Seriously.* London: Jessica Kingsley Publishers.

Davies, J. M. and M. G. Frawley (1994). *Treating the Adult Survivor of Childhood Sexual Abuse.* New York: Basic Books.

Dumas, A. (1998). *The Count Of Monte Cristo.* New York: Tor Books.

Elster, J. (1990). "Norms of Revenge." *Ethics*, 100: 862-85.

Fairbairn, W. R. D., Ed. (1943). The Repression and the Return of Bad Objects (with special reference to the "War Neuroses"). *Essential Papers on Object Relations.* New York, University Press.

Feiner, A. (1995). "Laughter Among The Pear Trees: Vengeance, Vindictiveness, And Vindication." *Contemporary Psychoanalysis.* 31: 381.

Genesis, in The Holy Scriptures. A New Translation. Philadelphia: *The Jewish publication society of America.*

Grand, S. (2000). *The Reproduction of Evil. A Clinical & Cultural Perspective.* Hillsdale, New Jersey: The Analytic Press.

Hagman, G. (1997). "Mature Self-object Experience." *Progress in Self-Psychology.* 13: 85-107.

Hegel, G. W. F. (1977). *Phenomenology of Spirit* (translated by A. V. Miller). Oxford: Clarendon Press.

Herman, J. (1992). *Trauma end Recovery.* New York: Basic Books.

Hopper, E. (2002). *The Social Unconscious: Selected papers.* London and New York: International Library of Group Analysis, Jessica Kingsley Publishers.

Howell F, Elizabeth (2002). "Back to the 'States:' Victim and Abuser States in Borderline Personality Disorder." *Psychoanalytic Dialogues.* 12(6): 921-957.

Klein, M. (1975). *Envy and Gratitude and Other Works.* New York and London: Dell Publishing Co., Hogarth Press.

Kleist, H. V. (1997). *Michael Kohlhaas.* Skokie, Il: Distribooks.

Kohut, H. (1972). "Thoughts on Narcissism and Narcissistic Rage." *Psychoanal. Study of the Child.* 27: 360-400.

Kohut, H. (1982). "Introspection, Empathy, and the Semi-Circle of Mental Health." *International Journal of Psycho-Analysis.* 63: 395-407.

Lansky, M. (2001). "The Problem Of Forgiveness In The Tempest." *Journal of the American Psychoanalytic Association.* 49: 1005 -1033.

Lansky, M. (2005). "The Impossibility of Forgiveness: Shame Fantasies As Instigators Of Vengeance In Euripides' Medea." *Journal of the American Psychoanalytic Association.* 53: 437-464.

Laub, D. (1985). "Prolog. Knowing and not knowing the Holocaust." *Psychoanalytic Inquiry* 5.

Laub, D. and N. C. Auerhahn (1989). "Failed empathy: A Central Theme in the Survivor's Holocaust Experience." *Psychoanalytic Psychology.* 6: 377-400.

Levi, P. (1988). *The Drowned and the Saved.* New York: Summit Books.

Melville, H. (2003). *Moby Dick.* New York: Barnes & Noble.

Mitchell, S. A. (1988). *Relational Concepts in Psychoanalysis: An Integration*. Cambridge, MA: Harvard University Press.

Ornstein, A. and. Gropper C (1983). “Shoplifting: An Expression of Revenge and Restitution.*” Annual Psychoanalysis.* 11: 311-33.

Rosen, R. I. (2007). “Revenge: The Hate That Dare Not Speak Its Name.” *Journal of the American Psychoanalytic Association*. 55: 595-620.

Searles, H. F. (1956). “The Psychodynamics of Vengefulness.” *Psychiatry*. 19, 31-39.

Slavitt, D. and P. Bovie, Eds. (1998). *Medea. Euripides* Philadelphia, University of Pennsylvania Press.

Socarides, C. (1966). “On Vengeance: The Desire To Get Even.” *Journal of the American Psychoanalytic Association*. 14: 356-375.

Steiner, J. (1996). “Revenge and Resentment in the ‘Oedipus Situation.’” *International Journal of Psychoanalysis*. 77: 433-443.

Stuckless, N. and R. Goranson (1994). “A Selected Bibliography of Literature on Revenge.” *Psychological Reports*. 75(2): 803-811.

Chapter 5

VENGEFUL WISHES: WHAT ARE THEY ABOUT? THE COMMUNICATIVE FUNCTION OF VENGEFULNESS

Miriam Berger

When I was an intern, a patient told me with a gleam in her eyes that each morning before her husband entered the bathroom to brush his teeth, she would dip his toothbrush in the toilet. She claimed it gave her strength to bear the many humiliations she suffered at his hands. "He thinks he is so smart going out all dressed up. It makes my day to know what shit he really dips in." I don't know whether she eventually managed to find more constructive strategies for self-development, but it seemed that that was the most she could do for herself at that point in her life.

Vengeful behaviors come in a myriad of shapes, depending on the function they are supposed to serve in any given relational context. As human ingenuity is endless, their nature can, at times, be expressed in rather peculiar ways.

A colleague with whom I discussed the subject of vengefulness told me that while attending a memorial for a deceased relative held in a cemetery, she came across the site of a would-be grave waiting to be used. The inscription that was to be engraved on the tombstone when the time came was ready and read as follows: "*Children I have reared and brought up, and they have sinned against me*" (Isaiah 1:2, King James translation; the original Hebrew can also be translated *"...committed crimes against me"*).

It seemed like a preplanned act of revenge: future mourners (the children?) who would attend the funeral of their relative (a parent?) were to be confronted with these words, shamed and devastated. The words were meant to leave them utterly helpless, with no possibility of redemption. It must have been intended to serve as a final "settling of the score," enabling the deceased person to "rest in peace" after having made his or her point so adamantly. I can imagine the relatives needing lengthy therapeutic interventions to help them recuperate from this vengeful attack.

These may be rather odd anecdotes, easily dismissed as too peculiar. It is not easy, however, to come to terms with the idea that vengefulness is actually part of our daily emotional repertoire, of relationships in general, including intimate relationships within families, between parents and children, between siblings, between friends and colleagues.

Since vengefulness as such is difficult to own, it can be displayed indirectly by quarrelsome interactions, accompanied by a sense of being targeted by the ill will of others.

The following vignette may be illuminating. Rosa, a patient in a mental health clinic, is irritable, argumentative, and given to outbursts of rage that threaten to cost her a job she badly needs. Rosa complains bitterly about various mistreatments she has been subjected to. Her ex-husband, for instance, is "inhuman." His misdeeds are innumerable: "he is a chronic procrastinator, a liar; he skips alimony payments; he is neglectful, mean and ungrateful; he just doesn't care about us." No, she does not wish him ill. She is not "like that"; she knows vengefulness is prohibited. If she had ill thoughts towards him, it would really happen to him: God would make her wishes come true.

What does she envision "would really happen" to him in that case, I ask. "Horrible things," she says, "you know, like curses: he might be run over by a car, break his neck, get sick, get fired, lose money, be cheated on by this fancy tart he spends a fortune on." No, she doesn't want to even think about "such things"; she might get terribly guilty if "it" happens to him.

Rosa's attempts to maintain health contain a not-so-unusual proposition, namely, that vengeful fantasies are a magical act that will damage her ex-husband and blemish her own soul with moral flaws for which she will end up being punished. Her effort to renounce thoughts about such "curses," to be good and righteous, represents the common belief that ill wishes towards others are tantamount to actually causing them harm, that vengeful wishes in themselves violate some moral code. (This echoes Boris' idea that vengefulness is a "plague of the mind.") Since vengeful fantasies are perceived as dangerous, Rosa opts for a "safer" alternative: she acts without thinking. However, it is evident that the solution becomes a problem in its own right; while she avoids those harmful fantasies, her stormy outbursts and irritable behavior really do cause damage, to herself as well as to others.

It may well be that releasing her "prohibited" fantasies from the demonic grip that subdues them, allowing them a legitimate access into her emotional world, would improve her ability to control her temper. Acknowledging her ill wishes towards others may set her free from the victimhood constellation in which she is stuck (Chapters 1-3 in this book). It may ameliorate some of the destructive interactions she is involved in and help her stay away from trouble.

It appears that Rosa would benefit from Goldberg's (2004) succinct suggestion:

> Revenge fantasies are important ***healing tools*** because they help us to use thoughts and feelings in the service of harnessing our impulses and controlling our actions (p. 6, my emphasis).

A comment I found in a footnote to Freud's *Civilization and its Discontent* provides unexpected support for my view of vengefulness as a legitimate feeling, a commonplace aspect of our daily musings, associations and fantasies:

> A great imaginative writer may permit himself to give expression—jokingly, at all events—to psychological truths that are severely proscribed. Thus Heine confesses: "Mine is a most peaceable disposition. My wishes are: a humble cottage with a thatched roof, but a good bed, good food, the freshest milk and butter, flowers before my window, and a few fine trees before my door; and if God wants to make my happiness complete, he will grant me the joy of seeing some six or seven of my enemies hanging from those

trees. Before their death I shall, moved in my heart, forgive them all the wrong they did me in their lifetime. One must, it is true, forgive one's enemies—but not before they have been hanged" ("Gedanken und Einfälle," Section I).

I assume that Heine, the renowned humanist, will not be accused of encouraging violent acts of revenge.[1] Heine's "confession" is nevertheless an act of revenge in its own right: Not only does he allow himself the freedom to imagine his enemies hanging from trees and says it would make him happy, he also announces it *publicly* through his writing. (I am stressing this combination—owning up guiltlessly to "evil" feelings *and* making these feelings public by letting others know about them—since I think that the vengeful act of "telling it to the world" is an essentially *relational* act. I shall address the topic of "telling it" more extensively in Chapter 6.)

Heine's personal confession about indulging in prohibited fantasies opens a space for some playfulness concerning vengefulness. From this perspective, vengefulness can be viewed as just one state of mind among many, a feeling like any other; it becomes a platform from which to explore relational experiences. One's openness to its many shades and meanings may even evoke creativity; it engenders new ways of relating, thinking and imagining; it frees one's imagination from constrictions imposed by reality.

This resonates with Goldberg's (2004) remark that *"revenge fantasies are a way of acting without acting"* (p. 5). Vengeful wishes provide us with a means of acting without actually causing damage, of getting even without really striking back. (Vengeful deeds, on the other hand, are usually best left for nights at the opera.)

This ability to sustain emotional pain and contain it within one's boundaries rather than thrash it around indirectly can release creative abilities and enhance the forming of a potential space for "play" (in Winnicott's sense). Getting in touch with vengefulness can be transformed into personal strength and emotional resilience, into an ability to fend for oneself in the real world. It can help pave the way to richer and more explicit communication between people. It can enhance "mindfulness," accountability, and, eventually, the mature capacity for mutual concern. I hope to illustrate these ideas through the clinical vignettes I present in some detail further on.

VENGEFULNESS: A RESTORATIVE/COMMUNICATIVE PROCESS

As I see it, the desire to exact revenge on another is neither an indication of emotional pathology nor a sign of flaws in one's moral character. On the contrary, vengefulness can be assigned a meaningful relational function. As a restorative/communicative process, it has a

---

[1] Christian Johann Heinrich Heine (born in Düsseldorf, 13 December 1797, died in Paris, 17 February 1856) was a journalist, essayist, and one of the most significant German romantic poets. His famous saying about the burning of books is prominently displayed in the Yad Vashem Holocaust Museum in Jerusalem and in the United States Holocaust Memorial Museum in Washington. Among the thousands of books burned in Berlin's Opernplatz in 1933, following the Nazi raid on the Institut für Sexualwissenschaft, were works by Heine. To commemorate the terrible event, one of the most famous lines of Heine's 1821 play *Almansor* is engraved in the ground at the site: "Dort, wo man Bücher verbrennt, verbrennt man am Ende auch Menschen." ("Where they burn books, they will ultimately also burn people.") Heine's original text refers to the burning of the Quran by the Spanish Inquisition.

double purpose: it informs us about basic relational needs that have been disrupted, while at the same time serving as a self-remedy meant to repair the disruption.

Following is an inconclusive list of the unconscious restorative/communicative messages "encoded" in vengeful wishes, fantasies, and thoughts:

- They sooth one's soul and "turn the tables" on defeat and misery.
- They restore dignity and personal pride.
- They maintain self-esteem, relevance and power.
- They sustain one's experience of being an agent in one's own right.
- They safeguard one's coherent identity.
- They maintain equality.
- They provide a shield against unbearable emotional pain.
- They safeguard remembering of wrongdoing, sustaining meaningful continuity between past and present.
- They prevent acquiescence to dismissal, discrediting, denial, and indifference.
- They maintain the hope that one can expect accountability.
- They sustain faith in a just, lawful world in which sins are punished.
- They "inform" about disruptions of reciprocity.
- They protest against humiliation and shame.
- They summon help and sustain the hope that one will be heard.
- They constitute a demand for recognition.

These unconscious "messages," when decoded, can serve as an "internal gyroscope" (Goldberg, 2004), part of an emotional regulatory system that draws our attention to experiences in need of consideration. In other words, they point out basic needs or "vital human concerns" that arise when mutual recognition is disrupted and needs repair. Vengeful wishes represent a mirror image of non-recognition: thwarted as they may be, they retrieve reciprocity, as if saying: "I can contribute to and enrich your life, just as I can injure you and make you suffer; I can renounce you, just as I can grant you my recognition; we are equals, despite your attempts to turn me into an object. *I do count*."

The events that evoke vengefulness as a restorative/communicative process run a continuum, from the mundane frictions permeating everyday human relationships to the most extreme forms of brutality that people can inflict on one another. This continuum of injuries, from the smallest to the largest, evokes a wide range of emotional responses, vengeful wishes included.

The creation, disruption, and repair of mutual recognition constitute a continuous relational process, creating a transformative basis for the making of "subject relations."

Avoidance of Vengefulness

Belonging, interconnectedness, and participation in a shared reality are primary human needs (Foulkes, 1964; Dalal, 1998). Avoiding vengeful wishes, thoughts or fantasies, renouncing or discrediting them may indicate that something in one's emotional regulatory system concerning these primary needs is amiss.

Non-recognition, when left unattended, may be envisioned as an invisible wound, causing internal bleeding in the tissue of human life and endangering one's relations with self and others.

Vengefulness is only one of several ways to activate, unconsciously, the process of healing those relational wounds, with the aim of reopening channels of communication and reconnecting broken tissues.

Since I attribute to vengeful wishes an informative/restorative function, I suggest that therapists should "hear" their absences as a meaningful clinical data. It may well be that we therapists ought to become more attentive not only to the presence of vengefulness but especially to the lack of it. One way of understanding the dynamics of such "absences" pertains to the idea that painful emotional experiences might not be "registered" in one's inner world; they sometimes undergo dissociation and constitute "non-experience." It is assumed that this process of avoidance is a survival strategy that spares the person unbearable emotional pain (Howell, 2005; Stern, 1987).

Since I suggest vengefulness is a coded communication about painful experiences that were dissociated from one's awareness, it may be that the absence of vengefulness signifies the existence of an additional level of protection against pain. It is as if a "double dissociative shield" has been erected within the inner world of the injured person, making his emotional experiences less accessible to him. The person's ability to communicate the pain he suffered is wiped out, along with the traumatic experiences that engendered that pain.

Such dissociated experiences do not just evaporate into thin air; they follow their own course of projection and disavowal, but may erupt unexpectedly and become destructive in unforeseen acts of revenge.

The presence of vengefulness that is merely implicit in wishes, fantasies or thoughts becomes explicit via the relational act of "telling it" to an other. In order to be effective, the act of "telling it" must involve human presence. It can turn "non-experience" into a shared reality felt and validated by all involved parties. The act of "telling it" can be seen as an emotional thread that points out basic relational needs, recognizing which can help repair the relational "fabric" (the "black holes") torn by post-traumatic experience. When this communicative thread is cut off, there is less hope for a healing process to start and take its course.

Discrediting, either social or personal, may silence the desire to get even. Since the regulatory "gyroscope" is shut down, it may turn wishes into vengeful acts that pull people apart and position them against one another. *Discredited feelings breed dissociative processes, both in the relational field and in people's inner world, and dissociative processes generate further discredited feelings in turn.* These self-perpetuating dynamic cycles generate relationships fraught with domination and subjugation, distancing, alienation, exclusion, and lack of mutual concern.

Since vengefulness represents hope for a just world, the lack of it may feed helplessness and despair. It may cause one to adopt a passive stance in the face of wrongdoing, resign oneself to a victim's fate, and forgo any attempt to protest or struggle to change one's life for the better.

Vengefulness as an Activation of Personal Resources

As mentioned, vengefulness, or rather the acknowledgment of vengeful desires, may become a developmental resource. Such acknowledgement can provide the strength and courage one needs in order to move away from a stance of helplessness and defeat and harness one's energies to the task of fending for oneself.

The following short vignette may illustrate this last point.

L., in her early thirties, heard that M., her ex-boyfriend, had a romantic relationship with one of her colleagues. It turned out that the couple had been living together for some time; apparently, their commitment was a serious one, as the rumor said they were about to get married. L. was extremely upset about this news.

L. had felt mistreated by M. when they were together and to make bad things worse, he was also the one who broke up with her: "He just walked away one day and that was it; dismissed me as if I were nothing." After the breakup, he ignored her numerous pleas to talk things out. She was mortified: "What a terrible mistake it was to allow him to do this to me. I should have been the one to sack him; he did not give me a chance to say the last word."

For months, L. was depressed about this sudden cutoff, humiliated by M.'s refusal to talk to her, by his recurrent criticism when they had been together: he used to tell her she "doesn't have it in her," that she was not able to really give of herself to a man, that she was not enough of a woman for him." It was a stormy relationship characterized by the humiliating sense that she was the needy one who couldn't bring herself to leave. Then, one day, he just quit. L. became withdrawn and silent. She already had a history of abusive relationships with men, and each fall worsened her emotional state.

Finally, after a long period of a painful withdrawn silence in therapy and impoverished energies to cope with her daily tasks, she started to respond to my encouragement by expressing the wish that he would "rot in hell," that he would end up old, lonely, desolate, that he would never be able to share his life with a woman.

Gradually, she picked up enough strength and decided to "show him which one is not capable of being in a relationship." As she started to sense the vindictive rage simmering in her, she became determined to stick it out with a man she had started dating—a man she would not have considered were she in a different state of mind since he seemed too "normal" for her. Her wish to make M. suffer, to make him regret terribly that he had missed out on his chance with her, became part of her inner motivation to withstand the difficulties she usually experienced when dating.

Recently, she moved in with her new boyfriend and came to feel better. She drew much strength from this success. In fact, I had the feeling it was a much more constructive choice on her part, with a potential to develop into a mature, warm and stable relationship in which she could really grow.

However, upon hearing the news about M.'s plans to marry, she reported being flooded again by uncontrollable rage and vengeful fantasies. This time she managed to be much more outspoken: she was seized with wishes to meet M.'s girlfriend and tell her what he was really like, to "warn" her about his "rotten character" of which the girlfriend was presumably not aware yet.

At times, it seemed she was on the verge of spoiling her newly formed relationship with destructive deeds that she would certainly regret. I empathized with her pain, while carefully exploring the shades and meanings of her vengefulness. She needed to trust my ability to protect her from harming herself or others and to support her in the arduous developmental task of distinguishing deeds from wishes. Our therapeutic relationship was a struggle against the danger that her unconscious emotional wounds might become a self-fulfilling prophecy, that she may indeed become the impoverished, helpless, vengeful, bitter person she often felt she was.

Our work turned to be constructive in this respect: eventually, her open rage, along with her readiness to share with me her vulnerabilities, enabled her to get in touch more fully with a sense of strength and self-esteem. She made meaningful decisions about her future with her current boyfriend. It took her a while to understand how anxious she unconsciously was about this new relationship and how much she really did appreciate her new boyfriend, not only as a replacement, but as a person she could love and respect. This process had a transformative value for her. It helped her recognize she had an active role in making the relationship work (as well as in spoiling it, as she almost did); she became more cognizant of her ability to contribute to creating trust between her boyfriend and herself, without feeling so desperately devoid of inner resources and self-worth. It helped her consolidate the relationship, with satisfying outcomes for both partners.

The point I am trying to stress through this brief vignette is that being in touch with one's own vengefulness can become a personal resource if processed openly. It generates inner strength and resilience and may be utilized to mobilize one's energies for self-development.

L.'s wish to "show him" was a way out of a state of humiliating defeats and shaming failures, which had repeatedly hindered L.'s personal growth. The wish to outdo the offender can play a meaningful part in freeing one's creative energies and "flexing one's muscles." In other words, one's growing pride and developmental achievements can be experienced as "sweet revenge." The desire to "show them" can thus play a part in consolidating one's developmental goals.

As mentioned earlier, the range of vengeful feelings is quite wide and includes rebelliousness and feistiness, which can help one overcome difficulties and cope with adverse situations. (It is said that Ivona Trump got a piece of advice in this spirit when dealing with her divorce from her tycoon husband: *"Don't get even,"* she was told, *"get everything!"*).

I do not suggest that the merits of acknowledging vengefulness need stop here; as I will show more extensively later on, such acknowledgement can be part of an evolving relational process. It is important to realize, however, that the wish to "show them" has its merits: it can fortify one's self-esteem and help regain trust in inner resources. It can generate personal growth and a sense of strength; it enhances one's determination to succeed "in spite of everything." As Holmes (2005) puts it:

> Success stories were able to give up the pleasure of destroying the object. Self-enhancement as a form of revenge then became an enticing alternative. *Cure, after all, is the ultimate revenge* (p. 61, my emphasis).

VENGEFULNESS: CLINICAL CONSIDERATIONS

An understanding that places the patient's behavior in a relational context is clinically productive, as it responds to the patient's subjective emotional reality without neglecting the emotional reality of others he or she lives with.

Such a stance demands that the therapist struggle with a twofold position. On the one hand, the therapist must have a firm hold on "real" reality, with the implication that injuries inflicted by others must be recognized as such. On the other hand, the therapist must believe no less firmly that the patient is capable of being an agent in his own right. Let me explain each of these in turn.

I think that the therapist's commitment to truth, his or her deep respect for "hard" facts, is essential to the patient's recovery. Even when it is not possible to hold the offender accountable, the therapist's acknowledgement of "real" reality represents symbolically his belief in society's moral obligation towards its members. Failure to acknowledge the validity of the patient's claims (which may be manifested by lack of detailed attention to what really happened out there in the objective world of facts) might constitute a recurrent trauma. The therapist's validation of the reality of wrongdoing provides the injured patient with a needed sense of safety; it is an emotional, relational, and physical anchor in stormy seas. It facilitates a process of retrieving basic trust in an orderly, sane world. It strengthens the patient's belief that "help is on the way" (Améry, 1980), that he or she is not alone yet again, helpless in the face of injustice.

If the therapist focuses solely on the dynamics of the inner world, the patient may feel abandoned, left to his or her own dwindling resources. Failure to hold the real other accountable may constitute a blow in its own right, replicating the patient's original trauma. Such basic values as accountability are the product of a shared reality. Since trust in such values has been disrupted, it becomes important to revalidate it through the therapeutic relationship. Frenczi's plea to trust the patient and believe his account of real abuse comes to mind here (Ferenczi, 1949).

This issue echoes the age-old psychoanalytical "wars" about the nature and origins of aggression and whether it's apt to place it inside or outside the world of the individual. As my work is embedded in relational concepts, I believe that inside and outside are counterparts of one another: none can be examined separately. The processing of vengefulness requires both perspectives.

In addition to validating reality, the therapist, as noted above, needs to believe that the patient is capable of being his own person. In other words, the therapist must recognize the patient as an active agent, as a person capable of owning up to his decisions without being merely reactive. The therapist must believe that the patient is able to exert his own power and make his own choices. This faith is a gesture towards validating the patient's value as an equal subject.

The therapeutic work has to identify and address the dissociative states that may be part of traumatic situations: that is, it needs to acknowledge the pain the patient suffers and the real difficulties she struggles with but also the real pain she may be inflicting on others (Bromberg, 1996; Howell, 2005). A one-sided identification of the therapist with the patient's afflictions alone (or with the "inner primal aggression" the patient supposedly needs to process) might have a damaging and weakening effect in the long run.

As stated above, addressing vengefulness along with its implied meanings can stimulate personal development. This requires a kind of double perspective that simultaneously explores two modes of relation:

1. The relations between patient and others.
2. The relations between different self-states in the patient's inner world.

Either of these two modes may become dominant and take over one's relationships with oneself and with others.

The patient's ability to acknowledge his desire to punish someone who has hurt him enables him to get in touch with an "active self," with the "*doer*" in himself, which may be less accessible for various reasons (including experiences of failed recognition).

Awareness of one's own desire for revenge can stimulate the sense of personal agency from which one has been detached. It restores one's sense of power and validates one's ability to have an impact, to "make things happen."

When avoidance and distancing are reframed as "actions" in their own right, they pave inroads into recovering one's relevance as a subject. Acknowledging the "*doer*" in the patient may enhance the patient's ability to effect productive changes in his life. The process triggered by such acknowledgement may balance off the paralyzing helplessness, despair and sense of passive defeat into which the patient has fallen.

The therapist's struggle to "hold in mind" both perspectives imparts the belief that the patient is an equal subject capable of being in charge of his world, responsible for his actions. It constitutes a gesture of understanding and identification with the wounded patient's emotional pain, while validating her power to affect her destiny. It conveys recognition of the patient's right for respect, as well as her obligation to respect others.

These two perspectives are interdependent and mutually reinforcing. The combination between identification and confrontation defines the therapeutic relationship as *"reciprocity in action"* (after Foulkes' definition of the analytic group as *"ego-training in action").*

As stated earlier, mutuality is a paradoxical process: The therapist's recognition is valuable only insofar as the patient perceives him as worthy enough to grant it, and vice versa.

Approached from this perspective, the therapeutic relationship enhances the patient's ability to internalize and encompass his own inner subjective experience, the other person's separateness, and the unique sovereignty of both. It restores trust in reciprocity and in a just world worth belonging to and struggling for.

WINNICOTT'S CONTRIBUTION: RUTHLESSNESS, CONCERN, VENGEFULNESS

I would now like to review briefly some aspects of Winnicott's notions about aggression, which seem to contribute a dynamic perspective to my thoughts about the value of recognizing vengefulness as a developmental asset.

According to Winnicott (1983), the "true self," the core of one's vitality and authenticity, is an "active self." This self is energized by aggression, which Winnicott defines as a life force, an innate resource that strives towards self-realization, towards "using" others creatively (where "using" is distinct from exploiting). The earliest aggressiveness is originally part of the infants' healthy appetite for life, or of some other form of instinctual love, which Winnicott terms as "ruthlessness." In Winnicot's understanding, the infant is endowed with a primitive ruthless self that predates the concerned self. One's ability to feel concern for others develops later if this passionate "ruthlessness" (or aggressiveness) is allowed to be expressed and is accepted as such. In other words, what happens to these aggressive energies and how they impact one's life is determined by the way the environment responds to them.

Winnicott (1983) replaces Kleinian "guilt" with "concern," which denotes a healthy sense of responsibility towards others. According to him, human care for others is based on the maturation of an innate primary love impulse (i.e., the desire to "devour" life ruthlessly and forcefully), not on shameful guilt or on "reparations" to the giving other that has been usurped. Concern is essentially not an outcome of atonement for harm done.

From this point of view, concern for others is rooted in the infant's acknowledgement of the mother's goodness, which leads the infant to the joyous realization that there is someone unique out there—different and separate from, yet similar, to it—who is willing to be involved in a creative, productive exchange with it (Ferenczi, 1949; Eigen, 1981). "Ruthlessness" is thus an expression of the infant's innate primary morality. Winnicott's "morality" is not rooted in compliance or inhibition; it is rather a manifestation of self-expression and of connectedness to personal desire (Philips, 1993).

I suggest that adding the notion of "mutuality" to Winnicott's "concern" positions it more firmly in an intersubjective context and enriches its clinical relevance and conceptual plasticity.

"Taking mutuality seriously" (after the title of Dalal's book, *Taking the Group Seriously*), I suggest that Winnicott's ruthlessness can be perceived as the baby's primary contribution to its relationship with others. It is a primitive form of contributing, of "pitching in," of bestowing the baby's creative energies, passionate interest and joyful curiosity on the mother. Ruthlessness is thus a primary form of "recognition" granted by the baby to the mother. From this perspective, the mother needs the baby no less than it needs her. (This is true despite the fact that their needs are very different; mutuality does not imply symmetry.)

From this perspective, Winnicott's well-known saying that there is no such thing as a baby without a mother is complemented by its reversal, "there's no such thing as a mother without a baby." The two define each other and form a primary model for reciprocal exchange between people.

In this understanding, if ruthlessness is accepted by the caretaker as rooted in a desire to contribute, connect and have a personal impact, if it is perceived by the caring other as a relational asset, then it can develop into compassion or ruth: It can eventually turn into mature concern for an other, into a capacity for accountability and social responsibility. It constitutes a moral foundation for human relationships; a basis for the development of a culture of mutual caring.

Winnicott believes that acknowledging aggression, ruthlessness, and even plain hatred can be transformative; it can deepen one's emotional experience of having a "true self" and enliven relationships, protecting them from alienation and numbness.

Winnicott's (1965) "concern" is a labor of love; it is a guiltless commitment to mature relationships with self and others (Philips, 1993). Winnicott's ideas about ruthlessness and concern can enrich our understanding of the dynamics of caring among people. In an intersubjective context, ruthlessness can ripen into a capacity for mutual concern: This occurs when people are attentive enough to processes of breakdown and repair in mutual recognition.

This type of ruthlessness, I suggest, includes vengefulness in its recesses. Following Winnicott, I contend that acknowledging vengefulness is a primary contact with reciprocal exchanges of "I can do to you what you can do to me" that create a first step towards intersubjective processes. It sets in motion one's sense she is her own agent, similar, yet distinctly different and separate from others; as such, it generates developmental transformations. When explored in the therapeutic relationship with this perspective in mind, it may help the patient reconnect to powerful feelings from which she had been cut off, harness her energy to self-fulfillment, and strengthen her ability for mutual concern.

Acknowledging vengefulness enhances a process of healing, helping one to emerge from the state of helplessness that "impingement" (which in my thinking is a form of non-recognition) has imposed. Helplessness in itself is not necessarily unbearable; it can be perceived as a state of being "un-integrated" rather than being utterly powerless (Winnicott, 1983). The dreaded annihilation anxiety that helplessness evokes has to do with experiences of being impinged upon, dismissed, overlooked, unacknowledged, whether one is an infant or an adult. The link I make between helplessness and vengefulness relates to the emotional impact that experiences of failed recognition have on one's development.

Winnicott's dictum that "there is no baby without a mother" can be understood as representing the belief that we are innately interrelated, that "there is no subject without an other." This human quality of interconnectedness makes us extremely sensitive to acknowledgment and reciprocity. The need to be seen, known, recognized, "held in each other's mind," constitutes a matrix of vulnerabilities on which vengefulness touches.

From this point of view, mutual concern and mutual recognition are interconnected. They are both part of the struggle towards creating a culture of caring.

REVENGE AND SURVIVAL: THE DANGER OF DISCREDITED FEELINGS

Winnicott considers vengefulness a relational danger inherent in the baby's existential helplessness and dependence. In his view, avoiding vengefulness is part of the "ten commandments" of close relationships: fathers should not take revenge against sons; therapists should not take revenge against patients, and so forth. It seems to me that his pronounced prohibition implies a belief that vengefulness does in fact play a part in close relationships. This prohibition may well reflect a genetically transmitted datum branded in human consciousness regarding the dangers inherent in human interdependence.

We may assume that the more powerful the prohibition, the more powerful the wish. Fear of revenge and the wish for revenge feed each other. The very need to warn against it may indicate that vengefulness is a widespread component of everyday relationships, especially close ones.

Goldberg (2004) provides us with a rare personal confession about her vengeful wishes, especially towards her child.

> Like everyone (hopefully), I live with revenge fantasies of murder daily. When I am imagining being alone, being away from those I love the most, my unconscious is on the subject of revenge and murder. There are times, for instance, when my daughter's

> demands are more than I can tolerate. I might be driving, and I imagine an auto accident—I am hurt or killed, and finally my precious, beloved daughter understands that she cannot make such demands on me. My revenge is my injury to myself (p.10).

Mitchell (2002) voices a similar thought, although he does not refer specifically to revenge:

> The momentary aggressive fantasies I generate in relation to strangers are nothing compared to the intensity of the homicidal fantasies I harbor toward those I live with and love most deeply. And the effectiveness and danger of aggression are directly proportional to how much one knows about its target...*If aggression is a key ingredient of passion, there is plenty of it to be found in long-standing relationships...* (p. 141, my emphasis).

These words disclose, I think, a meaningful emotional truth about intimate relationships in general. The "homicidal fantasies" to which both Mitchell and Goldberg courageously confess should thus find a more prominent place in the praxis and thinking of psychoanalysis.

The Desire to Make One Suffer: Can the Therapeutic Relationship Contain it?

It is possible that psychoanalysis' reticent and ambivalent attitude towards vengefulness has to do with their fear of experiencing its powerful emotional pull from up close. Therapists' anxieties about their patients' reactions may stop them from articulating interpretations that may seem to them too disturbing; such anxieties may even silence (unknowingly or otherwise) any discredited emotions and thoughts they might have, if these pose a threat to their role, or expose their personal world in an unfavorable manner. Perhaps they fear that their frustrated patients, exploiting the therapists' ability and obligation to contain hard feelings, would become vengeful towards them and engender counter-vengefulness in return. In addition, transference and countertransference processes invite, by definition, displacement of failed relationships. Therapists may find that they are faced with more "transference" production than they bargained for. Such excessive transference can overburden the therapeutic interaction and evoke anxieties that may be too overwhelming. Therapeutic relationships (perhaps all relationships) do offer the possibility of a corrective experience, but they have their own limitations.

The patient's vengefulness, I suggest, contains within its recesses a poignant question to the therapist: *Are you ready to suffer for me and with me?* It also implies a hidden hope that the therapist's participation in the patient's suffering and pain *will enable the patient to return from his or her emotional exile.*

The therapist's ability to "agree" to bear the emotional pain engendered by of the patient can become transformative: it can serve as a bridge to a reality of mutual concern. Suttie's (1960) definition of the therapist's role as that of a willing "victim" who takes it upon himself to partake in the patient's suffering expresses a similar thought:

> The therapist's role is neither the technical role of a doctor nor the God-like role of the perfect parent. It is more like the role of *the victim onto whom hatred, worries and*

> *distrust are put*. He is the catalyser through which the exiled soul is re-integrated into society again (p. 72, my emphasis).

I am aware, however, that the wish to inflict pain on an other, even if this "other" is a therapist who is ready to take upon herself painful experiences, is troublesome and rather difficult to accept (see the beginning of Chapter 1). In spite of all the above dynamic explanations about the developmental value of vengefulness and its functions in relationships, vengefulness still poses a threat that may at times be too overwhelming. Therapists are socialized "to do good." The process of opening vengefulness up for intersubjective exploration and contextualizing it in the therapeutic relationship requires, however, that we sometimes "agree" to feel "bad," i.e., to feel victimized by patients and vengeful towards them; it requires a readiness to become targets of vengefulness, stand-ins for the real offenders. It also requires that we let ourselves feel the same towards patients. While such exchanges may eventually have a redeeming quality, they require real faith in one's ability to survive them. Such claims for emotional presence, authenticity, and generosity may sometime exceed the zone of safety that the therapeutic relationship (or any relationship, for that matter) is able to afford.

Winnicott's thinking about hard (and discredited) feelings that evolve in the context of therapy can be helpful in this context. Referring to the attitudes of mental health professionals towards psychiatric patients, he says:

> One can forgive those engaged in this work if they do awful things. This does not mean, however, that we have to accept whatever is done … as sound according to principles of science. However much he (the psychiatrist) loves his patients, he cannot avoid hating them and fearing them and the better he knows this the less will hate and fear be the motive determining what he does to his patients (Winnicott 1975, pp. 194-5).

Vengefulness, I suggest, can be thought of and related to with a similar sensibility.

Clinical Example: Tammy

As stated above, identifying the restorative-communicative function of vengefulness in the therapeutic setting may aid the patient to process the painful feelings stirred by failed recognition; it may help ameliorate the destructive reactivity that locks an individual or a couple in dead-end traps.

The following case illustrates my suggestion that identifying and processing vengeful feelings in couple relationships may help both partners to grow and to become closer to one another. Though I will describe the case in some detail, I do not aspire to do justice to the relationship's full complexity but rather to illuminate the aspects related to vengefulness and its processing.

Tammy, thirty-seven years old, is married to David. Both are ambitious professionals with esteemed careers. Their three young children were born with the help of arduous medical procedures that extended over the first seven years of their marriage.

Through those years, Tammy suffered bouts of depressive moods, panic attacks, and periods of feeling overly anxious and lost. Since Tammy is usually a highly efficient bank manager, she was quite scared by these episodes of malfunctioning.

Her periodic downfalls were often evoked by occurrences that made her suspect her husband was being unfaithful to her. At times, she would find pieces of "evidence" that he was having affairs with other women. He used to deny it adamantly. In any event, sex was just another item on their endless list of daily chores. Their sexual encounters were mostly task-oriented, aimed at producing the wished-for pregnancies.

When she made attempts to confront David, he would supply extensive explanations of his whereabouts and tell her she had a problem with trust. She would calm down for a while and accept, uncomfortably, the thought that her moodiness and anxious queries were probably part of her faulty character. Her growing sense that something must be deeply wrong with her made her seek therapeutic help. She wanted to "understand the root of the problem and feel happy," as she should.

Apart from these episodes of anxious doubts and shakiness that overwhelmed her periodically, Tammy's family life was stable.

Gradually, therapy became for Tammy a significant relationship, long after the initial feeling of urgency had passed. It assisted her in coping with the many difficulties her pregnancies, births, parenthood and competitive career engendered. Tammy felt that she and David formed a fundamentally "good team." However, the sexual difficulties between them continued. It appeared that sex was fraught with anxiety, suspicion and tension. As far as she was concerned, it was David's job to initiate physical intimacy. However, he was "exhausted" quite often, seemed too reluctant or too distant. Despite the friendship between them, she feared she was not attractive to him, that he was not interested in her as a woman. She avoided approaching him physically as "he should show more enthusiasm about it." All their talks, explanations, understandings and fights concerning this issue brought them nowhere. He did not seem too bothered by the lack of sex between them and told her that "it just takes time."

Tammy's frustration grew steadily. This state of mind resonated in our relationship as well. Tammy would be depressed or angry, and I would feel lost and stuck. She wanted me to provide a "reason" for David's lack of interest in her. She felt that the key to the solution was in his hands and that she could not affect it. As for me, it seemed I slid unknowingly into Tammy's shoes: there was nothing I could say or do to make any difference. At times, when I managed to pull myself out from the grip of this enactment, Tammy would calm down and be willing to acknowledge that she actually had more impact on their relationship than she credited herself with; but those were fleeting moments.

Over the course of her struggles with fertility problems, I would suggest periodically that she may be denying her husband sexual intimacy as an attempt (albeit unconscious) to reverse roles and "pay him back" for his apparent lack of attraction to her. She would either ignore my suggestions or dismiss them as mostly irrelevant. As far as she was concerned, she approached him often enough, made it clear she was interested, was rejected by his passivity and was terribly hurt. It was "obvious" he should do something about it: How could I not see that?

As our relationship unfolded, I learned that my attempts to interpret her passivity as an (unconscious) active "doing" in the service of retaliation were perceived by her as a sort of betrayal: I was siding with David against her. My suggestions constituted empathic failures. I needed to acknowledge it, and I did. I realized that oftentimes I was acting too much out of my own frustration, out of my own sense of helplessness at my inability to release her from this impasse; I was hurt by her dismissiveness towards me and was filled with a wish to punish her when she made me feel irrelevant, useless, uncaring, or accused me of betraying her trust; "How could she dismiss my utter devotion to her well-being?"

Looking more closely into the inner fabric of those interactions, it seems that I was unknowingly bracing myself against the pangs of non-recognition. I had my own personal acquaintance with being non-recognized; apparently I was not too keen to let those pains touch me too much. My untimely interpretations must have been a dissociated way of "getting even" on my part. I was not going to give in to her "devaluations" of my good will. These countertransference distancing moves diminished my sensitivity to her emotional reality. Apparently, she needed my undivided identification with her position as unloved, and I had to open myself more wholeheartedly to the pain of her denied longings for approval.[2]

It was through these periods of hard feelings between us that I became more understanding towards Tammy's vulnerabilities in that specific stage of her life. Her most urgent need was to establish a safe, solid base for her family. The thought that she may have an impact on their relationship (including sexual intimacy), that she was actually "doing" things unknowingly, was too anxiety provoking. It caused an unbearable fear that she may be "too independent" and thereby lose David's commitment towards her. She needed to need him and to attribute to him a directive role in their relationship.

For Tammy, owning her personal desires meant that she might lose control over her life, become "weak" and helpless. She was afraid that she might need David too intensely, that he would dominate her like her father did when she was a girl. It felt too risky at that time. Although none of this was stated between David and her, she was unconsciously afraid that she may be either too dependent or too independent in relation to him. The balance she was able to maintain throughout her struggle with fertility problems, childrearing, and career demands was too precarious.

The therapeutic relationship evolved gradually, as did Tammy's family life. The babies grew into active toddlers, and Tammy felt strengthened, confident and more relaxed. Working out the stalemates between us was productive; it enabled her to be more trusting about the possibility of talking things out without losing the relationship.

It appeared that Tammy's attitude towards her difficulties with David became less defensive; she could now "hear" my reflections about her feelings in a different way. My suggestions that she was actually pushing him away, even though she did not attribute to herself any "doing," were accepted as " interesting"; the idea I put forth that she may be vengeful towards David, that she may be "settling the score" with him, evoked her curiosity. A space for mindfulness started to open up both between us and within her.

Tammy's suspiciousness towards me subsided, as did her accusations that I was blaming, criticizing or pressuring her to compromise, be more tolerant and forgiving towards David. The newly built trust between us, combined with the stable growth in her personal life, helped create a safer base for her self-esteem.

---

[2] It is possible to conceptualize these interactions as enactments of "doer and done to" cycles, or as processes of projective identification. My focus, however, is on exploring the dynamics of vengeful wishes as a relational process that is embedded in reciprocity between real people, rather than in relationships between container and contained, which is more in the Kleinian frame. At any rate, I believe that projective identification always includes a constituent of vengefulness as part of its restorative-communicative function.

Tammy's ability to feel that she was not only rejected but also actively rejecting was transformative. It constituted a starting point for a new feeling of ownership over personal initiative: Tammy was getting in touch with being a "doer" no less than David was, albeit in a very different context.

My suggestion to view her passivity ("it's his job to come on to me") as a way of punishing him for the pain he inflicted upon her was now accepted as an asset she possessed. It turned out she actually could "get even." She was not as helpless as she initially felt; she had her own ways to get back at him and make him feel unwanted and unloved.

Since the language of business transactions was part of her work, my idea that she was "managing" her personal life in terms of emotional transactions was appealing and useful. It strengthened her. Her earlier fears that I was abandoning her and siding with her husband made way for a desire to feel more of an active partner in their relationship. My readiness to identify with her being hurt by him, but at the same time not to overlook her vengeful acts against him, constituted a model she was ready to develop. Her rage and vindictiveness were now put into an understandable context we could experience and talk about. She was able to be a "subject" with actions of her own. The authentication and acknowledgment of both her vulnerability and her strength enhanced her self-esteem.

As we moved along, Tammy could "remember" that she had been careful not to undress in front of David, as she felt she "won't show him her body; he doesn't deserve it." Oftentimes, she would go around the house cold and aloof, pulling a sour face, avoiding his look, silent for hours, restricting their interactions to functional exchanges about necessary household affairs. David had been held as a culprit in more than one way; but now her own contribution to the distance between them became more available for exploration.

Gradually, Tammy came to the decision that she wanted to confront David and request he tell her the truth. She felt that all this while David was hiding things from her, and she was now determined to know the truth, whatever it may be. This kind of directness was too threatening for her earlier.

She made it clear to David that if he continued his "explanations," their relationship would be at stake. This time it was clear to him that "she meant business." He understood that they had come to a crossroads and that he might lose her and break up his family. Apparently, he also felt that the old situation was entrapping him. Maybe he was even hoping that the change would somehow come from her; that she would neither yield to him anymore nor give up on him as a full partner. He told her the truth: He did have other women, including during her pregnancies and after her childbirths.

Tammy was deeply shattered. She felt humiliated, ridiculed, abused, raging at his betrayal: "He took advantage of my trust, caused me unbearable grief, made me crazy." She was in agony: "He sold me his lies, and I bought them." She was full of contempt at herself for her "utter stupidity." She felt he had shamed her terribly. "Surely he was laughing behind my back with his girlfriends about my naiveté. Surely everyone at work knew; they were looking at me with pity and scorn." At the same time, she was scornful towards "his lack of values and integrity." This was not the person that merited her respect. She felt he was not worthy of her loyalty.

She disclosed to me her retaliatory "plans": to change the locks in their apartment, block his access to their home, leave him outside her door, desolate, looking for a place to stay, forced to "tell his lies" to friends and relatives. She had an urge to tell what he was really like to "everyone"—his parents, her family, his fellow workers. She knew David was extremely sensitive to what people thought of him; he was most careful to come across as a dependable and trustworthy family man. He cherished his reputation as a stable, decent businessman; it was his trademark in the firm he worked for. Exposing his "deceitful nature" out in public would shame him beyond repair. She knew it would hurt him where it was most painful. She wanted to make him look like "scum," so he "will know what it feels like to be so degraded." She wanted to hurt him, to make him lose face, to be utterly humiliated. She wanted "to make an idiot out of him, just the way he makes me look."

While her pain and rage were spelled out directly, she was also filled with relief "she had not experienced in a long time." The emotional distress, confusion and fogginess that had accompanied her for many months had dissipated. "Suddenly everything is falling into place. I've stopped being the one with 'the problem.' I've become grounded. Everything is more real. I can hate him openly, be enraged and scream without him telling me I am crazy. I have all the right to throw him out of the house now, if I want to."

Tammy did consider leaving him; although she reassured him that he was best off telling her the truth, she felt she may decide to end her marriage: "David was too much of a fraud." She wasn't sure he was worth the trouble of repairing the damage and rebuilding a relationship she could feel proud of. She wasn't at all sure she could really bear that much pain herself and still be able to open herself to him, even if she wanted to. The extent of the disruption and the shock it caused her was at times too much.

The fact that he decided to tell her the truth was most meaningful at this point. His willingness to take responsibility for his actions without resorting to any lengthy "explanations" or "stories" and his readiness to admit he was cheating all that time was crucial. He met her pain and rage with shame but without avoidance. I felt there was some chance that this would constitute a turning point in their relationship.

His acknowledgement ("Yes, I did this to you") meant to her that he was committed, ready to fight for them and to deal with emotional difficulties that were nearly "unbearable" for him. In any event, his agreeing to "be there" mattered to her and counted when her disdain and despair were at their worst.

His acknowledgment allowed her "to return to herself," to get in touch with her wounded self-esteem as a woman, to explore her own difficulties with intimacy, with trust, with letting herself go. She realized that intimacy, whether physical or emotional, evoked anxieties of which she had not been aware beforehand. She was afraid of being "weak," needy, and submissive, of losing her independence, even of losing her "good mind," which was her main asset in the struggle to gain the affection of her strict, demanding and domineering father; he would crush her mother's will if she dared express an opinion that was out of line with the "rules of the house" he endorsed. Tammy learned to protect herself from emotional closeness, and survived by being "brainy," distant, "tough" and rigid, just as he dictated. Her personal history of failed dependence needs was played out time and again on the stage of her relationships with others, but it was especially significant when it concerned her marriage.

This period in their relationship was stormy. They talked a lot. Despite the emotional turmoil they were undergoing, Tammy felt hope. She believed this crisis would bring them closer.

David went to therapy. For the first time in his life, he felt lost, anxious, in need of help. Tammy was important to him, and he wanted to save their marriage. In addition, he felt he had reached a dead-end with himself. He was being pulled too often into situations that were threatening and shameful to him. The confrontation with Tammy had made him painfully aware of the fact that he had lived a good part of his life underground, going into hiding in his own house, anxious about being found out. He was afraid he was injuring Tammy, causing damage to his family; at the same time, he was afraid she would seek revenge, destroy him and all he cared about.

Hiding as an emotional "strategy" to managing relationships with women was not new to him, but the turmoil it created and his inability to cope shook him. He certainly did not think he would need therapeutic help, as it was somehow "agreed" between them, half-consciously, that Tammy was the one with the emotional difficulties; he always managed to handle difficulties "lightheartedly." This "arrangement" came to a halt by her ultimate confrontation and his confession.

David is the son of Holocaust survivors. Since his childhood, he has been used to hiding his emotional needs (especially his vulnerabilities). Others in his family always seemed needier. Supposedly, he was the one who "always managed to land on his own feet"; he was "easy"—the one his parents did not have to worry about, the one who did not overly consume their resources—whereas his younger brother was "trouble."

Therapy has gradually enabled him to become aware he is more vulnerable than he had known. To be sure, he always does "land on his feet"; but the problems that this apparent self-sufficiency generates are no less costly than the ones it is intended to solve.

As things stand, David perceives Tammy as being "totally white" while he himself is "totally black." She is "conservative, not really into the sexual fantasies that turn him on; no chance she would ever become interested." He realizes he needs Tammy to be more enthusiastic about him, to approach him with a desire of her own. Her expressed passion would signify he is wanted and accepted. It would calm down his concealed vulnerability about his own self-worth; he is afraid he could be appreciated and loved only if he hid the "black" sides in himself, sexually and otherwise.

The confrontations with Tammy, their talks, and the therapeutic relationship he is involved in enable him to risk "coming out of the closet": "At forty–two, I want to stop hiding and know what it is I am doing."

This crossroads in their lives, despite (or perhaps thanks to) the great emotional difficulties involved, is still hopeful for both of them. They are able to share more openly discredited longings, needs, fears and wishes, vengeful fantasies included. Their relationship has become more real. On the individual level, Tammy feels she has gained a sense of self-esteem, strength and confidence that she initially lacked. Processing and exploring unacknowledged vengefulness has been conducive to consolidating her sense of being a subject. It released her from the hold that angry helplessness had on her.

Deeds and Doers: Is There a Link That Can Reconnect and Contain Them?

The transition from perceiving oneself as a passive reactor, an object, to perceiving oneself as an active agent with an impact on reality is a complex, ongoing intersubjective process.

The dynamics of "doer and done-to" (Benjamin, 2004) are not linear; they don't lend themselves to simple formulations of cause and effect. Actions evoke counter-reactions and vice versa. The "desire to see another suffer" is not readily available for scrutiny, especially when evoked in closed relationships. Dismissals, exclusion, denying care, warmth, love or sex, which may be related to unacknowledged vengefulness, are communicated in subtle ways. Since ***deeds*** are dissociated from ***doers***, it is rather difficult to detect who is responsible for what. Relational cycles of mutually discredited feelings create a state of emotional confusion and anxiety for everyone involved.

That is not to say that there are no doers or done-tos. The opposite is the case: as stated earlier, I believe that dealing with injured feelings in relationships requires a most detailed account of what actually *did* happen in reality. I claim that it is crucial to face facts, to acknowledge who has done what to whom, before any process of reparation can start to evolve. The realities of abuse and justified claims for retribution have to be authenticated by the therapist if any healing work is to be effected. That, in my view, is the case whether the patient is the victim or the perpetrator. Schafer's (1983) aphorism addresses this controversial point succinctly "It is not a departure from neutrality to call a spade a spade" (p. 4).

The confusion between facts and feelings is a well-known product of traumatic experiences (Howell, 2005; Herman, 1992). It is enacted in the therapeutic relationship in many forms and calls for a special effort to be "real," ready to open oneself to threatening feelings, including vindictive wishes towards patients who may be victims and perpetrators at the same time.

Mutual acknowledgment is based on a commitment to truth as an objective entity. It demands minute personal knowledge of the inner and outer realities of all involved parties. Nothing less can satisfy the need to repair the broken connectedness and restore the injured self-esteem.

Having said that, it is also relevant to look for those places in the above clinical vignettes in which there is no need to identify the "bad guy," no need to discover who "started it," who is to blame, what "really" caused the problem. These places are "earned" by painful processing: they constitute a breakthrough in the cycle of unacknowledged vindictive acts and open up a potential space in the relationship.

Betrayal is one of the most painful blows that a partner in a relationship can inflict. The intensity of the feelings it evokes and the personal meanings it acquires have to be recognized by all involved parties, including the therapist. Reality and truth are sobering; they are absolutely necessary for reestablishing a basis for trust and togetherness. Closeness can be reached, however, only after the actuality of wrongdoing has been properly explored and authenticated. In this respect, the therapist is an essential, involved witness who does testify before metaphoric judges.

We are not used to perceiving avoidance, absence, lack of doing, or passivity in close relationships as "actions" in their own right. They are experienced mostly as "reactions." Anxiety tends to toss "action items" into the domain of the other. The "ping pong" dynamics of projections and counter-projections can be transformed into a shared reality, however, through awareness to processes of mutual recognition.

INCONCLUSIVE REMARKS

I would like to recapitulate some of the main points raised in the clinical illustrations in this chapter:

1. People in close relationships punish each other for their painful experiences much more often than they are aware of. That does not mean that close relationships cannot be curative and reparative. Mitchell's (1997) idea that becoming part of the problem is how we become part of the solution catches the spirit of this complexity.
   It is clinically useful to detect such cycles of mutual "punishment" and vengefulness, in order to enhance each party's ability to take personal responsibility for his share in producing the distance and enmity generated by such unknowing "punishments." Processing these behavioral cycles, while keeping in mind that unacknowledged vengefulness may be at work, is productive. It helps alleviate the estrangement that may destroy the relationship. In addition, it strengthens each party's personal development and capacity to exert influence and effect a desired change.
2. Behaviors known to us as "passive/aggressive" include a hidden dimension of vengefulness. The advantage of acknowledging this dimension lies in its relational significance, in the ability to place such processes in an intersubjective context. Vengefulness presupposes an "other" that is the recipient of vengeful desires, an "other" who is the cause of the disruption and whose recognition is absolutely required in the process of reconnecting and creating a shared reality.
3. Since vengefulness is a discredited feeling, it is difficult to identify and process. To acknowledge it is to admit that we have ill wishes towards others, including others in our charge and close to us. Vengefulness evokes anxiety, guilt and shame; it threatens one's self-esteem and the belief in one's sense of essential goodness. Therapists are especially prone to disconnect from vengefulness, since their socialization prioritizes positive feelings like compassion and caring rather than aversive ones like hatred, resentment or enmity.
4. Awareness of vengeful behavior in therapy can lead to transformation. It may release personal energy that is otherwise curbed. Owning up to vengefulness may be empowering and may validate one's relevance as a subject.
5. The therapist's ability to be fully present in the therapeutic relationship, to explore his own vengefulness and his own fear of the patient's vengefulness, enhances the process of mutual recognition and promotes the emotional development of both patient and therapist.

The developmental, restorative and communicative value of hard feelings, the ability to "admit" them into the therapeutic interaction, to acknowledge their impact, to explore and re-integrate them into one's relational matrix, is not entirely new in psychoanalysis. (Winnicott's concepts of aggression and hatred and Kohut's understanding of narcissistic rage are classic examples.)

As one of the most "banished" emotional experiences, however, vengefulness merits much more attention than it has received so far in our therapeutic endeavors. Its potential for becoming destructive is matched only by its potential for enhancing personal growth and for deepening mutual concern and accountability. Acknowledging the prevalence of vengeful wishes and opening ourselves to the emotional tribulations they evoke may assist in integrating them into our clinical practice as one meaningful type of feeling among others.

What makes dialogue (let alone intimacy) possible is the readiness to take part in the arduous process of mutual recognition. From this perspective, "stepping on each other's toes," hurting one another, wishing to strike back, to "regain balance"—when coupled with the ability to stop, to take a look, to pay attention, to accept responsibility where needed and to make amends—can be transformative. One's capacity for coexistence with others involves the daily task of negotiating to reconnect fractured links and retrieve mutual acknowledgment. As Mitchell (2002) puts it, "paradoxically, the survival of romance depends not on skill in avoiding aggression but on the capacity to contain it alongside love" (p. 120).

I suggest that vengefulness constitutes a significant (albeit unrecognized and discredited) part in these processes and is woven into the fabric of all relationships, including therapeutic ones. The therapist's awareness of the intersubjective meaning of vengefulness may provide *both parties in the relationship* with more detailed knowledge about their assets and vulnerabilities. Such awareness adds a perspective to our understanding of the nature of stalemates in the therapeutic relationship and of possible ways to untangle them.

By acknowledging the normalcy of ill wishes towards others, and by being emotionally receptive to the patient's vengefulness as well as to their own, therapists can enhance the healing of problems caused by discrediting, whether social, personal, or interpersonal.

References

Améry, J. (1980). *At the Mind's Limit: Contemplations by a Survivor on Auschwitz and Its Realities.* Indiana University Press.

Benjamin J. (2004). "Beyond Doer and Done to: An Intersubjective View of Thirdness." *Psychoanalytic Quarterly*. 73: (1): 5-46.

The Bible (King James Translation), Isaiah 1-2.

Bromberg P., M. (1996). "Standing in the Spaces: The Multiplicity of Self and the Psychoanalytic Relationship." *Contemporary Psychoanalysis*. 32: 509-535.

Coleridge, S. T. (1950). *The Portable Coleridge*. New York: Viking Press.

Dalal, F. (1998). *Taking the Group Seriously*. London, Jessica Kingsley Publishers.

Eigen, M. (1981). "The Area of Faith in Winnicott, Lacan and Bion." *International Journal of Psycho-Analysis*. 62: 413-433.

Elster, J. (1990). "Norms of Revenge." *Ethics*, 100: 862-85.

Feiner, A. (1995). "Laughter among the Pear Trees: Vengeance, Vindictiveness, and Vindication." *Contemporary Psychoanalysis*. 31: 381.

Ferenczi, S. (1949). "Confusion of Tongues between Adults and the Child." *International Journal of Psychoanalysis*. 0: 225-230.

Foulkes S. H. (1964). *Therapeutic Group* Analysis, Karnac Classics.

Goldberg J. G. and (2004). "Getting Even: Fantasies of Revenge and the Stabilization of the Ego: Acts of Revenge and the Ascension of Thanatos." *Modern Psychoanalysis*. 29: (1) 3-21.

Herman, J. (1992). *Trauma end Recovery*. Basic Books.

Holmes, L. (2004). "Hell Hath No Fury: How Women Get Even." *Modern Psychoanalysis*. 29: (1) 49-61.

Howell E. (2005). *The Dissociative Mind.* Hillside, NJ: New Jersey Analytic Press.

Mitchell, S. (1997). *Influence and Autonomy in Psychoanalysis*. Hillsdale, NJ: New Jersey Analytic Press.

Mitchell, S. (2002). *Can Love Last?* New York: Norton.

Philips, A. (1993). *On Kissing, Tickling and Being Bored.* Cambridge, MA: Harvard University Press.

Stern, D. B. (1987). "Unformulated Experience and Transference." *Contemporary Psychoanalysis*, 23: 484-490.

Schafer R. (1983). *The Analytic Attitude*. New York: Basic Books.

Suttie, I. D. (1960). *The Origins of Love and Hate*. London: Penguin Books.

Winnicott, W. D. (1965). "The Development of the Capacity for Concern." In *The Maturational Processes and the Facilitating Environment Studies in Theory of Emotional Development.* Madison, Connecticut International Universities Press. pp. 73-83.

Winnicott, W. D. (1975). "Hate in the Countertransference." *In Through Pediatrics to Psychoanalysis*. New York. Basic Books, Inc.: pp. 194-204

Winnicott, W. D. (1975). "Aggression In Relation To Emotional Development." *In Through Pediatrics to Psychoanalysis*. New York. Basic Books, Inc.: pp. 204-219.

Winnicott, W. D. (1983). *Playing and Reality*. London and New York: Tavistock Publications.

Chapter 6

"AM I MY BROTHER'S KEEPER?" VENGEFULNESS AS A LINK TOWARDS RECONNECTING

Miriam Berger

This chapter examines some of the more "public" aspects of vengeful wishes, in particular their role in preserving *valued collective ties*, a *sense of belonging*, and *social recognition*. Knowing and remembering are major components of the process of recognition; they play a part in defining personal and social identity and in promoting the hope for justice, accountability, and mutual concern. Vengeance should, therefore, be understood in relation to the dynamics of knowing and remembering.

VENGEFULNESS, REMEMBERING, KNOWING

Remembering is a multilayered, complex emotional-cognitive process. I will discuss it only to the extent that it touches on the issues at stake: vengefulness, accountability, and related matters discussed in the previous chapters.

As stated above, remembering and knowing are central dimensions in defining personal and collective identities. They delineate the boundaries of a coherent shared reality and sustain a needed trust in the continuity of one's group for generations to come. Like threads woven into a fabric, remembering and knowing constitute a collective history that binds members of a group to each other. Each member's personal biography is thus made part of the community's common history, which shapes it in many unconscious ways. Volkan's (2001) views about the role of historical events in the formation of collective remembering and in defining group identity come to mind. According to Volkan, "chosen traumas and chosen glories" serve to form ethnic and religious common identities: by defining the group's shared mental representations of meaningful historical events transmitted through the generations, they serve as a "tent" containing the group's mental resources.

Knowing and remembering, I would like to suggest, play an important part in the process of mutual recognition as well.

Referring back to the biblical tale of Cain and Abel, it is significant to note that when God asks Cain "Where is Abel thy brother?" Cain says, "I know not: Am I my brother's keeper?" His denial, his "not knowing" is not accepted by the higher order he attempts to evade. God's rejection of this answer becomes constitutive: one cannot claim innocence in the face of evildoing against one's fellowman, a "brother" metaphorically or otherwise. We thus find in this tale, as I understand it, an ancient foundation for a culture of accountability (an idea to which I will return later in this chapter).

Unacknowledged realities stand in danger of being erased from the record of authenticated facts; consequently, they may also erase personal and collective emotional experiences, become "non-facts" ("acts without an actor"), generate "non-experience" (Puget, 2002), and, eventually, even become a decisive factor in the obliteration (or, to use a cruder term, the "extermination") of people's physical existence. To say it differently, with a dynamic perspective in mind, they become dissociated entities, both within one's inner world and in outer social reality (Howell, 2002).

A blatant instance of attempts to annul "facts" and consequently to annul accountability is the denial of the realities of genocides, whether Jewish, Armenian, or other. I believe that the road to the physical annihilation of people is thickly paved with the obliteration of factual reality. Améry expresses his protest against the dangers of this kind of oblivion in few acute words:

> My book is meant to aid in preventing precisely this [i.e., false conciliatoriness based on a denial of the dreadful realities witnessed by Améry]. … *What happened, happened. But* that *it happened cannot be so easily accepted* (Améry, p. x1; my emphasis).

Acts of "*non-re-cognition*," such as forgetting, ignoring, denying, not knowing, distorting or evading the truth, may weaken one's hold on reality in many ways and facilitate real violations of human rights and dignity; they may even endanger lives. Edmund Burke allegedly said that "all that is necessary for the triumph of evil is that good men do nothing." To that I would add: "or *know* nothing." The popular saying, "what you don't know won't hurt you," which is sometimes meant to soothe one's suspicious fears, can acquire the more sinister meaning captured succinctly by Baudelaire: "It is the Devil's cleverest guile to convince us that he does not exist."

To claim that what happened did *not* happen constitutes an attack on one's sanity. It discredits one's mental existence, confuses cognition, distorts one's emotional "gyroscope," and may eventually sabotage one's capacity to survive. Such a denial of reality can shut down the "alarm system" that regulates one's functioning and safeguards life, preventing it from summoning help in the face of danger.

According to Moses (1982), groups and communities may be subjected to similar processes when their history is denied or distorted, namely, when they are attacked by the "hurtful weapon of non-recognition." Underlining chronic political conflicts, Moses claims, are dynamic processes in which both sides show "the ubiquitous use of that most narcissistically hurtful international weapon: non-recognition" (p. 56).

As stated earlier, vengefulness can be perceived as part of the emotional "alarm system" or "gyroscope" that contributes to processes of recognition, on the personal as well as on the social level.

My special attentiveness to questions of acknowledgment may be due to my own firsthand experience of being de-legitimized: I keep my false birth certificate, along with my other "Aryan Papers," from "there," in a special drawer in my dresser, as a significant reminder that social recognition is a precious human asset not to be taken for granted.

Améry states that *"Dignity is the right to live granted by society"* (Améry, 1980, p. xiv, my italics); since it is "a right to live," its denial by society (or others) may be likened to a death sentence. Améry's relentless, probing study of victims' "resentment" or vengefulness attests, then, to the crucial significance that recognition by others plays in one's life, personally and socially.

The state of Israel, which was to become my homeland after I had wandered in post-war Europe as a refugee, was established by an international vote—an act of social recognition that had international as well as the most personal dimensions. This act of recognition was meant as a reparative gesture towards the Jews who had survived genocide. Tragically, however, the same course of events that finally granted the Jews a home and a legitimate citizenship also deprived their Palestinian neighbors of these same rights and became their calamity.

Since then, I have been living in a country torn apart by conflicting claims for recognition by two peoples that have found it extremely difficult to allow a process of mutual recognition and reconciliation to develop between them. Consequently, life for everyone is endangered by a continuous state of war.

Israelis and Palestinians alike seem to maintain a seesaw-like balance that, time and time again, recreates dynamics of "Us and Them": victims and victimizers exchange places continuously, obstructing opportunities for reciprocal and cooperative solutions (Berman et al., 2000).

Regrettably, the chronic state of war in which Palestinians and Israelis engaged over the last century is a living proof that mutual recognition (or its absence) is a decisive factor on every level of people's lives.

VENGEANCE: SOCIETY'S MORAL MEMORY

Acknowledging wrongdoing signals that what has been done cannot be dismissed and that, consequently, the person (or the group) to whom it has been done cannot be dismissed either (Laub et al., 1989).

From this perspective, vengefulness may be regarded as an unconscious mechanism that reverses the danger inherent in "not-knowing." It offsets the tendency to discredit, overlook, exclude, ostracize, or de-legitimize others (Berman et al., 2000)

German sociologist Wolfgang Sofsky, who has explored the aftermath of social violence, believes that the combination of memory and revenge is essential to preserving social values:

> …vengeance is a part of society's *moral memory*... The modern devaluation of revenge has failed to take notice of its moral perseverance. Revenge does not know forgiveness nor does it fall into oblivion. Time may pass by but vengeance is keeping an eye on its

> aim. It has a long memory and does not know any prescription. It is waiting with patience for the moment of fulfillment. The memory of the deed does not extinguish. In the flow of time, revenge thus is a moment of duration. It is keeping the past present; it bears the dead in mind and keeps faith with them. It wants to continue where the dead are no longer able to do so. The deed shall be rescinded. *Vengeance, therefore, is a leap out of the impotence of suffering into liberating action* (Quoted in Sievers, 2006, p. 58; my emphasis).

Vengefulness, when perceived as a coded communication, can be understood as a dynamic relational process safeguarding the hope of the excluded ones (whether individuals or groups) to be re-included, to be readmitted into the society from which they were banished.

Vengefulness, thwarted as it may be, aims to renew a sense of social belonging. It "keeps an eye" on the prospects of "coming home" that the excluded person or group is nurturing. It is a coded signal representing the de-legitimized person's (or group's) request to regain rights to dignity, equality, sovereignty and power. It opens a path back from an experience of helplessness and irrelevance. It is a call to impose accountability, paving the road back to re-cognition and re-inclusion; it offsets the wrongdoing and constitutes a triumph of justice over the forces of evil which threaten people's emotional and physical existence.

Gosford Park: The Revenge of Discredited Selves

As stated earlier, social discrediting turns into an inner dissociation of the discredited individual or group, and vice versa. In this respect, social and personal realities reflect and shape each other in a myriad of ways. These processes, within and without, combine to increase the alienation and loneliness of the injured person: he is further banished from himself, from his personal resources and from essential ties to his community.

Popular entertainment oftentimes depicts urgent topics in a light-hearted, stylish way that is easy to digest and reflect upon. Robert Altman's suspense film "Gosford Park" is one such work, depicting in an elegant manner certain facets of the connection between social discrediting and revenge. Like innumerable suspense movies, it hinges on revenge for seemingly long-forgotten past injuries. It is a tale of crime and punishment that reinforces our implicit conviction (not to say, our essential need) that evil deeds will eventually be revealed and justly penalized.

The film operates on two interlocking levels. On the one hand, it portrays the relationships between two groups of people, masters and servants, assembled for a weekend at a country estate. On the other, it is a suspense story about the murder of their host, the estate's owner.

The film's plot unfolds as follows: A gathering of British gentry (and one American) comes together for a weekend of hunting at a country estate. The noble guests arrive with their entourage of personal servants; the "masters" are led to the upper rooms of the house, while their servants are sent down to the basement, where the storage, laundry, kitchen, cooking, etc., takes place.

The servants have no personal names; they are called by the names of their masters. Thus, Weiss's servant is called Weiss "for the sake of order and efficiency." In a similar vein, it turns out that the servants have no notable personal histories that deserve sharing in public.

When they all sit down for their common meal in the kitchen downstairs, they are amazed at the American valet's question: "Were any of your parents also servants?" His attempt to make a personal contact, to get to know the others more closely, much in the same way the gentry upstairs does, embarrasses the other servants. This is obviously not an acceptable subject for a dinner conversation down in the basement. Apparently, they are not supposed to have any subjective lives of their own and are expected to be defined basically through their role of catering to the needs of others. It seems that the group downstairs serves as a receptacle for the emotional realities that the group upstairs rejects; the servants function as an "anti-group" for the masters, and perhaps even vice versa (see Nitsun, 1991).

As the plot unfolds, it becomes apparent that that same silenced subject—the servants' personal histories, their ties to the past, and the constituents of their identities—is the central motif around which the drama revolves. "Masters" and "Servants" are intertwined in secret relationships that are doomed to come to a closure with a violent death. As it turns out, the host was murdered conjointly by the male servant he failed to acknowledge as his legitimate son and by the servant's mother whom he molested years earlier when she was a poor young laborer in one of his factories.

The mother, now the manager of the "downstairs" estate servants, describes herself as "the perfect servant." She has no inner life and no subjective existence she can claim as her own; she is the ultimate "non-person," the embodiment of an individual "evicted" from her own personal being. One might speculate that the absolute domination her boss had over her body when she was young and very much at his mercy reverberates in the radical inner negation to which she has subjected herself ever since. It is as if she has emptied herself from within and filled the void with his wishes. She claims that she knows his wants and needs even before he identifies them for himself. In this respect, "master and servant" make a perfect negative match. Theirs may well be a good depiction of a "marriage made in hell." I can see them as the reverse image of mutual recognition, as non-recognition in action.

Her utter subservience and self-abnegation ripen over the years into revenge, culminating in murder: she serves him a poisoned drink, while her son stabs him in the back. The cycle that began with a violation of the young woman's dignity, and continued with a disregard of both mother's and son's claims for a legitimate place "upstairs," ends with the killing of the offender. The account of domination and self-abnegation has been settled; an "eye-for-an-eye" primary morality has reestablished the disrupted social order.

In the film, many years have gone by since the original abuse, but the humiliation has not subsided just because "time heals." Quite the opposite turns out to be true: the wounds "become sour," and the desire to redress a lifelong shameful existence ripens into an intricate premeditated murder.

"Gosford Park" represents quite elegantly the powerful hold that suppressed past injuries can have on people's lives over time. It is also worth noting that this tale of personal violation and revenge is interwoven with the social realities of class, status, and power, along with the rigid hierarchical structures embedded in them. One could go on and examine how issues of gender, class, wealth, etc., are played out in this film, but those subjects merit a separate discussion.

Revenge Cinema: Scenes of Comic Relief

Proceeding beyond this cinematic depiction, I am reminded of a popular aphorism that tells us that "revenge is best served cold." That, in my mind, is where trauma meets remembering: remembering in this context may become a tool for "freezing" the wound, waiting for the right moment to get even (See Sofsky's quote above).

Lack of recognition is the ultimate injury; it is felt as a negation of one's unique subjectivity, one's right to have a history and a name of one's own. It generates shame and humiliation, which in turn give rise to vengeful wishes. If the denigration is not properly exposed, acknowledged and authenticated, it causes unbearable emotional pain that demands vindication.

This process may turn into viscous cycles of vengeful attacks and counterattacks. Relationships within families, groups and whole societies can be locked into dead-end traps unless this destructive reactivity is attended to.

To illustrate this point, let us take a brief look at another group of films, the Godfather trilogy, whose unprecedented popularity is partly due, I think, to the fascination as well as the horror that unleashed vengefulness holds for us.[1]

The Godfather trilogy depicts an endless sequence of vengeful attacks and counterattacks between family members, rival clans, and competing gangs. These actions are mostly presented as either "business transactions" or familial duties, essential to maintaining the tribal boundaries of loyalties and betrayals. The protagonists claim to be compelled to engage in these actions by some objective necessity, supposedly in the family's best interest.

This bloodshed amounts to a "plague" transmitted from one generation to the next. Traitors, victims, villains, and heroes exchange places as the plot develops. All parties are trapped in a seemingly uncontrollable web of violence, indiscriminately taking the lives of loved ones and passersby alike.

Movies reflect reality and structure it; but at the same time, they also take us away from it. This may be part of their function, akin to interludes of "comic relief" that ease the tensions in Shakespeare's tragedies. There is no way, however, that fiction can surpass the devastation and chaos that unbridled violence creates in reality.

Vengefulness: The Hope That "Help is on its Way"

Questions of belonging and recognition, with the vulnerabilities they involve, are so central for us, I suggest, partly because they play a fundamental role in human survival.

In a paper about the dynamics of retaliation, Goldwater (2004) defines two human needs he considers essential and connects them to revenge: "As a feeling of connection and a feeling of esteem, or worth, are the two most basic psychological needs, their negation—abandonment and humiliation, respectively—are the two most profound psychological injuries. 'Revenge is sweet' in response to these injuries" (p. 23).

[1] The Godfather trilogy, directed by Francis Ford Coppola, is considered by many to be the one of the most critically and artistically successful film series in movie history. The legendary Don Corleone, with his familial dynasty, has become an all-time cultural icon since the early seventies when the first movie came out.

As I understand it, the "sweetness of revenge" is a measure of revenge's crucial role in maintaining one's need to feel relevant, to be able to make a personal impact on reality, and to belong to one's community. This "sweetness" offsets the danger of "bitterness" that denigration and exclusion may cause. Needless to say, these are unconscious "coded" communications that need deciphering within a relational frame.

Human beings, I take it, are to a great extent tribal creatures, "group animals" whose ability to survive individually depends on connectedness to others. It is assumed that in primordial times, being part of a cohesive group maximized the resources available to each member for survival and reproduction (Freud, 1921).

If this thought has substance, threats to belonging and to reciprocity endanger survival. Being deemed deserving of respect and being part of the fabric that binds a community together are—literally—lifelines. Acts of ostracizing, ignoring or dismissing one's relevance can be experienced as cutting off life supplies. These are probably the dynamic processes that make excommunication feel like a death sentence. Acts of excommunication exclude their targets from crucial emotional and physical communal resources, depriving them of their right to be sustained and protected by the community's rules and norms.[2]

The multiple meanings attributed to inclusion in- or exclusion from one's group are, I suggest, major aspects of human life. I touch upon this issue through the notions of revenge, recognition, and accountability, though I am aware that this is only one perspective out of many. Here again, Améry's (1980) simple and moving words are telling:

> The expectation of help, the certainty of help, is indeed one of the fundamental experiences of human beings, and probably also of animals... It is as much a constitutional psychic element as is the struggle for existence (p. 28).

These words express Améry's belief in the "protective shield" inherent in belonging, in being included in the network of obligations that members have towards each other. He is a living witness to the catastrophic consequences of exclusion from the human community, a moral spokesman for all victims of brutal abuse.

For many years after the war, Améry held onto his "resentment" (in the form of vengeful wishes) as an emblem of hope that "help is on its way." It is painful to know that he finally despaired of that hope. It is probable that he ended his life when he could no longer sustain the hope that the European community, "the world" at large, and the Germans specifically would recognize their share in the genocide of the Jews and assume accountability for it. The hope for recognition of evildoing and for accountability is, I believe, a hope society cannot exist without.

Social belonging and acceptance provide a needed sense of safety, a protective shield that enables the person to trust that "help is on its way." Being part of a reciprocal exchange system enables people to develop their unique subjectivity and to depend on self and others as resources of help, empowerment and growth (Foulkes, 1975; Dalal, 1998).

---

[2] In a study about the dynamics of scapegoating among children, Twemlow (2000) explores processes of ostracism in schools; he sees it as one of the fiercest punishments an adolescent may be subjected to by his peers; it is a source of many violent interactions among youngsters and poses a continuous threat to growing up in communities and neighborhoods. The subject, Twemlow claims, requires more thorough understanding and research. ("The Roots of Violence: Converging Psychoanalytic Explanatory Models for Power Struggles and Violence in Schools." *Psychoanalytic Quarterly*, 69 (4): 741-785.)

The attentive, concerned look of an "other"—what the Hebrew idiom *lassim lev* literally renders as "putting one's heart"—has evolutionary value. It symbolizes "mindfulness" towards others, the recognition that separate sovereign others do exist out there in real reality and ought to be taken into account as such. The existence of an "other" that can "see" the person constitutes a basis for a context of approval and acceptance; it is an invitation to partake in processes of reciprocity and mutual recognition (Fonagy, 1998).

Alternatively, the absence of this "look" of recognition is felt as depriving the person from essential life provisions; it may be harmful and even destructive, making people "invisible" in many ways. The issue of "invisible" people and of the psychological and sociopolitical implications of their status merits a separate discussion. Let me just mention, as one example, the many thousands (if not millions) of illegal aliens who live a marginal existence on the fringes of western societies, deprived of the legal rights and obligations conferred upon citizens, disturbing and perhaps even posing an insidious threat to the established social order.

Seeing, knowing, remembering, and recognizing are essential in granting personal and social relevance and legitimacy, while the lack of them may be weakening and threatening to one's well-being and even his very life.

Remembering As Vengeance

Sofsky's suggestion to view vengeance as "a part of society's moral memory" has its counterpart in Bergman's proposal to view remembering as a sublimation of prohibited revenge (Bergman, 1985).

In a paper about remembering as a meaningful function in the lives of Holocaust survivors, Bergman claims that if we were to ask a primitive tribe what it was that the victims of murder demanded of them, the immediate answer would be revenge. But if we posed this "tactless question" to Holocaust survivors—if we were to ask them what it was that the six million dead demanded of them—the overwhelming reply would be that *they want to be remembered.* This remembering is supposed to *bear witness* to what had happened, to confirm that the victims' deaths were not senseless after all, that they did not die in vain, that their suffering would continue to be acknowledged by the generations to come as having some human meaning. Replacing vengeful acts, this kind of remembering serves in a sublimated form the quest for justice and accountability; it confirms the crucial belief that a future does exist for the victims' offspring despite the attempt to annihilate them (p. 14).

From this point of view, remembering as a form of sublimated vengefulness is a projection of hope into the future. It has the important function of sustaining belief in the survival of an orderly world that, in the long run, evil cannot defeat. In doing so, it foresees the reestablishing of a just society. In this respect, remembering is a form of "re-membering," of reclaiming into "membership" that which had been cut off, annihilated, "dis-membered" and wiped away.

Furthermore, this understanding of remembering indicates that the implementation of justice or of any other moral norms of conduct is a collective issue, not to be limited to the personal sphere alone; it belongs to the public dimension of human life. As the saying goes, justice has to be ***seen***, not only done. The presence of *others* is always implied in such formulations. The function of "being seen" safeguards the collective value system.[3] Being seen is tantamount to being known by others. Such "seeing" is a symbolic act of acknowledging the other's subjectivity. The "other" is the essential witness whose "seeing" provides one's life with a solid foundation of emotional and ethical validity, making one a relevant member of one's community.

Winnicott's ideas about the constitutive function of the mother's "mirroring" come to mind here as a conceptual framework providing a dynamic link between the inner personal world and the real concerned caretaker . I may be overstretching Winnicott's thinking a bit, but it seems to me that his belief in the crucial role of an "other" who recognizes the baby as a sovereign subject contributes some depth to the issues at stake; I dare say that the ideas presented here would not be foreign to his notions, although Winnicott is basically a devout individualist. The "whole world," which (it is hoped) will know, remember, and acknowledge one's experience, can be encapsulated in the act that Winnicott calls "mirroring"—that act of seeing and hearing, of listening to the other, on which redemption depends.

Vengefulness: An Act of "Telling it" to the Whole World

Roiphe (2000) is adamant about the value of making wrongdoing publicly known and acknowledged. She stresses the act of "*telling it*" to others, claiming it has a therapeutic function as it entails witnessing and the validation that accompanies it. In a poignant article on the writing of childhood memoirs, she claims that every memoir is an

> ….act of witnessing [that] contains within its resonances ... the not-so-civilized hope for revenge. It serves as a child's cry, 'I will tell on you'. This witnessing, sometimes many years after the insult, is the last resort of the powerless, the child for example. It contains the message that what you have done will not be hidden, I will expose it for the entire world to see. Then you will be revealed for what you are and held accountable for what you have done… This desire for revenge is a spark to the memory, sets the mind on its backward path, spurs the effort of writing and ensures the final act of publication… Anger is behind the need for revenge and anger is the handmaiden, the husband, the bride, the mother of revenge. We tell ourselves other things… but behind that lies the child's voice, 'I'll tell on you, I really will' (p. 1011).

As noted above, "telling it" positions the "other" as an essential witness, one whose emotional participation authenticates the injurious deeds. The witness's presence salvages the victim from the danger of being isolated, dismissed, and de-legitimized.

Améry's describes his "little book" as a testimony that has to be heard for a process of humanization to take place:

> Let this book then be a witness not only to what real Fascism and singular Nazism were, but let it also be an appeal to German youth for introspection. ... I describe the state of someone who was overcome; that is all… I sometimes hope that this study has met its

[3]It is interesting to mention in this context that in the 12th century, King Henry II established the doctrine that crime is not simply an offence against a private person requiring reparation in the form of money or blood, but a disturbance to the well-being of the king himself and therefore an offence against the state (Elster, 1990).

> aims; then it could concern all those who wish to live together as fellow human beings (Améry 1980 p. xiv).

Wounds caused by others can be cured by others. The loneliness, alienation and subjugation one has suffered can be made accessible and understandable by the acceptance and identification of others. Their readiness to participate in the "telling" makes possible a process of mourning for the victim's suffering and losses, paving the way to a restored shared reality and to recovery.

Améry expresses vividly his desperate need for the Germans' willingness to accept their responsibility and to recognize their accountability for what he had gone through. His hope is to see

> the two groups of people, the overpowered and those who overpowered them … joined in the desire that time be turned back and, with it, that history become moral… The spiritual reduction to pulp by the German people, not only of the books, but of everything that was carried out in those years (between 1933 and 1945), would be the negation of the negation: a highly positive, redeeming act. *Only through it would our resentment be subsequently pacified and have become objectively unnecessary* (p. 79, my emphasis).

The desire to be known and remembered, to be acknowledged by future generations as persons who sacrificed their lives to die in dignity, was also the vision motivating those who organized the uprising of the Warsaw ghetto. In a book documenting the accounts of some of the last living fighters of that battle (Grupinskaya, 2002), the translators write in their introduction that some of the insurgents prepared themselves for the fighting many months in advance, knowing it was to be their last battle. Their passionate desire was to die while holding onto their weapons. This passion to die as fighters symbolized an outcry, a protest against the inhumanity to which they were subjected.

For a long time before the uprising, the insurgents recorded in writing both the atrocities they witnessed and their own plans, including a meticulous account of the process of gathering arms and planning their combative moves. *The uprising was meant to be seen, remembered and known.* As the translators state, a person does not write a memoir, does not set out to revolt and to fight a doomed battle, unless he believes in some way that justice will prevail and that the rule of evil will eventually come to its end. Underneath the desire to avenge the Germans, there must have been faith in society's ability to redress this evil, to retrieve the continuity of a history with humane values. The rebels meant their battle to be a symbol of faith in the ability to stand up against obliteration.

Their wish has been fulfilled to some extent, as the uprising has come to represent an act of freedom in the face of brutal oppression. It was meant to make future generations remember and know that trampled dignity can be retrieved and that hope was alive, despite everything. Judging by the place history has allotted to the Warsaw Ghetto uprising, it seems that their voice has found some echoes in our collective memory of the holocaust.

Primo Levi (1988), whose *Survival in Auschwitz*, an account of his time as an inmate in the death camp, has been described as one of the most important works of the twentieth century, expressed his devastation at the indifference he met upon returning home: his "ghastly tale" had no place in post-war Europe.

Levi's choice to quote Coleridge's *Ancient Mariner* in the epigram of his book *The Drowned and the Saved* (a sequel to *Survival in Auschwitz*) speaks for itself:

Since then, at an uncertain hour, that agony returns: And till my ghastly tale is told, this heart within me burns.

The Rime of the Ancient Mariner is perhaps the most widely recognized story of the return from hell and the compulsion to speak about it. Coleridge's Mariner comes back from the depths of human suffering and frailty, wrecked, stunned, and obligated as both witness and victim. The Mariner returns to tell his story. This telling, the Mariner says, "left me free"; but he is compelled, again and again, to speak of his experiences.

For Levi, however, there was no return. For him and for many others who survived the atrocities of the Holocaust, liberation was in many ways a new trauma; the victims of evil were received with suspicion and disbelief. Their sight aroused unbearable feelings of dread, shame and collective guilt, which were dismissed along with the people who signified them.

VENGEFULNESS: THERAPEUTIC CONSIDERATIONS

Therapy can provide an arena in which these issues are reactivated and receive a chance to be redeemed. It makes possible the act of "telling it" publicly, validating one's social relevance and personal truth. It offers a renewed opportunity to deal with past injuries, humiliations, and vengefulness, with the aim of restoring trust and a needed sense of belonging. The therapeutic relationship constitutes a social microcosm that recreates within its boundaries issues of "central human concern" (Chapter 1).

Since I am a group analyst as well as a clinical psychologist, my conceptual framework includes the perspectives of group and individual therapy alike. I believe that combining these two perspectives contributes to our understanding of the issues at stake and enriches the clinical implications that concern us when treating hurt patients.[4]

Considering the analytical group, I suggest that the group and the group therapist represent the ultimate "collective other" with whom and through whom we shape our personal world. This "collective other" can grant the needed recognition and thus help restore one's self-esteem, connectedness and sense of belonging.

Only once the "whole world" knows what has happened can the pact of silence that isolates the patient and seals his loneliness be dissolved. The therapeutic group can be perceived as such a "world," which gathers to witness the evil deeds, share in the suffering, validate the patient's reality, and join in the demand for culpability.

Each group member acts as a witness for the other; each accepts responsibility for the other's suffering (although he or she is not the real-life offender). This communal participation, acknowledgment, and authentication have a redeeming quality; they initiate the arduous process towards healing and create a relational space for its unfolding (apparently it was in this sense that Foulkes defined the dynamic interactions in the analytic group as "ego training in action").

---

[4] As stated earlier (Chapter 1), psychoanalysis does not address vengefulness very often. Since vengefulness is essentially a "social" feeling, group analysts would seem to be natural contributors to exploring its dynamics and its impact on group processes. However, going over volumes by Foulkes (1948, 1964, 1965, 1975) and Bion (1961), two major figures in the field, I could not find any discussion whatsoever of vengefulness and its vicissitudes.

Elster (1990), who studies norms of revenge from a socio-philosophical perspective, contends that "honor is a *triadic* rather than a *dyadic* relation: *A gains honor by humiliating B in the presence of C*; hence the insistence of feuding societies that killings be publicly recognized" (p. 884). This perspective contributes a meaningful social dimension to psychoanalytic thinking about dignity and self-worth: one's sense of dignity is determined not only by one's relation to the people with whom one directly engages (i.e., complementary pairs of "doer" and "done to"), but also by the involved presence of third parties or "witnesses." In this sense, *dignity is a triadic construct in the same way that all "social feelings" are*: it is determined by the collective relational matrix and born out of it. Witnessing represents public recognition—one can say it is actually "public recognition in action"; it safeguards the preservation of human dignity and upholds the values that connect people to each other.

In view of these ideas, I would like to suggest that one of the central curative elements that group therapy provides is the very arena it creates—an arena for the act of "telling it," including the act of "telling on *them*," the essentially *vengeful*, punitive act of shaming and naming the offenders. Group therapy creates the arena in which, as Roiphe (2000) puts it, what "you have done will not be hidden… [but will be] for the entire world to see."

Providing such an arena may well be one of the main reasons for prescribing group therapy for grieving individuals who suffered traumatic experiences, especially when the injury is manmade. Joining a therapy group evokes the hidden wish to "tell on them," to reveal publicly the true face of those who injured, humiliated, shamed, mocked, dismissed and excluded the wounded individual. Joining a therapeutic group is an act of faith; it evokes the expectation that *this* time one will be heard, that the abuse and injustice one has suffered will finally become known and recognized. It reawakens the hope that this time, one will not be abandoned to face one's aggressors alone; this time, one will be re-included in the communal circle with other fellow humans.

The matrix of group connectedness creates a framework that provides a "holding environment" in which a continuous process of negotiations about personal relevance, acceptance, and inclusion can take place. The group serves as a witness, a "collective eye" that acknowledges the wrongdoing, validates the knowledge that what has been done cannot be dismissed; it embodies a commitment to reparation by its very emotional participation in the "telling." It is as if the group becomes a symbolic "ombudsman" that upholds the norms, values, and obligations regulating human social lives.

Some may argue that the act of communicating that which cannot be communicated, of telling one's story through behaviour when one is unable to communicate through language (which requires more sophisticated symbolic functioning), can be captured by the Kleinian concept of projective identification or by the Freudian conceptual framework of repetition-compulsion processes. I feel, however, that traditional Kleinian or Freudian concepts do not convey sufficiently the real essence of my argument, nor do they address the social dimensions that play a part in the processes I describe. They do not encompass the *ethical* significance that I believe is inherent in human connectedness, as I attempt to explicate throughout this work. A related issue—although rather different—pertains to the fact that I choose to work from within the intersubjective perspective in psychoanalysis; its cultural sensibilities are closer to my belief that the most significant relevance in the "burning need" to "tell one's story" is that it enables a vital re-connectedness to a receptive, empathic listener who is ready to become an engaged partner to the telling and to take upon himself the teller's pain.

AMCHA: A CLINICAL VIGNETTE

An illustration from group supervision conducted at Amcha (an organization for the psychosocial treatment of Holocaust survivors and their families) can be helpful in demonstrating the clinical relevance of some of the above thoughts. I believe that the dynamic processes in the supervision group reflect and echo the ones that occur in the therapeutic relationships presented in the group; this reflection enables the unfolding of emotional states that operate in the therapy in an unconscious manner, making them accessible for explicit exploration (Berman and Berger, 2004).

Before I present this clinical vignette, a word about Amcha would be in place. Amcha was established in the late 1980s, as an act of public recognition aimed at a hitherto mostly invisible population, namely, Holocaust survivors. Its creation was part of the process of breaking the "pacts of silence" to which the Holocaust and its aftermath had been subjected in Israel—a process begun in 1960, with the bringing to trial of Adolph Eichmann.[5]

Prior to Eichmann's trial, people avoided getting close to "those" emotional realities; they mostly kept the ones that came from "there," from the Holocaust – whether neighbors, family members, or others – at a safe distance from themselves. They did not want to know what had happened "there." It took Israeli society almost 40 years after the end of the Second World War to finally start the arduous process of acknowledging the colossal dimensions of the destruction brought by the Holocaust. The presence in Israel of more than 400,000 Holocaust survivors, silent unto themselves and silenced by others, began to rise to public and private awareness only after 1960.

The lives of those survivors, along with the lives of their children (the so-called "second generation") were heavily marked by what they had gone through. Alerting the public to their need to be heard, seen, and recognized was one of Amcha's declared purposes.

5 After World War II, Nazi war criminal Adolf Eichmann fled from Austria and made his way to Argentina, where he lived under the name Ricardo Klement. In May 1960, Israeli Security Service agents seized Eichmann in Argentina and took him to Jerusalem for trial in an Israeli court. Eichmann testified from a bulletproof glass booth.

The Eichmann trial aroused international interest, bringing Nazi atrocities to the forefront of world news. Testimonies of Holocaust survivors generated interest and horror in Israel and outside it. The trial prompted a new openness in Israel; many Holocaust survivors finally felt able to share their experiences as the country confronted this traumatic chapter.

The charges against Eichmann were numerous. After the Wannsee Conference in January 1942, Eichmann (aided by Alois Brunner, Theodor Dannecker, Rolf Guenther, Dieter Wisliceny, and others in the Gestapo) coordinated deportations of Jews from Germany and elsewhere in western, southern, and northern Europe to "killing centers." Eichmann made deportation plans down to the last detail. Working with other German agencies, he determined how the property of deported Jews would be seized and made certain that his office would benefit from the confiscated assets. He also arranged for the deportation of tens of thousands of Roma (Gypsies). Eichmann was also charged with membership in criminal organizations—the Storm Troopers (SA), Security Service (SD), and Gestapo (all of which had been declared criminal organizations at the 1946 Nuremberg trials). As head of the Gestapo's section for Jewish affairs, Eichmann coordinated with Gestapo chief Heinrich Mueller on a plan to expel Jews from Greater Germany to Poland, setting the pattern for future deportations. For these and other charges, Eichmann was found guilty and sentenced to death. On June 1, 1962, Eichmann was executed by hanging. His body was cremated, and the ashes were spread at sea, beyond Israel's territorial waters. Eichmann's execution remains the only time Israel enacted a death sentence.

An exposition of this organization's history and its psychosocial functions, meanings, and implications is beyond the scope of this paper; suffice it to say that over the years, it has become the largest provider of psychological services for Holocaust survivors in the world.

A personal note about my own place in the organization may be relevant, however, to the issues at stake. Although I was one of the first (and few) psychologists to start these services, it took me a long time to realize that I myself was struggling personally and professionally, from deep within, with the aftermath of the Holocaust.

I invested a lot in developing a program of psychosocial care that would respond adequately to the needs of this population. Yet, nothing in my professional knowledge and experience had prepared me for the intensity of the impact that the direct encounter with the raw feelings engendered by the traumatic histories of my patients' as well as my own had created. Getting to know personally, from up close, the long-term psychic damage caused by that war was at times too devastating, even in the protected space that the therapeutic setting provided.

I knew "about" my history, but did not "know" it as a living part of myself, in the sense marked in the Bible as carnal knowledge; I was not fully aware of the extent to which my being born into that war cast its shadow on the therapeutic interactions I was involved in and responsible for in real time. Through the work in Amcha I realized keenly, time and again, that I was one of "them," though different in my role as psychologist. Polish being my mother tongue, I could speak it with some older patients; at times it was even a necessity as their command of Hebrew was minimal; our use of a common language revived in me painful experiences of growing up as a child of uprooted refugees whose struggle to find a safe hold in reality was their main daily preoccupation; speaking Polish opened an access to a host of intimate, "banal," everyday details, which only the use of one's primary language (of what Améry calls "incarnated words") can make possible. Someone once defined me as an "internal outsider," which, I realized was true in more than one sense.

It was there, through intimate encounters with my patients, their inner world and their struggle to create a life worth living after the war, that I became aware of the crucial significance, for the victim and for those close to him, of other people's readiness to bear witness, to be fully present, to "be there," especially when the emotional experience touch on the unbearable. I thus became preoccupied with issues of vengefulness, recognition, accountability, and concern.

Clinical Example: A Supervision Session at Amcha

The following clinical example is derived from one of the many group supervision sessions that were part of my daily clinical routine at Amcha. The group I present consisted of six to eight therapists who met weekly to discuss their caseloads.

One of the therapists presents a 71-year-old woman, a Holocaust survivor. She sought professional help because the depressive feelings that had accompanied her for many years had grown heavier lately; she found it increasingly difficult to cope with everyday chores.

Her life is a sad tale of sequential traumatizations, going back to her childhood in the Holocaust in Poland. Without going into detail, let me note shortly that she survived abandonment, starvation, beatings, numerous sudden uprooting from one hiding place to another and brutal separations from attachment figures. Despite this history of hardships and loss, she managed to make a life for herself, though she does not perceive it as an achievement she can be proud of or feel happy about.

She married, started a family, and raised three children with whom she has had complex relationships fraught with bitter conflicts and periodic cutoffs. She lives with a chronic sense of disappointment and bitterness about close relatives who are "indifferent" to her plight; she feels maltreated, victimized and abandoned by family members who "just do not care." She is alienated from her very old, sick mother and has an estranged son who now lives in Europe.

The psychologist presenting the case gives a lengthy, detailed description of what this woman has gone through. Her tone is matter-of-fact as she neutrally and dryly recounts horrible events, including lists of names, persons, places, dates, and minute circumstantial data that are supposed to clarify the patient's history and her current problems. It is a long, traumatic sequence. The group responds with a heavy, seemingly endless silence. Someone goes out for a cup of water. "I couldn't breathe in here," he says upon returning.

After some more silence, I comment that the patient seems to have taken all the air out of the room. I suggest that the participants share some of their associations with the group.

Gradually, the atmosphere softens, and they begin to talk. They recall their encounters with other patients whom they experienced as exhausting and exasperating. The feeling of having the air "taken out" is passed on from one member to another as the circle of sharing widens.

One therapist starts talking about a woman he saw in therapy, a child survivor, who overwhelmed him on their first session with ghastly details of her family's history during the war, when they were in hiding: eight of them were squeezed into a tiny cellar, terribly fearful as the Gestapo was in the midst of one of their shooting "hunts" on the streets of the ghetto. She told him that her then two-year-old sister, who started crying, was almost choked to death by an uncle, because her crying threatened to reveal their hiding place.

The group space becomes dense with this horror, flooded with anxiety that practically makes it difficult to breath. The atmosphere is now heavy and tense. The group sinks into another silence.

My associations wander to an experience a patient once told me about. She filed a charge against her husband who had beaten her. She was badly bruised, and the scars were still showing. The police officer who interviewed her then said "jokingly" that her husband should be more careful next time and learn the art of "dry blows" (the Hebrew expression for painful blows that leave no visible signs on the body surface), since they are hard to detect and would not incriminate him. She was shattered by receiving such a response from someone who was supposed to protect her. Her wish to retaliate and redress her humiliation was a major issue in our talks.

Returning to the reality of the group, I have a sense that this memory can be productive and shed some light on feelings that unknowingly burden the group members; it appears that they are bracing themselves against a threat inherent in the violence they have been touching on from so close up. It is as if their patients' traumatic pasts are coming alive within the space of the group and get played out in that arena. Therapists thus feel caught in the victim-victimizer trap; it is as though they can be cast only into one of those two complementary roles and become either victim or victimizer. The capacity to inhabit a potential space (and create a so-called analytical third) collapses.

Following my last association, I remark that they seem to receive “dry blows” from their patients.

Reluctantly, some more direct talking starts to emerge. The therapists begin to describe the impact that their close contact with victims of atrocities has had on their lives and on their therapeutic relationships; they disclose hesitantly that at times they feel afraid of their patients, angry with them, bored or detached.

They are shamed by these responses and become guilt-ridden. It is “awful and inhuman” to feel that way towards any patient, but hatred towards Holocaust survivor verges on the unbearable. It brings them too close to feeling sadistic themselves, “sliding into the shoes of Nazi torturers.” They report that quite often they feel helpless, paralyzed, irrelevant, dangerously lacking in human empathy and concern.

I realize we are caught in the grips of enactments that abusive relationships can cause quite powerfully (Meissner Davies, 1997). Amcha’s professed aims "to be there" with emotional presence and readiness as human witnesses to what happened seem to collapse under the colossal dimensions of the destruction of that war; it casts its heavy shadow on all of us, insidiously molding the therapeutic interactions into extreme polarized poles that cannot occupy a shared space.

I suggest that their silence may be an expression of forbidden vengeful wishes that are denied conscious access to therapists and patients alike. Both parties unknowingly keep a pact of silence about some of the darker aspects of the violent reality of the victim’s emotional life and relationships.

The psychologist who presented the case seizes my comment about “dry blows” with apparent relief: “I can relate to that,” she says. “Thinking back, I feel that I actually wanted to make you all gasp for air. She (the patient) chokes me every week. I just needed to choke you back as well. I realize she hates me with my ‘empathic’ silences; it must be hell for her not to be able to talk about how utterly helpless, humiliated and vindictive she feels, towards ‘them’ and towards me."

It becomes apparent that her dry and lengthy presentation has reactivated in the group some of the feelings her patient evoked in her. During their sessions, she often becomes numb and detached, unable to identify that she is being attacked, “hit” by her patient’s “dry blows.” She is often seized by a (forbidden) desire to get rid of her patient, along with the unbearable realities she brings forth.

The hidden vengefulness of her patient has been recreated in the group, “blocking the air.” As it becomes acknowledged by the psychologist’s authentic response, the “choked” morbid silence in the group gives gradually way to honesty and openness. Group members share with each other hidden dissociated emotions they experience daily; their own fears, vengefulness, and sadness resonate with their patients’. A process of mourning, understanding, and containment begins to unfold within the group (Berman and Berger, 2004).

It should be noted again that vengeful wishes are especially unacceptable by therapists, whose socialization fosters empathy and compassion rather than “hard” feelings like helpless rage, hatred, or the desire to get even. Ill wishes towards others, especially others who are in one’s charge as patients, are strictly prohibited.

However, dissociation from these feelings leaves the patient and therapist locked in their loneliness; they are the stuff that pacts of silence are made of. The same can be said about group members and conductors, in therapy or in supervision. The clinical example presented above illustrates my point that pent-up vengeful wishes against patients often hold a clue towards untangling an impasse. The more silenced and anxiety provoking these feelings become, the more one needs to get in touch with them, acknowledge and process them. These dynamics are especially meaningful in the treatment of patients who, like Holocaust survivors, suffered prolonged sequential trauma.

Speaking in a different context, Archbishop Desmond Tutu puts it this way:

> True reconciliation is not cheap. It cost God the death of His only begotten Son. So, in the real world, those who seek to avoid the pain, the shame, or the loss they have suffered can remain caught in cycles of revenge (Tutu, 1999, p. 270).

Therapists and patients constitute together the "matrix of pain and hope" that this work is all about. The ability to be in touch with these feelings constitutes the transformative process of mourning, so essential for a process of reconciliation and forgiveness to evolve (see Urlic's chapters in the present volume).

THERAPY, A PROMISE THAT CANNOT BE FULFILLED: THE LIMITS OF REPARATION

Since I am placing such an emphasis on the therapeutic value of acknowledging hard feeling like vengefulness, it behooves me to point out I have some reservations about this process. The following thoughts serve to balance off the danger of idealizations that may "creep" unknowingly into my arguments and provide an unrealistic promise that cannot be delivered. Since what I've described in this chapter is mostly the dynamics of group therapy and group considerations, I will confine my remarks to that framework, though I believe they can be relevant to other therapeutic relationships as well.

The group fulfills several contradicting functions. On the one hand, it represents the public sphere, the town square, the court of justice and the jury, all rolled up in one. The group, its members and its conductor are (interchangeably) the "other" whose recognition is so vital for restoring the individual member's "trust in the world," his faith in accountability and his need to feel that he matters. On the other hand, the group represents the very same "other," or community that caused the injuries each member has suffered. As such, each member must bear the consequences of inflicting that old pain and partake in the emotional burden such responsibility generates, despite the fact that the group members are not the real-life offenders in the outside world.

I am aware that this twofold function that group members serve for one another can be discussed in terms of transference-countertransference or displacement; but I do not think that these terms alone can truly encompass the meaning I wish to attribute to the complex emotional reality of the therapeutic encounter in the analytic group. As already mentioned, I believe that our psychoanalytical understandings and practices need to include a moral desire.

In the introduction to her book about the psychoanalysis of evil, Grand (2000) says she has found that

> ……mental health is not simply about the capacity to love and work. It is the struggle to behave with ethical strength on behalf of the other, and for oneself. Repudiating

> moralism, but unabashedly embracing morality … freed me to articulate my own clinical and moral perspective on issues [concerning evil and the nature of the analytic treatment of malevolent patients] (p. xi, my addition in parenthesis).

I find that her remark strengthens the case for the notion that therapeutic praxis cannot confine itself to "neutrality" devoid of moral dimensions. As I see it, the therapeutic relationship is a process imbued with values; it strives to implement a humane ethical base for one's life with oneself and with others.

The needed process of atonement can evolve when group members share in one another's suffering yet are also able to remain authentically close to themselves, without losing sight of difference and separateness.

Each group member has a double role; he is both himself and an "other," each with his own respective functions. Group members authorize and validate each other's unique experiences; each one becomes keenly aware both of his connectedness to others and of the limits of this connectedness. The disappointment embedded in the nature of this reality is painful for all involved; true witnessing entails emotional receptivity to suffering, along with the realization that there is a limit to our ability to be with one another. *As much as this is an encounter with the redeeming quality of sharing and togetherness, it is also an encounter with our essential loneliness.*

As said before, the therapeutic framework is not a Forum or a High Court of Justice. Bearing witness, opening oneself to unbearable emotions, is a necessary but insufficient condition for reparation. In a way, the therapy group initially holds out a promise it cannot fulfill. As Feiner (1995) emphasizes, this internal contradiction between what therapy can offer and what the injured individual needs is distressing and painful for all concerned. It is an authentic encounter with the limits of therapeutic relationships (or of relationships in general), no matter how understanding and considerate they may be.

The common recognition of the limits of reparation is connected with the realization that there are always many relevant perspectives that both constrict and redefine one another in a constant process of negotiations.

Bearing in mind these constrictions, it is evident that deeds done cannot be undone; what has happened in the past cannot be changed, and what has been lost cannot be retrieved. The wish to avenge, to actually "get even," cannot be fulfilled. That is not to say that loss cannot be worked through, mourned and transformed.

Mourning is the process through which the reality of loss can be acknowledged, incorporated and contained in the consciousness of the individual and the community who suffered it. It takes presence, identification and the emotional participation of others.[6]

Améry says he wants to "nail the criminal to his deeds" (p. 72) so that the pain that the perpetrator inflicted on him would become a "moral reality" for the criminal and as such will redress the victim's loneliness. This "nailing" would constitute the transformative move Améry longs for. It would signify for him a commitment to reestablishing a just world, one based on accountability and mutual concern—a world that would accept his feelings,

---

[6] The Jewish tradition prescribes that prayers for the dead be done in a group of at least ten men. This seems to represent an ancient wisdom about the deep connectedness between the personal and the public. The acknowledgment of private pain by the "collective other" has a redeeming quality: one cannot do it by oneself alone.

acknowledge the legitimacy of his grief, respond to his gnawing "resentment" and to the "disturbing grudge" he has borne in his heart since the war.

However, this quest for "nailing" may have tragic consequences for the avenger as well, if his need cannot be satisfied by what is possible to achieve in a given reality. If the desire for revenge cannot be satisfied adequately (for whatever reasons), the would-be avenger may become trapped in an impossible demand to turn back time, to undo what has been done. Thus, he may place himself at a chronic distance from a reality that in actuality could offer him some warmth, comfort and compassion, despite its limitations. As therapists, our understanding of these vicious cycles can help release one's relationships from these cycles' powerful and damaging grip.

If the nature of the above constrictions is taken into account and acknowledged, the "resentful" person's desire to regain his position as a valued and equal subject can be comprehended and contained. The isolation and alienation that hang over group participants may gradually dissipate with mutual recognition and understanding of the feelings involved. These can be transformed into a renewed link to a shared reality and a much-needed sense of belonging for all.

WHERE DOES VENGEFULNESS HIDE? DECODING "SIGNALS" OF VENGEFULNESS IN THE THERAPEUTIC RELATIONSHIP

If vengeful wishes are so difficult to relate to, so elusive and evasive in nature, then how are we to identify them? How are they manifested in the therapeutic relationship? How are we to track the traces left by the injuries inflicted on the patient, if those traces are not explicit? Which "signals" are supposed to call our attention to the existence of wounds that await healing?

As I said earlier, vengefulness is a form of communication that aspires to "tell on them." It can be viewed as a symptom indicative of unbearable emotional experiences born in utter loneliness. Foulkes tells us that "the symptom mumbles to itself with the hope to be overheard." This notion may be useful: it guides us to become more attentive listeners, careful to respond to elusive "mumblings" and to attempt to transform them into meaningful communication.

I suggest we hear those hidden vengeful feelings in the lengthy, stubborn silences that invade many therapeutic hours; in expressions of self-negation, in rejection and indifference to others, in reticence and isolation, in chronic blaming, bitterness and cynicism; in denigration towards self and others; in manifestations of disdain for and mistrust in the capacity of others to make any valuable contribution; in chronic complaints about feeling stuck and bored.

Addressing this question, Feiner (1995) suggests that "[w]hat is in the 'blackness,' or the 'cancer ball,' or the 'unnamable,' or the 'burning agony,' or the 'deadness,' or the 'emptiness,' is most likely the vindictive rage that needs no stranger's labels, clichés, or interpretations" (p. 390).

Another "hiding place" for vengeful wishes is found in the syndrome that Berman (in this volume) terms "Victimhood." My suggestion is that underlining some of the masochistic (or abusive and hostile) traits and behaviors that comprise the category of "Victimhood" are those pent-up vengeful feelings that are denied access into the shared space of self and others.

Unacknowledged abuse can "turn the tables" and become calcified into "Victimhood" syndromes in the following way: A person can become a walking emblem of the demand for retribution, justice, and reparation for the injuries he had suffered. The self-state that demands revenge takes over; the injured person becomes possessed by his humiliation and by a consuming desire to undo what has been done; in this sense, he is caught in the grips of dynamics defined as "the identification with the aggressor" (Ferenczi, 1933; Frankel, 2002) and loses sight of the destructive relational cycle he actively (albeit unknowingly) partakes in; he becomes entrenched in a state of helpless righteousness that sets him apart from others whom he sees as bad and powerful; he may become blind to the pain he inflicts on others that are far from being his real offenders. When these self-states dominate relationships, they hamper development and obstruct process of transformation into a culture of mutual acknowledgment and mutual concern (Howell, 2005; Bromberg, 1996).

As I see it, these relational formations may be communicative messages that need to be deciphered and understood. They suggest the possibility that covert revenge wishes await recognition. Touching on painful experiences and the feelings generated by them, **vengefulness included**, may assist in retrieving these experiences from the emotional exile into which they were banished. A process that ensures a safe spaces in which openness about these silent entities can evolve helps build a bridge that "the spiteful ones" can cross on their way to rejoin their communities.

Cain And Abel: "I am My Brother's Keeper"

The biblical tale of Cain and Abel, I suggested earlier, is engraved in our collective memories as a formative myth about the nature of accountability in men's lives. (See the entire biblical tale quoted in Chapter 1.) Such accountability binds all members of society into a commitment to abide by the rules on which communal life is morally based; it constitutes a culture of interconnectedness and reciprocity, in which each person is a symbolic "brother" to the other.

The ancient question, "Am I my brother's keeper?" calls attention to the idea that a commitment to mutual care and responsibility is both a basic tenet of human life and a relational achievement that demands continuous emotional efforts.

In the biblical tale, Cain kills his brother Abel because the Lord "had not respect" for his offering. It is a vengeful murder stemming from Cain's envy of the appreciation afforded to his brother's gift and denied to his own. Cain's offering was not acknowledged: God did not "respect" his contribution. As a result, "his countenance fell" (the countenance, or face, being the mirror of the soul). God's disregard and dismissal proves to be a mortal wound for Cain. He kills his brother in revenge: he avenges God's disregard by killing God's beloved son. The killing of Abel may be understood as symbolically representing the emotional obliteration experienced by Cain when God ignored his offering, as well as his reactive vengefulness against Abel, who is actually an innocent stand-in for God (since the supreme power is not accessible to human revenge).

God is there to remind Cain he is accountable, however. He symbolizes the demand for personal responsibility. "What hast thou done? The voice of thy brother's blood crieth unto me from the ground." Cain admits the murder and confesses: "My punishment is greater than I can bear." God witnessed his deed and thereby assured that anarchy will not prevail. His "seeing" makes the crime known and retrieves it from the danger of obliviousness. It prevents Cain's attempts to deny his deed, to "get away with murder." It enables Cain to acknowledge the reality of his terrible act, to atone for taking the life of his brother. It makes him truly "see" himself as capable of doing evil and owning up to it; as a result, he grows in stature and is granted the position of founder of society. It is as if Cain's question "Am I my brother's keeper?" receives a simple, self-evident answer: "Yes, you are: you are your brother's keeper."

It should be noted that in the Hebrew original, Cain's reaction to his sentencing by God is in fact open to two diverging interpretations. It can be understood (as it is in most English translations) as "my punishment is greater than I can bear"; but it can also be read as "my crime is greater than I can bear," which radically alters its meaning.[7] If the latter interpretation is true, then the Cain's transformation—from the question "Am I my brother's keeper?" to the recognition that "my crime is greater than I can bear"—is especially dramatic and meaningful. It signifies a transformation from a culture of indifference, of "every man for himself," to a culture of mutual concern and of commitment to the well-being of others. It sets the stage for recognition of the implications of our interdependence and our utter need to be regarded as lawful members by our community.

Cain's recognition of his culpability is thus "set for a sign" on his forehead in order to safeguard the continuity and coherence of social constructions. This sign "nails" him to his slain brother in a moral bond, while protecting his own life from the retributive vengeful acts of others. The destructive cycle of murder and counter-murder, which might have resulted from the denial of accountability, is thus amended and blocked. The sign God sets on Cain's forehead symbolizes the value of owning up to one's deeds personally and collectively. It emphasizes the significance of mutual recognition and mutual concern in human life. It formulates, right at the beginning of history, the foundations for a society in which each person is his brother's keeper.

End Notes: Vengeful Wishes are Not Vengeful Acts

I would like to recapitulate the arguments made throughout this text.

Feelings are not actions. What I explore in these chapters is vengeful wishes, fantasies, dreams, wants—not acts.

The capacity to recognize the difference between feelings and deeds, between inner and outer reality, between fantasy and fact, is a product of personal development and a mode of interpersonal relatedness. Both domains along with their interrelations need our continuous attention.

[7] Whereas most English translations of the Bible render the Hebrew avon as "punishment," in modern Hebrew, the word usually takes the meaning of "crime." At any rate, traditional Jewish interpreters of the biblical story disagree on its meaning (and, consequently, on the meaning of Cain's response), some (for example Abraham Ibn Ezra) reading it the first way, some (for example Nahmanides) the second.

The capacity to accept feelings, any feelings, as legitimate expressions of relationships with self and with others can contribute to the moderation of vengeful acts, if not prevent them altogether. This capacity to process feelings and contain them is one of the most valued human assets. It is an ongoing relational process.

Vengeful wishes are a normal, expected response to injuries to one's "social feelings," namely, those feelings that pertain to one's dignity and self-agency, to one's need to have an impact, to count, to be a "subject." These feelings are relevant only in the context of relationships; there is no point in exploring them as products of one's internal world alone (which would be akin to Buddhist riddles that invite us to hear the sound produced by the clapping of one hand). Furthermore, these "social feelings" have a moral dimension and denote our existence as human beings that are bound to each other ethically as well as physically and emotionally.

Vengeful *acts*, by contrast, are destructive. They can trap all parties involved in an uncontrollable vortex and become a "plague" that spreads death indiscriminately, attacking victims, perpetrators, and innocent bystanders alike.

We Middle East inhabitants, Israelis and Palestinians alike, have a firsthand experience of this "plague." There is not one person in the land I live in who has not been injured in some way, affected by the chronic state of war that infests all of us. Each side keeps an account of the wrongdoing of the other, while dissociating itself from its own share in causing suffering. The results are endless cycles of bloody feuds fuelled by non-recognition and lack of mutual concern.

Every society develops its own procedures for stopping cycles of violence. Rituals of atonement are effective as long as they are agreed upon and accepted by all parties. They usually consist of admission of guilt, peace talks, signing of agreements accompanied by exchange of presents like flocks of sheep or money to rehabilitate the damage done and compensate for losses. I think of such procedures as ritualized forms of mutual recognition: all involved parties acknowledge the reality of suffering, accept responsibility for doing harm, make a commitment to restore peace, and renew their obligation to create decent lives for everyone.

In this context, the ability to perceive vengefulness as part of our personal and social fabric is humanizing. Hopefully, it contributes to the effort to develop a culture of accountability, mutual concern, and forgiveness.

References

Améry, J. (1980). *At the Mind's Limit: Contemplations by a Survivor on Auschwitz and Its Realities.* Indiana University Press.

Benjamin, J. (1990). "An Outline of Intersubjectivity: The Development of Recognition." *Psychoanalytic Psychology.* 7S (Supplement): 33-46

Bergman M. S. (1985). "Reflections on the Psychological and Social Function of Remembering the Holocaust." *Psychoanalytic Inquiry.* 5: 9-20.

Berman, A. and Berger, M. (2000). "The Division into Us and Them as a Universal Social Structure." *Mind and Human Interaction*, 11: 53-72.

Berman, A. and Berger, M. (2004). "Matrix and Reverie in Supervision Group." *Group Analysis*, Vol. 40 (2): 236-250.

Bromberg P., M. (1996). "Standing in the Spaces: The Multiplicity of Self and the Psychoanalytic Relationship." *Contemporary Psychoanalysis*. 32: 509-535.

Dalal, F. (1998). *Taking The Group Seriously*. London: Jessica Kingsley Publishers.

Messler-Davies, J. (1997).Dissociation, Therapeutic Enactment, and Transference—Countertransference Processes: A Discussion of Papers on Childhood Sexual Abuse by S. Grand and J. Sarnat. *Gender and Psychoanalysis* 2: (2) 241-257.

Elster, J. (1990). "Norms of Revenge." *Ethics*, 100: 862-85.

Feiner, A. (1995). "Laughter Among The Pear Trees: Vengeance, Vindictiveness, and Vindication." *Contemporary Psychoanalysis*, 31: 381-397.

Ferenczi, S. (1933). The confusion of tongues between adults and children. *Int. J. Psycho-Anal.*, 30: 225-230.

Fonagy, P. and Target, M. (1998). "Mentalization and the Changing Aims of Child Psychoanalysis*." Psychoanalytic Dialogues*, 8 (1): 87-114.

Foulkes, S. H. (1975). *Group-Analytic Psychotherapy: Method and Principles*. London: Gordon and Breach.

Frankel, J. (2002). Exploring Ferenczi's Concept of Identification with the Aggressor: It's Role in Trauma, Everyday Life, and the Therapeutic Relationship. *Psychoanalytic Dialogues*, 12:101-139.

Freud, S. (1921). "Group Psychology and the Analysis of the Ego." In The Standard Edition of the Complete Psychological Works of Sigmund Freud, Volume XVIII (1920-1922): Beyond the Pleasure Principle, Group Psychology and Other Works, 65-144. *The Standard Edition of the Complete Psychological Works of Sigmund Freud,* Volume XVIII. The Hogarth Press and the Institute of Psychoanalysis, London.

Goldwater, E. (2004). "Getting Mad and Getting Even." *Modern Psychoanalysis*, 29 (1): 23-36.

Grand, S. (2000). *The Reproduction of Evil: A Clinical & Cultural Perspective*. Hillsdale, NJ: The Analytic Press.

Grupinskaya, A. (2002). *Around and Around*. Mapa Publishers.

Howell, E. (2005). *The Dissociative Mind*. Hillside, NJ: The Analytic Press.

Laub, D. and. Auerhahn, N. C. (1989). "Failed Empathy: A Central Theme in the Survivor's Holocaust Experience." *Psychoanalytic Psychology*, 6: 377-400.

Levi, P. (1988). *The Drowned and the Saved*. New York: Summit Books.

Messler Davies, J. (1997). Dissociation, Therapeutic Enactment, and Transference—Countertransference Processes: A Discussion of Papers on Childhood Sexual Abuse by S. Grand and J. Sarnat. *Gender and Psychoanalysis* 2: (2) 241-257.

Moses, R. (1982). "The Group Self and the Arab-Israeli Conflict*." International Journal of Psycho-Analysis*, 9: 55-64.

Nitsun, M. (1991). "The Anti-Group: Destructive Forces in the Group and Their Therapeutic Potential." *Group Analysis*, 24: 7-20.

Puget. J. (2002). "The State of Threat and Psychoanalysis: From the Uncanny that Structures to the Uncanny that Alienates*." Free Associations*, 9D (4): 611-648.

Roiphe, A. (2000). "A Discussion on a Memoir of Early Childhood Loss." *International Journal of Psycho-Analysis*, 81: 1011-1014.

Sievers B., Redding R. et al. (2006). "The Economy of Vengeance: Some Considerations on the Etiology and Meaning of the Business of Revenge." *Human Relations*, Vol. 59 (2): 241-259.

Tutu, D. (1999). *No Future without Forgiveness*. New York: Doubleday Press.

Twemlow S. W. (2000). "The Roots of Violence: Converging Psychoanalytic Explanatory Models for Power Struggles and Violence in Schools." *Psychoanalytic Quarterly*, 69 (4): 741-785.

Volkan, V. (2001) "Transgenerational transmissions and chosen traumas: An aspect of large-group identity," *Group-Analysis* 34: 79-97.

PART THREE

Chapter 7

To Live with Enemies and the "Impossible" Task to Think on Forgiveness*

Ivan Urlic

Disfigured Picture

My soul
is torn apart
by horrible crimes
of aggressor in my village.

The crush of shells
is deeply carved
in my mind.

The pale face of a killed child
at the corner of my street
is freezing my blood.

My breath was taken away
in a panic fear
when our house
was surrounded.

What then was happening
remains closed
at the bottom of my soul.
I can't remember. Only a dull
pain
in my insides
tells me
that something horrible was happened.

The death and
destroyed feelings

happened to
my family.

The house in ruins.
The heart in turmoil.
The future in darkness.

Why have they
done it to me??

I am searching for the voice
to console me,
the hand
to save me,
the heart
to sympathize with me,
the eye to see my
deep
hidden wounds,

the ear
to hear my
untold pain.

Will
the monster's madness
ever change?
To transform
in a face
that talks to me
about
the real humaneness.

Christoph Horn (Catholic priest from Switzerland, while organizing medical help during the war in Croatia and Bosnia and Herzegovina).

Kriegsgedichte—Friedensgedichte, (Private edition, Horw, Switzerland), October, 1993.

The essential idea in writing about the culture of forgiveness and reconciliation processes was to describe them in the frame of dynamics of the encounter with deep narcissistic wounds within the sequence of confrontation with the trauma suffered and mourning of the losses, enabling the need for forgiveness and possibly even reconciliation to occur. In following chapters, all clinical examples have remained in the ambience in which they were born and have taken some of actual features—the difficult atmosphere of war and its aftermath, and in the psychotherapeutic frame of reference. Therefore, throughout my contributions in this book, I am following the developmental line of my experiences with tragic consequences due to the war events. Psychosocial help, and psychotherapeutic processes, always bearing in mind the desired therapeutic aim—attaining the level and creating the space for the culture of forgiveness to develop, opening up the possibilities of reconciliation with oneself and with the other(s).

In that way, I am strongly supporting the necessity to parallel these (therapeutic) processes with the work of mourning for the losses and unattained wishes. I am suggesting that only through the thorough mourning process, the possibilities of forgiving and reconciling can become attainable achievement and constructive aim of psychotherapeutic and psychosocial interventions.

1. Introduction: Enemies, Conflicts and Armed Clashes

To speak about ongoing hostilities is a quite complex and difficult task. The more so is the fact and necessity to live with enemies of all kind. It is always possible to ask ourselves, time and again, where is there a space for a mutually exchangeable and recognizable phenomena that we would call reality, and where do we enter the space filled with prejudices, judgmental positions, cultural stereotypes that block curiosity and questioning, and very often represent the space for aggressive, destructive expressions. The latter paves the way for unlearning processes to become blocked, and the new knowledge and insight result unable to enter the scene. So, the ghosts of the past and present times are often occupying the place that the open-mindedness would serve much better.

There is anecdote that had a great echo in ex-Yugoslavia and was often retold as very characteristic for the close type of mentality of people. Some decades ago, in Belgrade, there were demonstrations in front of the American and British embassies. People were throwing stones against windows. One man came in front of the Turkish embassy and was throwing stones against its windows. A friend asked him what he was doing, and he answered: "I remember them from the time of the battle of Kosovo." The joke was considered to be very witty. But, the mentioned battle was over 600 years ago. There is the drama of the phenomenon we could recognize as a heavy narcissistic injury, the military defeat that brought about five centuries of Turkish domination of Serbia.

We might presume that the wounds of the past can have very long shadows and, if not metabolized properly, may represent the burden that is transmitted through generations as a heavy weight. At the level of one's nation's cultural tradition, as well as each member's level, such trauma with all its pathetic content and additional meanings can start to live its own life, transforming itself into a myth that becomes not only a national, but also an individual way of seeing historical and actual perspective, especially articulated in the cultural and political scenes. Though that, transformation and transmission of a myth can serve the purpose of national pride and unity using the mechanisms of turning into opposite, denial and projection.[1]

The OUN statistics show that almost every day, there are more than a hundred armed clashes and wars in the world. What a remarkable monument to human uncontrolled aggression!

According to reliable data (Gleditsch et al., 2002, p.615), in the period 1946-2001, there were 225 armed conflicts, and 34 of them were active in all of or part of 2001. Armed conflict remains a serious problem in the post-Cold War period. For three decades, the Correlates of

---

[1] Parts of the topics and some clinical examples were elaborated in some other author's publications, cited in references. I thank Profs. Ljiljana and Alan Moro and Prof. Matko Marušić for their helpful suggestions during the early phases of the manuscript, Mrs. Antoslava Vukas for her dedicated work on the technical preparation of the text and Mrs. Margaret Casman-Vuko for her sensitive and meticulous language editing.

War project has served as the main supplier of reliable data used in longitudinal studies of external and internal armed conflict. The COW datasets on war use the relatively high threshold of 1,000 battle-deaths. The Uppsala dataset on armed conflict has a lower threshold, 25 annual battle-deaths, but has so far been available for only the post-Cold War period. This dataset has now been backdated to the end of World War II.

According to Eriksson et al. (2003, p.593), a total odd 226 armed conflicts have been recorded for the years 1946-2002. Of these, 116 were active in the period 1989-2002, including 31 in 2002. There were five wars in 2002. Both numbers were the lowest for this period. Seven interstate-armed conflicts were recorded 1989-2002, of which one was still active in 2002. In 2002, a larger proportion of complex major armed conflicts were resolved, compared with new and minor armed conflicts. Although these data on armed conflicts suggest that there is a decline in the use of armed force, there is an increased feeling of fear and insecurity in many parts of the world, especially because of terrorism incidents.

Harbom and Wallensteen (2005, p.623) write that in 2004, there were 30 active armed conflicts, up by one from 2003. Despite this slight increase, the number of armed conflicts remains lower than at any time since the early 1970s. While seven of the conflicts from 2003, were no longer active, one entirely new conflict broke out, and seven conflicts restarted, three with action taken by new rebel groups and four by previously recorded actors. A total odd 228 armed conflicts have been recorded after World War II, and 118 after the end of the Cold War.

Twentieth century in Europe was marked by two world wars, clashes of two totalitarian ideologies and rises and falls of empires of different colors. It was believed that the lesson about unleashed human aggressivity was learned and that another war in Europe would be highly improbable. As a matter of fact, the last of European empires, the red one, fell without a bullet shot. It started with the fall of the Berlin Wall and continued with dissolution of Czechoslovakia and the Soviet Union itself. But, the last decade of twentieth century in Europe had to pass through another war experience, the one that marked the dissolution of Yugoslavia. The unimaginable has become reality.

On the other side, the heritage of the twentieth century regarding all kinds of clashes and conflicts continued to spread throughout the whole world, becoming ever more numerous and complicated in relation to possible resolutions. The Middle East, an extremely complicated puzzle about political, geostrategic and ethnic/religious issues, might be the most obvious example of controversies this world is confronted with at the beginning of twenty-first century.

The rational meaning of these data is quite clear. But to go through experience of war and its aftermath leaves an inner turmoil in every society and in the majority of its members that takes time to elaborate it and to work through. This inner turmoil is even worse in societies were the state of war has become chronic, or the state of "no war no peace." Numerous researches done so far indicate that coping mechanisms might get exhausted on personal and much wider levels, and that there are limits to possibilities to adjust to always new terrorist attacks, armed assaults, and many other forms of threats to the bare human existence.

2. Reactions of People in War Situations: Some Croatian Experiences

“The war is the woe of human nature,” wrote the Renaissance writer from Dubrovnik Marin Držić (1979, p.10). The Croatian experiences at the end of the twentieth century had to pass through another woe of that kind, after having suffered two world wars and experienced three entirely different political and social systems. The research was following therapeutic efforts in order to better understand how the warfare influences the entire human personality and the society.

At the beginning of the war in Croatia in 1991, and in Bosnia and Herzegovina in 1992, it was very popular to quote the Chinese curse: “Might you live in interesting times.” These times in Yugoslavia started to evolve a decade before the war broke, culminating in the armed conflict. The “usual” dynamics of life became an “interesting” one, bringing about deep changes, leading to death and destruction in personal, social and cultural spheres, as well as in construction of some new independent states, different organizations of these societies, and the possibilities for them to reaffirm their specific cultures and cultural heritage. The coping mechanisms of all kinds were set in motion, and many couldn’t confront such deep and even radical changes in an efficient way.

After the end of the war in Croatia, I received from one veteran of war the following letter:

> Dear Dr. Urlić,
> I am feeling very badly, it’s unbearable. I feel devoid of any sense. Nothing can make me feel happy and satisfied. I would prefer to stay the whole day in bed because I can’t struggle all day against anxiety and fear. What is left in me is only nausea and something like a cramp in my chest. I am in the middle of great fears, panic and phobias. I have fear of open space, an unhealthy, shameful fear of people. Diverse irrational fears of some catastrophes, disasters, fear that the house where I am living will collapse, fear from sudden rumors, voices, fear that I’ll fall from some high place...
> Arising from these fears, I feel very uneasy and I can’t stay on my legs. Please, could you correct or adjust the therapy and find for me some medicine that will consolidate me so as to enable me to re-enter the normal life? Or some injections, or anything, some experienced therapist, or anything that could catch away my fears?
> Yours faithfully ...

This letter, as so many other intimate stories of sufferings caused by experiences of war, uncovers the hidden worlds of those affected by the Post-traumatic Stress Disorder (PTSD), the disorder still not understood enough or fully recognized. Numerous persons experience psychologically traumatic stressful events that are “outside the range of usual human experience,” but not many develop PTSD. A diagnosis of PTSD requires, according to Greist and Jefferson (1995), “the presence of substantial disruption in functioning or suffering associated with re-experiencing the trauma; persistent symptoms of arousal, and signs of numbing and avoidance” (p. 277).

There is an old, wise saying that tells us that time heals all wounds. It might be said that PTSD is the result of a failure of time to heal all wounds. The memory of the trauma is not integrated and accepted as part of one’s personal past. Instead, it comes to exist independently of previous schemata (Urlić, 1999, p.487).

In trying to understand post-traumatic stress more fully, I would like to quote the proposal exposed by Joseph et al. (1997) that “a traumatic event presents an individual with stimulus information that, as perceived at the time, gives rise to extreme emotional arousal but interferes with immediate processing” (p.32). Representations of these events’ stimuli are held in memory, due to their personal salience and to the difficulty they present for easy assimilation with other stored representations. These event cognitions take two forms, corresponding to the dual representation theory of Brewin et al. (1988)—information that is not available to conscious inspection and information that is deliberately retrievable and can be easily edited. Event cognitions provide the basis for the re-experiencing phenomena or intrusive recollections of the trauma, which are sometimes full and realistic enough to be very intensive, experienced as if the events were really happening again (flashbacks). The traumatic cognitions will idiosyncratically reflect the individual’s prior experience, personality, basic assumptions and the specific components of an event that presented the individual with the greatest subjective threat. Intrusive ideation is, therefore, influenced by personality and/or representations of an earlier experience.

Many of these features, re-exposed by the stimulation of the individual psychotherapy or the group setting arena, and protected by the therapeutic (group) structure and discretion, can be re-experienced, shown and recognized, named and approached, and finally worked through in a different way than it was usual for each individual. It should be added that the group psychotherapeutic approach appears to be the therapy of choice for persons suffering from PTSD.

Regarding experience from the war in Croatia and its aftermath, I have become aware, together with many Croatian colleagues, that the further away we are from times of war, the more we are able to use this distance to try to make better understanding of the past experiences that were outside the range of usual human experience.

The warfare situation is an extraordinary one and stimulates seemingly peculiar behavior patterns. Observing refugees from Bosnia and Herzegovina that were coming to Croatia in 1992, it was possible to see on one side persons dressed in their best dresses, as if prepared to go to a party, and on the other side of that spectrum persons in morning-gowns, as if being caught by surprise; nevertheless, the war was already ravaging the whole country. At that time, it was almost impossible to encounter people that were somehow prepared to flee their home, city, country. Anyhow, it is generally assumed that the war stimulates primarily the necessity to survive. In that respect, it stimulates defense systems to organize and coping styles to evolve.

How do people react in war situations? As the observation is suggesting, there are extreme reactions that might be expected, primarily panic that might be expressed either through over agitation or withdrawal and wordlessness. That phase is usually followed by depression and separation anxieties. The syndrome of multiple losses is likely to appear. The expression of aggressive feelings is often intertwined or can appear as overwhelming emotion and behavior. Regression, considered to represent the general tendency of psychic functioning, is observed almost regularly in various degrees in war-provoked situations. Nevertheless, in war time, as in any other adverse situation, there is space for constructive and creative behavior. Under intensive stimulation of warfare, the capability for organization and leadership can be uncovered, many defensive and humanitarian actions carried out, as well as many other self-helping and other(s)-helping undertakings. In extreme situations, self-esteem is very often heavily tested. In our experience, it proved to be true for almost entire populations having to sustain the war and its aftermath.

3. On Stress-Related Disorders and the PTSD

Stress-related disorders encompass a wide range of disruptions of the normal process of adaptation to stressful life events. According to the Horowitz (1976, p.279) model, the person experiencing stress passes through regular stages of response, including outcry, in which the person protests that what was happened cannot be true; intrusion and denial, during which the person is either painfully aware of or oblivious to the new reality; working through, when the person becomes better able to integrate the event; and completion, which is marked by function at or above the pre-stress level. In adjustment disorder, this process of adaptation does not proceed to completion. The presumed cause is psychic overload, i.e., a level of intra-psychic strain that exceeds the individual's ability to cope. The feeling of continuity of the personality is disrupted. Some persons become caught in a seemingly endless stage of denial, as the stressful event(s) have never occurred, avoid all reminders of the stress, and remain emotionally numb or isolated. In others, intrusive symptoms predominate. The persons become very painfully aware of the stressor(s), that they are unable to sleep or control the flood of incoming emotions and images associated with the event. Some others oscillate between symptoms of intrusion and denial, with no overall change in psychological assimilation of the stressor(s). Any of these patterns is more often than not accompanied by difficulties in personal functioning and interpersonal relationships, as well as in his/her activities in a wider social sense.

During history, all these processes suffered by populations and soldiers caught by the warfare have called rather little attention; nevertheless, there are descriptions found on ancient Egyptian scrolls, and in old chronicles, poetry and novels. Kolb (ibid, 36-119), reviewing the evolution of notions of impacts that stressful event(s) exert on people, writes that the nineteenth century views about the serious consequences to the individual exposed to emotional-psychological trauma still remain with us. That means that continuing psychological and physical distress from such experiences, which have to be reassessed, are understood by many merely as malingering, rejecting, "non-accepting." The kind of attitude is often characteristic for officials and some clinicians that do not share the psychodynamic and psychophysiological views of the etiology of the PTSD.

World War I brought about the recognition of the acute war neurosis among the psychiatrists throughout the western world. Also, as Kolb states, for the more enduring anxiety symptoms and those related to states of guilt, shame, and anxiety, individual psychodynamic treatments were commenced in special treatment units. The positive therapeutic outcomes stimulated the interest in psychoanalysis and psychodynamic theory that followed the war. When the then-Freud's students returned from the front line and reported the frightening repetitive nightmares suffered by their patients, he was induced to remodel his theories regarding sexual conflict as causative of the neuroses, and that dreams represented wish fulfillments, and to assume that the neuroses represented an unresolved conflict in the ego.

Almost two decades later, Kardiner (1941, pp.35,37) stated that the post-traumatic states differed from the neuroses of peacetime and that they should be regarded as a "physioneurosis," underlying the importance of startle reactions and the process of "conditioning." His observations of the long-term consequences of the war neuroses became reinforced after W.W.II. Many researchers have found that symptoms connected with stressful war experiences were persisting after twenty years and more. The most striking feature was that the symptoms failed to habituate when soldiers returned to their familiar surroundings and their habitual pre-war life patterns. In ex-prisoners of war and concentration camps survivors, severe personality disorders were observed. Niederland (1964, ibid. pp.94,120), followed by many other researchers, described personality changes and the "survivor guilt" of these survivors. Krystal (1978, ibid p.84.) described the personality disturbances of Holocaust survivors, as well as the extraordinary effects upon the transference relationships encountered in attempts at intensive therapy with them. From these therapeutic experiences came the very important suggestion that such persons should be initiated into psychotherapy through a group, in order to attenuate transferential distortions leading to the perception of therapists as persecutors. My experiences from wars in Croatia and Bosnia and Herzegovina will clarify these observations through several clinical vignettes, later in this chapter.

After the return of Vietnam combatants, the professional and wider public opinion had to take notice of some important difficulties these veterans of war were struggling with, attracting growing attention. Nevertheless, veterans were often seen as malingerers, neurotics or psychopathic personalities, or were labeled as psychotics or as chronic alcohol or drug abusers. The consequences of stressful event(s) related to warfare and other extraordinary stresses, through research, treatment experiences and more comprehensive knowledge finally brought to a formulation of the PTSD in 1980, DSM-III classification of the American Psychiatric Association.

Post-traumatic stress disorder was defined as a severely stressful event that could be expected to cause great stress in almost anybody. The most prominent features to diagnose the PTSD consist of:

- Existence of a recognizable stressor that would evoke significant symptoms of distress in almost everyone;
- Re-experiencing of the trauma, often in the form of intrusive ideas accompanied by unbidden and unwanted feelings;
- Reduced involvement with the external world or a numbness and inability to respond to social stimuli, and constricted affect;
- At least two of the following symptoms that were not present before the trauma: hyper-alertness or exaggerated startle response, sleep disturbances, survivor guilt, shame feelings, memory impairment or trouble concentrating, avoidance of activities that arouse recollection of the traumatic event, intensification of symptoms by exposure to events that symbolize or resemble the traumatic event.

The most usual forms of trauma that may precipitate post-traumatic stress disorder are those that propel the person into a sudden unaccustomed state of helplessness and extreme danger. PTSD is apparently more severe and longer lasting when the stressor is of human agency (see Ch.10).

The DSM-IV classification (1994) brought some changes into diagnostic criteria for PTSD: "The person has been exposed to a traumatic event in which both of the following were present:

1. The person experienced, witnessed, or was confronted with an event or events that involved actual or threatened death or serious injury, or a threat to the physical integrity of self or others.
2. The person's response involved intense fear, helplessness, or horror."

The other criteria did not change substantially from previous ones. It was further specified that an acute PTSD is diagnosed if duration of symptoms is less than three months, chronic if duration is three months or more, and with delayed onset if the appearance of symptoms started at least six months after the stressor.

The exposed criteria were of a great help to me and my colleagues when organizing psychological support and treatments for refugees and displaced persons, for soldiers and later for war veterans, ex-prisoners of war, victims of torture, for understanding and helping family members of persons with PTSD, as well as when occasionally it was needed to explain that kind of mental health problems to the government officials and to the wide audience through special broadcasts.

In my and my colleagues' experiences, the psychological help for refugees and displaced persons was first organized simultaneously with the help for soldiers that later became war veterans. Together with the therapeutic attempts at various levels, the research was done to enable psychiatrists, psychologists and other psychological helpers to understand better the population they were working with. I am suggesting that it is of essential importance to use both the psychological and psychosocial helping approaches with research, in order to better understand dynamics that are unfolding not only on a rationale but on individual and social unconscious levels.

4. Refugees and Displaced Persons: Reality, Despair and Mechanisms of Defence. Results of a Research

When the whirlpool of war started, general anxiety and tension increased with each report of terrorist actions and military operations by which the enemy pressured the Croatian population to leave their homes. The growing flow of refugees moved towards the more secure regions of Croatia. In the beginning, mostly children and adolescents arrived, especially from the northern plains of Croatia near the Danube, bordering with Serbia. Soon they were joined by the displaced persons from north Dalmatian regions and Dubrovnik. From March 1992, new waves of refugees from Bosnia and Herzegovina started to seek refuge in Croatia. The wave of the displaced brought many people to Split (the second largest city of Croatia), where they were accommodated in hotels, tourist camps, various homes or private houses, or by their relatives. The data and experiences that will be exposed here were obtained by the network for the psychosocial help organized in the region of Split.

Although Split was relatively spared from war destruction, it could not escape the war operations completely. Numerous military bases and the headquarters of the Federal Yugoslav Navy have been located in Split. Frequent air raid alerts, shooting, sieges of military facilities and shelling from the sea created an atmosphere of immediate war danger, which soon became everyday reality.

In order to ascertain the main traumatic factors and basic characteristics of reactions of certain refugee groups (children, adolescents, and adults), which dominated in the situation of acute war trauma, with special emphasis on the most frequent defense mechanisms of adults, all the refugees first were interviewed (Tocilj-Šimunković and Urlić, 1995, p. 253-261). All the data were fully compiled for 199 children, 177 adolescents and 107 adults.

Regarding displaced children, most frequent traumatic events were shooting (85%), shelling (67.4%), bombing (23.8%) and other stressful events (15.5%).

On the other hand, the most frequent reactions to the trauma were fear (which is the basic response to a traumatic event), crying, increased need for closeness with other family members, intensified tension, panic and inability to express any emotional response.

Reactions to the war-related stress in the group of parents could be classified into four subgroups: fear (61.1%) and tension (40.4%), sadness (23.85%) and anxiety (18.15%); panic (16.6%) and composure (16.1%); desire for action (5.7%) and rage (4.7%).

Children's responses in relation to their parents' reactions to the war-related stress were assessed by six parameters: panic, fear, crying, tension, increased dependence and "complex" behavior, which could be subdivided into three groups. Most frequent reactions were fear (89.9%), crying (47.7%), increased need for closeness with parents (45.1%) and, finally, tension (26.9%). The third subgroup included extreme reactions to stress: the child remained "calm" without showing any particular reaction to the event (14%) or they overtly panicked (13%).

Regarding displaced adolescents, most of them were exposed to bombing (69.5%) and shooting (64.4%), while other possible stressful events were not identified.

Then we compared the adolescents' feelings during earlier separation from home with their feelings provoked by the exile. Earlier separation from home was accompanied by satisfaction (61.6%), excitement (13%) and anxiety (7.9%), while the last three on the frequency scale were sadness, fear and anger (each of them in 6.2%). Contrary to the emotional reactions to their earlier separation from home, displaced adolescents were aware of the following characteristics of their emotional state: anger (42.4%), sadness (21.5%), fear and anxiety (19.2% each).

In the group of adult-displaced persons, two basic types of reaction to the acute trauma could be observed. One type included reactions tinged with affection: anxiety (57%) and depression (38.3%), and the other included psychomotor reactions, such as agitation through shooting and putting the blame on the aggressor (48.6%), and stupor (33.6%).

In both groups of the displaced, common traumatic elements were war activities and psychic suffering. The answers revealed differences in their traumatic awareness of their damaged, demolished or burnt homes. This was present primarily in those who reacted with sadness and anxiety, while those with a prevailing psychomotor aspect of the reaction to the war-related stress did not identify with the fate of their homes very often, at least on a manifest, verbal level.

Defense Mechanisms of Adults Mobilized by War Trauma and Displacement

Tocilj-Šimunković and Urlić (1995) also studied the frequency of various defense mechanisms mobilized by our subjects in order to cope with the traumatic event. The therapists could register one or more defense mechanisms for each subject. In the initial phase of accommodation, various combinations of defenses were observed.

Out of nine defense mechanisms observed during the initial interview, rationalization (60.7%), projection (53.3%), regression (51.4%), repression (48.6%) and negation (41.1%) were present. Less mobilized defense mechanisms were identification (28.8%), idealization (19.6%) and reactive formation (13.1%).

5. Group Therapy as a Method of Choice

In the case of a total war when nobody can feel safe, the experts of the World Health Organization calculated that the existing psychological and psychiatric facilities in Croatia could satisfy only two to three percent of needs of the population. Group methods were recommended as methods of choice. For the group-analytically oriented therapists, it represented a challenge to modify the usual approach and technique in order to meet the needs of a population in despair.

In these circumstances, medical and social services in the region of Split tried to organize help on various levels. A group of 32 therapists, psychiatrists, psychologists, special teachers, speech pathologists and social workers set out from the institutions where they were employed to the places where displaced persons and refugees used to be placed. During first months, group therapists worked with DPs and refugees in places of their accommodations on a daily basis. In those days, quite frequently, group therapists had to go to the shelter together with the group members. In the periods of general alert, the groups met irregularly. The supervisory-consultation work with all therapists was done every day because of the dramatic pressure of tension, anxiety and uncertainty not only upon the DPs and refugees but upon the therapists, too. Psychological work in the war situation was a completely new experience to all of us.

Nevertheless, the group analysis has its roots in Northfield, England, from the first experiences with soldiers traumatized by warfare; as a method, it is primarily designed for therapy of neurotics. Very soon, we discovered that amidst massive projections, anger, fears and feelings of uncertainty and helplessness, it was of outmost importance to allow and facilitate the verbal expressions of facts and feelings, enabling refugees to be heard not only by therapists but by the other peer members of the group. This represents the first necessary step in trying to reach possible traumatic experiences in order to create some structure in the chaotic state of mind. Losing firm roots of their identity, they were feeling lost in space and time, becoming nobody and completely out of control of their destinies.

Croatian psychiatrists found themselves in the midst of that turmoil of war in our country with stirred up emotions, but with the conscience that we should help others who were suffering under shelling, bombing, shooting ... At the beginning of war between Croats and the enemy Yugoslav army, it was with great consternation that we had to witness bombing and shelling of the ancient city of Dubrovnik, the city unarmed and under the protection of

UNESCO as the world cultural heritage. The besieged city was accessible only by sea. As part of psychosocial help organized for citizens and defenders of the city, I was impressed by the bitter comment of one citizen when we were talking with them in one meeting: “If we survive, we should put a stone memorial with all names of enemy soldiers on the road they came to destroy the city and to annihilate us in order to put lasting shame on them, to make their children and grandchildren feel shame about their fathers’ misdeeds.” In these circumstances, it was for the first time that I heard the notion of shame expressed in such an unequivocal way, and I heard it as bearing stronger emotional and ethical charge in relation to war misdeeds than the notion of guilt. I believe that this very episode in the frame of the total war situation immersion has made a decisive impact on my understanding that the most appropriate aims of any psychotherapeutic work should try to attain the possibilities of forgiving and reconciliation.

It is very common to think and judge in terms of culpability: who is guilty for the armed conflict, persecutions, torture, destruction. Thinking in this sense, there were many realities, projections, negations and projective identifications that set in motion under the stress of war situations.

On a social level, as well as on personal one, the sense of shame is very often overshadowed by the sense of guilt. It is difficult to create the therapeutic atmosphere were the sense of shame could find its expression or even the name (Urlić and Tocilj-Šimunković, 2009, p. 166). On the other side, the experience from professional activities in war time has taught us that the group setting is the treatment of choice for suffering people that were caught up in war situation. And, the war that started in 1991, in Croatia spread in 1992, in neighboring Bosnia-Herzegovina, bringing more suffering and new waves of refugees. People that didn’t escape either had become soldiers or prisoners of war put in concentration camps, and some of the population was locked up in enclaves surrounded by enemy army. The life space, generally speaking, had collapsed.

Under such circumstances, Durham (2000, pp.74-75) said that some degree of hatred is inevitable, and it may be looked upon as an ingredient in the individual’s emotions that may also subserve adaptation and personality organization (connected even to victimization and vengeful feelings described in previous chapters).

6. The Therapeutic Mirroring of Traumatic Hatred

In the psychotherapeutic ambience, individual or group, there is the possibility to develop feelings of safety bringing about disclosure in a confidential way of difficult emotions that overwhelming experiences are provoking. Speaking about the group arena, there is a possibility for every participant to identify with other group members and to share many important parts of his/her difficult experiences. In that atmosphere, they feel protected and understood. It is in a psychotherapeutic setting that many horrible events find their verbal and emotional expression. Otherwise, hidden emotions and repressed images exert their lasting influence inside one’s personality, and the impossibility to express stressful events might bring about a shift in emotions, giving way to traumatic hatred, feelings of victimization, and revengeful fantasies. Some clinical vignettes from individual and group psychotherapy from various phases of wartime therapeutic experiences will uncover many kinds of inner world sufferings of people caught in very stressful events.

Clinical Vignettes

1. In the Beginning of Warfare: The Shock of War

The First Soldier Asks for Psychiatric Consultation

At the very beginning of the war, one soldier told me with bitterness when asked about what was causing his frequent insomnia, headaches and nightmares: "They (enemies) made me become killer... It is not fair...If I survive all this, I am quite aware that I will never be the same person again." It proved, certainly, to be difficult to identify with that position of a killer, but it was part of everyday reality in the war. The soldier was very unwilling to talk and explained that nevertheless, he was a farmer; he couldn't support seeing blood, which made his position as a soldier additionally extremely difficult.

Mirroring of War Experiences in Group Setting: The Dream of a Female Soldier

One group of veterans of the war in Croatia in the beginning was composed of four men and three women. Later on, the number of members increased to 12: ten men and two women. Their active participation in war was at least two years, but some of them were volunteers from the onset of clashes. The group was meeting once a week for 90-minute sessions. The group work started after the war operations ended, from January 1996, on. All participants have had some previous individual therapies with the same therapist. The development of the group process will be presented through some clinical vignettes.

In the session from the beginning of the group psychotherapy for war veterans, a female group member told her dream. *In that dream, there was football stadium filled with spectators. There was a football match. She turned with her face outwards toward the stadium, and she knew, she was looking with something like the third eye, what was going behind her back. When she turned herself towards the stadium, the very strange scene appeared: all players of both teams were spread dead on the grass, the arbiters didn't do anything, and the public was leaving the seats in silence.*

Commenting spontaneously on her dream, she said that after awakening she was feeling confused and angry—confused by such a scene and angry because nobody was apparently doing anything to clarify the situation.

It was obvious enough that the dream reflected attitudes of the international community toward the war in Croatia. The interpretation was that the dream bared the intuitions and understanding very common in Croatia at that time of the circumstances that favorized the war conflict to start and develop (a kind of social dreaming). The group had some difficulties to accept that kind of understanding, because it seemed that some members, at that level of development of group process, couldn't fully follow the symbolic way of expressing emotions and facts, especially through a dream.

Working With Refugees and Displaced Persons in a Group

The group of refugees and DPs was organized soon after they were placed in a new shelter. The group members originated from the region with a mixed population, Croatian and

Serbian. Apart from being neighbors, many of them were connected by family links. Now they were recollecting how in the last two years before the war broke, their Serbian neighbors were changing attitudes towards them and had some secret evening meetings (the prince Lazar's bones adoration, among other rituals). The bitterness was caused by the feelings of having been betrayed by Serbs from their villages.

Then one group member, Marko, was identified as Serbian, and the aggressive feelings were projected on him. "All of you are alike; you did all this behind our back. Shame on you!" shouted Pava, and many others were shouting, too. Marko was feeling lost, trying to say something, but in that atmosphere, he was not permitted.

The intervention of the therapist was aimed at distinguishing general considerations and projections about Serbs from an individual person. The comments of disbelief were soothed by Marko's tears: "I am here with all of you because I did not share their views (thinking on Serbian ultranationalists—Chetniks). My wife and myself were severely criticized, and they threatened our lives. Now I am lost, not knowing where to go with my family."

Silence in the group, many sighs and hidden glimpses towards Pava and the therapist.

"Now I see (Pava said) that you are one of us who suffer under their aggression. If I could only find that Milošević (Serbian President) I would take him by his neck and kill him like a chicken," showing with hands what she would like to do. Some others were agreeing, and the massive aggressive feelings were projected outside the group.

"But (said the therapist) Milošević is far away, beyond reach... Let us suppose that I am Milošević... What you would say to me in that case... ?"

There was a moment of surprise in the group, and many members said: "It is not possible, you are not Milošević, you are helping us...."

Then they started to differentiate friends and enemies on a more realistic basis, thus reducing projections.

In these circumstances, the way of reducing denial, projections and projective identifications is very difficult to open and very slow to develop, the reality being too harsh to be acknowledged and confronted. In Kleinian terms, it might be said that group psychotherapy was aimed primarily at enabling the refugees to shift from paranoid-schizoid to depressive position in order to allow the mourning processes to unfold, and the more realistic understandings to develop.

The Case of an Ex-P.O.W.

A young man in his early twenties was complaining that he could not participate anymore in the country's defense. He was crying and expressing his deep feelings of being ashamed by his weakness. When the first armed clashes started, he was feeling ready to stand for the defense of his homeland and against injustice. Being in mountains and not having defined rows, the situation was very confused. One night, he was with two other soldiers on patrol. They were ambushed by an enemy unit and tried to find shelter and escape. So, he found himself being lost in the woods and trying to find his way towards valley, where he could see a village. The village was deserted by population. But, all of a sudden he felt that enemy soldiers were encircling the village, cutting all possible ways out. The only solution he found was to lay down in a trough for porcs. He was hiding there for three days, drinking water that remained after livestock. Then he decided to surrender to whomever he found.

The enemy soldiers put him in a concentration camp. He was very reluctant to describe his experiences from these two months, because this was an "indescribable" experience filled up with all kinds of tortures, fiscal and emotional. When rape was mentioned, as some people were telling there were, he just nodded and said that "some people were even raped...." Sweating and wringing his hands, he was unable to say anything more.

He accepted the possibility to join one therapy group of people traumatized by war but after several sessions, he concluded that for him "to continue to live here was impossible," and he decided to go to the USA. He asked me to refer him to one of my colleagues, which I did. It happened that even on another continent, he was not able to speak more freely about his most dramatic war experiences. When he returned back to Croatia, he was feeling deeply submerged in the position of being an irreparable victim of torture. Avoiding social contacts because, as he said, he was "unable to feel himself," he was expressing pitiful feelings toward himself and very intensive hatred toward his torturers and the nation they belonged to.

As it was proven through time and repeating situations, helping people with deep wounds from catastrophic situations for them had a limitation when the core self was destroyed by putting persons in unthinkable situations of fear, humiliation, and shame. This represents one of the most common causes of victimhood attitudes to develop.

2. During The War

The Escape from Bosnian Hell

From the refugee camp, one 18-year-old young man was referred because he was overwhelmed with great fears that he would become mad and irresponsible for his behaviour. At first, he was unable to speak, could not even a glance at me, and was shaking with all his body. It turned out that he was Muslim, from Eastern Bosnia. Serbian nationalists encircled the small town and started to kill the population and rape young women. He was living in a large family. In that situation, he joined one group that found the way to the mountain. There, in a small valley, there was a farmer's house. They rushed to find some shelter, but someone from inside started to shoot at them. Finally, they discovered there were friendly people from the same town that let them enter. There, he found his eldest brother, armed, heavily wounded in his right arm. He was trying to adjust the machinegun toward his head to shoot himself. The brother shouted that they were encircled by enemy soldiers, that for him there was no escape, and was pressing his young brother to help him shoot himself and then he should try to escape...He refused to help his brother to shoot himself. Shooting started, a shell exploded, the youngster found himself in the woods again...After three days of wandering in woods, he was found by some people and brought to one gathering point for refugees. Helped by the Red Cross, he was brought to Split, but he did not even know where exactly he was. Desperate, not knowing the vicissitudes of other family members and whether somebody survived the massacre, he was uttering his dilemma: should he have helped his wounded brother die, instead letting him at the mercy of enemy soldiers; how he could have killed his own brother; whether he will ever find some family members...And, where to go now...?

In front of such despair, it looks like an impossible task to try to help with any possible word or action. It is my belief that what can connect people in these situations might be deep compassion, containing, listening, understanding. But words prove to be far too weak to enable a real dialogue. Perhaps the example from besieged Dubrovnik is another episode indicating how in situations of extreme danger and destruction, it is only despair, vengeful needs and feelings, and survival strategies that are filling the frame of collapsed space and time. In these cases, the empathic listening might be seminal in preventing vengeful fantasies from becoming acts.

3. After the War

The Dream: Enemy Soldiers are Running After Him

In the group setting, one veteran of war was in deep silence most of the session. Then, he found courage to share with the group his last night's dream. He was in the woods, alone, feeling fearful and insecure. In the middle of the woods, there was a phone cabin. The phone was ringing; he knew it was a call for him....Next dream picture: he was surrounded by ten Chetniks (enemy soldiers). He started to behead one by one....Next dream picture: ten of their heads were on spits....

The picture was in accordance with the tradition dating from centuries of Turkish occupation, when that way of treating enemies and traitors was customary. In dream spaces, it remained lively, as so many transgenerationally transmitted notions, pictures, attitudes, as well as the long dreamed of fulfillment of needs for revenge many family members that perished or were killed during previous wars or after them during repressions that followed.

Female Soldier Walking with Her Mother

There was another dream that was announced to the group as "silly." Vedrana was walking with her mother along the seaside. She was wearing military dress, but it seemed to be normally accepted by passersby. She and her mother were looking at the ferry entering the harbor. Mother was admiring the nice boat, but Vedrana knew that there was a coffin on the boat with her corpse in it. She was feeling indifferent to that. In the next scene of the dream, the coffin was brought out and the mother was commenting: "Poor young person." Vedrana didn't feel anything. She wondered how she had no feelings, knowing that corpse in the coffin was her.

Numbing, dissociation and denial of fears was very often observed as a reaction to the exposure to extreme situations and dangers for one's life. All members of the group were nodding, recognizing their own experiences.

In the group, there were many who complained time and again that they were able to hear only the beginning of stories of other members of the group. They were able to listen to the others only formally, but inside themselves, they were going through some personal experiences. One group member said that she was invited at a wedding party and had to go. She was forcing herself to stay there physically, but all that music and happiness, all that was far away from her.

Thus, the splitting emerged between reenactments of their own experiences connected to the past and actual happenings of ongoing life where they were unable to include themselves. It seemed like the group member-war veteran was leaving her body at the party, while in her soul, she was submerged by anxieties, tensions and flashbacks…

Aftermath of the War: Interethnic and Interconfessional Strifes and Identity Issues

Vinko was on military training together with Bosnians. They had to sit together and to shake hands, which he didn't want to do. Members of each ethnic group (Croats and Bosnians—'Bošnjaks') were gathering on a different floor. He said: "The Americans have good salaries and are training us....Everyone speaks about the war that will start again... Christians and Muslims can't live together... There is too much hate..."

Further associations between Croats and Bosnians spilled over into the football match, which took place that day. The therapist compared the football match with the "war game." These associations uncovered the confusion and oppression pertaining to the old regime's policies toward Croatians. The group members agreed about the impossibility of coming to terms with the enemy.

One member confronted the group about the dialogue of Pope John Paul II with his would-be assassin. In the group, the aggression turned toward greed and barriers of some administrative services when veterans want to obtain their rights.

The therapist summarized the group process by confronting the feelings of hate and judgement directed towards certain nations or certain groups that represent it. On the other side, there are individuals, like Pope John-Paul II or his would-be assassin, who act on their own behalf. Perhaps now the group is struggling between identification with our ethnic group and its beliefs and one's own moral values...?

One group member, Tony, said that there are prejudices among people: "If I get acquainted with a Serbian, I could like him as a person, but I don't want to have any connection with him." The others agreed.

The Indian poet wrote: "People are horrible, man is good" (Tagore, 1920). That sentence summarizes the essential dichotomy between individual and the large group that was so thoroughly mirrored in the group process. On the other hand, the power of prejudices was acknowledged as overwhelming.

Dramatic Confrontation and Transgenerational Transmission of Recollections and Emotions

Another vignette from the end of the first year of group therapy with war veterans discloses the struggle to master the evil.

In the group, there were many personal stories to unfold, very dramatic in content, covering episodes from war times and persecutions of their own and of their parents and grandparents. One of the most dramatic was told by Domagoj, who spent four years in the war. During one battle, he was leaving his unit to protect him from backside while he was crawling through a minefield to come to the machine-gun nest. The commander of that enemy position happened to be his school friend; they were even sitting in the same bench. He liquidated them all; there were six persons. The school friend said: "You don't want to kill me," and he answered: "You will be the first! You wouldn't spare me, either." During his telling of the story, his ticks have become something like atetoid movements and sudden jerks, and he remained in high tension like everybody else...

In the group springs out all mistrust towards Serbs that in the families was talked about, all misdeeds that they have done to various members of their families, together with the statement that "all of them are alike." There was the atmosphere of bitterness and disgust prevailing.

The group moved in the direction of opening not just very anxiety-provoking, but direct, aggressive, feelings connected to family stories about killing family members of previous generations done by Serbs. Living with all these stories, many of them were ashamed that their family members were "killed like sheep" and were longing for revenge.

Intergenerational transmission of wounds covering aggressive feelings was showing an unusual strength and resilience when the attempts were made to confront and interpret them.

One group member was recollecting the killing of one Chetnik on Orthodox Christmas. He said that now, for Christmas or some other festivity, the episode comes to his mind. He said that he didn't feel pity for him (and he was blushing), asking what he (the enemy soldier) was searching for on soil that was not his, and on his Christmas...If it were on any other day, his destiny would be the same...

Silence in the group. The therapist commented about shadows being spread over holiday atmospheres after that event. The war veteran said: "I don't know why, but it is somehow that way. There were others I have killed on front line, but this one especially remained in my memories..."

It seemed like the rude aggressive feelings and heavy anxieties were finding their ways to start the mourning processes. The group is able to speak more openly about sadness, not only about feelings of emptiness and boredom. Episodes like this one were indicating that sadness could be approached and felt but still not named.

According to Basoglu et al. (JAMA, 2005; pp.580-90), relative to controls, PTSD and depression in war survivors appear to be independent of a sense of injustice arising from perceived lack of redress for trauma. Fear of threat to safety and loss of control over life appeared to be the most important mediating factors in PTSD and depression. This finding may have important implications for reconciliation efforts in postwar countries and effective interventions for traumatized war survivors. In these situations, as Kernberg (1994) wrote, vengefulness is a typical characterological form of hatred.

Gladston (1987) states that his contention is that the development of the abilities to hate and to get over hating are two major accomplishments in the ego's growth toward the mastery of aggression in relating to the object world. Hatred can lead to forgiving the trespasser, foregoing revenge and forgetting the offence. By letting bygones be bygones, the ego is enabled to detach aggression from the obligatory pursuit of an object lost through disappointment and to retrieve energy for new endeavors. He also stated that in addition to the work of mourning to retrieve the lost libido, the patient must do the work of hating to liberate his aggression from continued service to the past. Forgiveness is accomplished by recovering the aggression that had been preempted by the desire for revenge and redirecting it towards a new goal. The work of forgiving allows for the symbolic blending of aggression and libido into an endeavor created to replace a hated object. With forgiveness, the blocking introject loses its significance. The goal of revenge passes. Comfort in a stronger ego allows the patient the prospect of a future freed of hatred from the past. I am supporting the idea that freedom of hatred from the past has a meaning of the regained ability to sublimate aggressive feelings, thus choosing human relations to continue in a more productive and positive way.

In her book *The traumatic roots of destructiveness: From pain to violence*, de Zulueta (1993, pp.30-31) wrote that "in the field of ethology, those who believe human violence to be innate are essentially followers of Konrad Lorenz. As he is an ethologist of considerable repute, his views on human aggression are still accepted by many as scientific truths. He sees aggression as an instinct that helps to ensure the survival of both the individual and species. However, in man, this same instinct becomes destructive because our cultural evolution has, so to speak, outstripped our biological evolution. Rapid technological development, particularly in the field of weapons, has given man a destructive power that is no longer kept in check by appropriate inhibitions. Our future thus depends on how we can channel our dangerous and redundant aggressive drives."

We might once again put the question where are all human hatred, violence and other aggressive behaviors are coming from, and what provokes and supports that way of relating to others? And, how to articulate all therapeutic procedures to enable the grieving process and the forgiving process to unwind, in order to try to heal deep narcissistic wounds, destruction of self and interpersonal relations? In other words, how to reconcile with oneself and the others?

Inability to Move beyond the Unforgiving Attitude

Patient attitude, active waiting for the psychotherapeutic (individual or group) process to unfold bringing about moving from victimhood, vengefulness, and other encapsulating behaviors, many times is not enough for the forgiving attitude to approach. The bleeding wounds prevent its development. What can be found in these situations is the denial of the possibility to forgive, sometimes even "forever."

Although no "gold standard" definition of interpersonal forgiveness exists, there is general agreement among theorists and researchers about what forgiveness is not: It is not pardoning (legal term), excusing (implies good reasons for offense), condoning (implies justification), denying (implies unwillingness to acknowledge), forgetting (implies failed memory, something outside conscious awareness), or reconciliation (McCullough, Pargament, & Thoresen, 2000, p.8).

Unforgiveness has been defined by Worthington & Scherer (2004), Worthington et al. (2000), and Worthington and Wade (1999) as a combination of delayed and chronic negative thoughts and emotions (i.e., resentment, bitterness, hostility, hatred, anger, and fear) toward a transgressor.

Unforgiveness is viewed as distinct from the immediate emotional response to a perceived injustice, such as anger. Instead, unforgiveness occurs in situations that remain hurtful for extended periods, such that one is stuck in a chronic hyper-aroused stress response, primarily through continuing rumination. Clearly, not everyone who is offended or hurt experiences unforgiveness (Worthington & Scherer, 2004). Forgiveness involves both the reduction of unforgiveness and an increase of positive emotions and perspectives, such as empathy, hope, or compassion.

Spiers (2004, p.261-263) asked a question: is a subjective state of unforgiveness harmful to the victim? In one study, psychological markers of stress were measured during the expression of either forgiveness or unforgiveness. Volunteers were given information about real aggressors and were then asked to cultivate either forgiving or unforgiving thoughts. Subjects who cultivated unforgiveness had significantly higher blood pressures and heart rates, as well as increased corrugator muscle activity than subjects cultivating forgiving thoughts. Furthermore, these adverse effects persisted after the stimulus was removed. It is theorized that persistence of the state producing these effects may lead to physical illness.

Another study measured levels of forgiveness in 197 college students. The Enright Forgiveness Inventory (EFI) measured forgiveness, and the Beck Depression Inventory and the State-Trait Anxiety Inventory measured psychopathlogy. There was a strong negative correlation between EFI scores and psychopathology index scores. Students in a state of unforgiveness may, therefore, be at increased risk of developing psychiatric illness.

Other studies have reached similar conclusions. The South African Truth and Reconciliation Commission undertook a study of 134 victims of human rights abuse. Each subject participated in a structured interview where the violations they experienced were recorded. Subjects also completed the EFI and the Composite International Diagnostic Interview Post-traumatic Stress Disorder module. Ninety percent had suffered abuse, 80% had witnessed abuse to friends or relatives, and 72% had experienced both. Sixty-three percent had a current psychiatric diagnosis, most commonly depression (55%), followed by post-traumatic stress disorder (42%). The study showed that participants with low forgiveness scores had a much higher rate of psychiatric disorder.

These studies suggest that unforgiveness is a significant risk factor for developing psychiatric disease.

Writing about the therapist's encounters with revenge and forgiveness, Durham (2000 p.63-64) described one of probably the most striking examples of the inability to forgive, which was recounted by Simon Wiesenthal. In his book *The Sunflower* (1976), he offers a stunning example of the discomfort in assessing issues of forgiveness. In a concentration camp during the Holocaust, Wiesenthal relates an encounter with a dying young SS officer who confessed of unspeakable atrocities toward Jews and asked Wiesenthal for forgiveness, a request that Wiesenthal could not bring himself to grant. In *The Sunflower*, he describes his predicament, his continuing self-doubt concerning his reaction, and the responses of thirty-two mature individuals of a variety of religious and professional backgrounds to the question: "What is your reaction to my refusal to forgive this dying perpetrator?" Obviously, not every question has to be answered, at least not immediately. Sometimes we might make better use of it by taking it as a starting point for thinking about and use our knowledge and experiences.

By the same token, associations go to apartheid and its aftermath. The essential point of the Truth and Reconciliation Commission was that there is no point exacting vengeance now, knowing it will cause future vengeance by the offspring of those we punish. Vengeance leads only to revenge ...Vengeance destroys those it claims and those who become intoxicated with it. It seems clear that if we don't deal with deep conflicts, they don't disappear. You can't cover the cracks forever. Forgiveness is not nebulous, unpractical and idealistic. It is, in fact, thoroughly realistic. It's realpolitik in the long run (Durham, 2000, p.6)

In this context, it is important to distinguish between hatred and rage. According to Kernberg (Durham, 2000, p.75), "hatred, is a complex, structured derivate of rage that expresses the combined wishes to destroy a bad object, to make it suffer, and to control it on the part of an enraged self. In contrast to the acute, transitory, and disruptive quality of rage, it is a chronic, stable, usually characterologically anchored affect. The object relationship framing this affect expresses concretely the desire to destroy or dominate the object. An almost unavoidable consequence of hatred is its justification as revenge against the frustrating object, and revengefulness is a typical characterological form of hatred." This represents one of the major reasons for psychotherapeutic, psychosocial or political interventions aiming at elaboration of hatred and prevention of vengeful acts, even of fantasies.

It is important that the patient and therapist realize that a solution is forthcoming: forgiveness. Otherwise, the insights are serving only the purpose of letting the patient know how miserable he/she is. Insight alone will not solve the problem created by injustice. During the process of understanding the affects that were nominating one person that was hurt by violence and injustice, the patient has to touch the seven layers of pain: anger, shame, depleted energy, cognitive rehearsal, comparison between offender and oneself, the possibility of permanent injury, a more pessimistic philosophy of life. Each person will have a different pattern of these seven layers, varying in number and intensity for each. Individuals with PTSD tend to be the most aware of both their anger and who their offenders are.

The Israeli psychiatrist M. Kaufman (1984, p.187) was the first to link forgiveness to the courageous act of "the readiness to bear pain" caused by the offense. He did not mean that the patient permanently must accept the debilitating emotions of anxiety and depression, but instead implied that the patient begins to mature as a person by accepting what happened.

In spite of growing evidence that thinking of forgiveness and reconciliation is an attainable aim in psychotherapy, social and political ambiences, there are doubts left over. Whether forgiveness therapy produces results superior to traditional approaches is not yet clear. That forgiveness can take its place alongside well-established techniques such as (support) group therapy is important, especially given the long history of support groups and the relatively short history of forgiveness as an explicit aim within therapeutic tasks.

Although healthy assertiveness is important, it can have limited value because mere words or behaviors often cannot compensate for the depth of pain and anger from a significant hurt. Also, the expression of anger rarely results in a true sense of justice or in freedom from the desire for revenge. In contrast to revenge, healthy assertiveness in association with forgiveness is an important aspect of the treatment of those with GAD (generalized anxiety disorder). The growing experiences from psychotherapeutic work with PTSD and otherwise heavily stressed people, psychosocial help, as well as other forms of interventions intended at healing deep hurts that provoke pain, anger, shame, guilt, hate, and many other difficult feelings indicate that unforgiving attitude should be approached, confronted, understood and worked through, in order to prevent severe psychic damages and behavioral distortions, as shown in some of clinical examples in this chapter. The aim to reach, according to my experiences, is the possibility to attain a forgiveness attitude that will enable reconciliation processes to unwind toward oneself and the other(s).

References

Brewin, C. R. (1988). *Cognitive Foundations of Clinical Psychology*. London: Erlbaum.

Basoglu, M. et al. (2005). *JAMA*. 294(5):580-90).

Držić, M. (1979) *Djeka. Zagreb: Liber*. P.10.

Durham, M.S. (2000). *The Therapist's Encounters with Revenge and Forgiveness*. London, Philadelphia: Jessica Kingsley Publishers, pp 63-64.

Eriksson, M., Wallensteen, P., Sollenberg, M. (2003). *Armed Conflict*. 1989-2002.
Department of Peace and Conflict Research. Uppsala University.

Gleditsch, N.P., Wallensteen, P., Eriksson, M., Sollenberg, M., Strand, H. (2002) Armed Conflict 1946-2001: a New Dataset. International Peace Research Institute, Oslo (PRIO), Department of Sociology and Political Science, Norwegian University of Science and Technology (NTNU), Department of Political Science, University of Oslo & Department of Peace and Conflict Research, Uppsala University. *Journal of Peace Research.*

Greist J.H., Jefferson J.W. (1995). Anxiety Disorders, In H.H Goldman (ed.) *Review of General Psychiatry*. Norwalk: Appleton and Lange; p.266-282.

Harbom, L., Wallensteen, P. (2005). *Armed Conflict and Its International Dimensions*, 1946-2004. Department of Peace and Conflict Research, Uppsala University.

Horowitz, M., (1976). J. of Stress Response Syndromes. Jason Aronson. In: Greist J.H., Jefferson J.W. (1995). Anxiety Disorders, In H.H Goldman (ed) *Review of General Psychiatry*. Norwalk: Appleton and Lange; p.266-282.

Joseph S, Williams R, Yule W. (1997). Understanding Post-traumatic Stress. *A Psychosocial Perspective on Post-traumatic Stress Disorder and Treatment.* Chichester: J. Wiley.

Kardiner, A. (1941). On essential pathology of combat neurosis. In: Herman J.L., *Trauma and Recovery*. New York: Basic Books, 1992.

Kaufman, M. E. The Courage to Forgive. *Isr J Psychiatry Relat Sci.* 21(3)1984:177-187.

Kolb, L.C. The Psychology of PTSD: Perspective and Reflections on the Past, Present and Future. *J. Traum. Stress.* 6(3):293-304.

Krystal, H. In: Herman J.L., *Trauma and Recovery*. New York: Basic Books, 1992.

McCullough, M.E., Pargament, K.I., Thoresen, C.E., (Eds) (2001). *Forgiveness, Theory, research, and Practice.* New York—London: The Guilford Press.

Niederland, W. In: Herman J.L., *Trauma and Recovery*. New York: Basic Books, 1992.

Spiers, A. Forgiveness as a secondary prevention strategy for victims of interpersonal crime, Forensic Psychiatry. *Australasian Psychiatry*. Vol. 12 No. 3, September 2004, 261-263.

Tagore, R. (1920). *Poems from Tagore*. (translated into English and with an introduction by C.F. Andrews). Calcutta: Macmillan.

Tocilj-Šimunković, G., Urlić, I. (1995). War Trauma: Emotional Responses and Psychological Defenses of Displaced Persons. *Croatian Med. J.* 4(36):253-261.

Urlić I. (1999). Mirroring of Psychogenic Autistic Barriers and Neurotic Boundaries in Group Process. *Group Analysis*. 32(4) 533-546.

Urlić, I., Tocilj-Šimunković, G. (2009). Working Through Shame in Groups for Victims of Trauma and War. *International Journal of Group Psychotherapy*. 59(2):165-178.

Zulueta, F.D. *From Pain to Violence: The traumatic Roots of Destructiveness*. London: Whurr Publishers 1993.

Chapter 8

MOURNING AND FORGIVENESS AS PARTS OF A HEALING PROCESS

Ivan Urlic

LIKE ONCE

Sometimes, while looking through the window at the tree,
and the wind is playing with young leaves,
it comes to my mind, yes that is the same street
- like once.

Sometimes, while looking at you sleeping,
and your face having carefree expression,
I feel you in myself,
- like once.

Sometimes, while day is fresh and light,
and nothing seems impossible,
I believe in tomorrow,
- just like once.

Sometimes, while looking at the sea,
and the sun is starting to show its gold,
it comes to my mind, that is a meadow in front of my house,
- like once.

Sometimes, while it is raining day by day,
and grayness is blending with smell of earth,
I feel sadness of the world on my shoulders,
- like once.

A poem of the refugee woman from North of Croatia, written several weeks after the end of war (and after four years of refugee life with her husband and three children).

THE CONCEPT OF FORGIVENESS

"Everyone says forgiveness is a lovely idea, until they have something to forgive..." (Lewis, 1942, cit Legaree, Turner, Lollis, 2007, p.192).

Legaree at al. (2007, p. 192) wrote that "for centuries in Western societies, forgiveness has been viewed as an important component of both personal and relational healing" (DiBlasio, 1993). Apology and forgiveness are phenomena encountered in virtually all human relationships. Repairing relationships is a major reason why people seek therapeutic services, and often the problem they are hoping to resolve relates to feelings of betrayal or victimization (Pingleton, 1989; Sells & Hargrave, 1998).

Forgiveness seems to be a complex concept for several reasons. One reason is that forgiveness is usually treated as a social, philosophical or religious phenomenon and as such seems difficult to approach by experiment.

That common element is the "letting go," giving up or cessation of emotion connected with memories of a hurtful act.

The history of forgiveness in psychology and the social sciences can be divided into two periods (McCullough et al., 2001). The first of these periods, roughly spanning the five decades between 1930s and 1980s, consisted of many theoretical papers and modest empirical work designed to shed light on aspects of forgiveness. A second period, roughly spanning the three decades from 1980 to the present, reflects more intensive and serious consideration of the concept of forgiveness (pp 3-10).

Finally, one might point to the fact that the 20th century has been the bloodiest and probably the most unforgiving century in human history, perhaps leading people to conclude that forgiveness constituted little more than a nice sentiment.

In the fields of mental health (ibid, p.3), little attention can be found with regard to the phenomenon of human forgiveness from authors such as Carl Jung, Karen Horney, Alfred Adler, or Viktor Frankl. Wang (2005, p.1) wrote that it is perhaps because of its religious implications that psychoanalysis has historically avoided speaking of forgiveness, although playwrights have often depicted forgiveness as a psychological mechanism than can help resolve cycles of anger and revenge.

Adding to the apparent complexity of forgiveness, there are polar opposite vantage points from which to interpret it. At one pole is a victim or an offended person, and at the other pole is a perpetrator or offender. Each suffers a different set of emotions. The victim feels anger and resentment, while the offender might feel guilt, shame, and possibly fear of consequences. Sometimes, both have feelings of shame.

Forgiveness is central to healthy human development and may be one of the most important processes in the restoration of interpersonal relationship after conflict (Urlic, 2004, pp.466-470). The common imperfection in the ability of human beings to relate to one another gives rise to frequent offense and consequent negative affective, behavioral, and cognitive responses in interpersonal relationships. Unaddressed, these negative responses can lead to impaired social functioning. Forgiveness involves the reduction of negative response to offense. It does not involve seeking retribution or restitution and does not require further vulnerability. Rather it allows accountability.

Theoreticians and researchers disagree about the definition of forgiveness.

Enright et al. (e.g., Enright, 2008, pp. 23-28; Enright & Fitzgibbons, 2008, pp.29-36), view forgiveness as a process through which negative thoughts, feelings, and behaviors towards a transgressor are replaced with positive thoughts, feelings, and behaviors. McCullough et al. (e.g., McCullough, Fincham & Tsung, 2003) view forgiveness as a redirection of negative motivations and the development of conciliatory motivations toward a transgressor. Worthington & Scherer (2004) make the distinction between *decisional forgiveness*, in which motivations change, and *emotional forgiveness*, in which negative emotions are replaced with more positive, other oriented emotions (e.g., empathy). Although progress toward definitional and conceptual clarity is being made, much more work needs to be done before we can choose a single formulation as better defining the subject. In my view, forgiveness is a process that, either decisional (rational) or emotional, represents a very slow re-working of deep internal wounds into better contextualized and more comprehensive frames of reference, eventually putting both sides on some kind of common human denominator, nevertheless preserving some moral judgment most of the time. A work of at least partial sublimation of negative feeling could be distinguished from the beginning of the process on.

Thus, although growing, empirical data regarding forgiveness are lacking, and there is a gap between the encouragement of forgiveness by clinicians and sufficient scientific knowledge of its underlying mechanisms (Toussaint and Webb, 2005, p.674), more work is needed to determine who will benefit from forgiveness and what factors will lead to its constructive use.

Neuroscientific research data indicate, according to Clark (2005, p. 649), that the cornerstone hypothesis is that before forgiveness takes place, memories periodically arouse fear stemming from the amygdala. This fear drives a pattern of anger and fight-or-flight readiness. Under appropriate circumstances, the frontal cortex interrupts the pattern and quells the fear response in the amygdala. The resultant relaxation of muscular tension signals the cortex that forgiveness has occurred. In addition, the memory pathway from the rhinal cortex and hippocampus to the amygdala is inhibited. Finally, a tangible act confirms that the memories no longer stimulate the amygdala, and the pattern of anger and stress do not recur.

In this growing area of research and therapeutic treatment, two concerns repeatedly raised by many researchers are the need of conceptual clarity and the development of appropriate measurements. The Enright Forgiveness Inventory (EFI) is an objective measure of the degree to which one person forgives another who has hurt him/her deeply and unfairly (Orathinkal et al., 2007,P.110).

Toussaint and Webb (ibid, pp. 681-682) were researching gender differences in the relationship between empathy and forgiveness. Much research has shown that women are more empathic than men. Yet, women and men are equally forgiving. However, it is not clear whether empathy is more important to forgiveness for men or for women. The results of the research showed that women were more empathic than men, but no gender difference for forgiveness was apparent. However, the association between empathy and forgiveness did differ by gender. Empathy was associated with forgiveness in men but not in women.

It is likely that an ability to understand others, to relate to others, and to treat others as one would like to be treated would enable a person to forgive others. The empathic person tends to focus on other's experiences in a fairly objective or unselfish manner rather than focusing on one's own experiences in a selfish manner. Empathy is a variable that is important in promoting forgiveness. As indicated above, theoretical and empirical works support this notion.

An integrated neuropsychological model of forgiveness

The Self during the forgiveness Process	**Neurophysiology Associated with the Forgiveness Process**
SELF (Memory of previous self-world orientatrion)	Mediated by the parietal, frontal, and temporal lobes, with input from the sensory system and hippocampus for memory
Injury to Self	Via sensorimotor system
INJURED SELF (Altered conspecific congruence)	Mediated by the limbic system (with negative affect), hypothalamus, and sympathetic nervous system.
Cognitive-Afectice Processing	Temporal, frontal, and parietal lobes with limbic system input
RECONCILED SELF (Restored conspecific congruence)	Parietal, temporal, and frontal with hippocampus for memory of new self-world orientation resulting in limbic system with positive affect
Forgiveness (Directed outward)	Mediated via limbic system with positive affect and motor function to control behavior.

Figure 1. Neurophysiological model of the forgiveness process (simplified, according to Newberg, d'Aquili, Newberg, and deMarici, 2001).

Webb et al. (2006), writing about dispositional forgiveness and adult attachment styles wrote that "a person's capacity for forgiveness may be associated with both mental and physical health." Yet researchers' understanding of the dynamics of forgiveness remains largely unclear (Brown, 2003; Worthington, 1998). McCullough et al. (2000) highlighted a fundamentally psychosocial element in forgiveness, defining it as "intra-individual, pro-social change toward a perceived transgressor that is situated within a specific interpersonal context" (p.509). Other researchers have noted the possibility of developmental influences in the capacity to forgive, and some researchers have begun examining developmental variables in forgiveness. According to Feeney, attachment research may prove a fruitful venue for this investigation of forgiveness, because previous research has indicated the possibility that attachment style reflects the ability to regulate negative emotion in the context of relationships. For example, securely attached adults show greater ability to deal with relationship distress in constructive ways than insecurely attached adults.

As noted by Worthington, Sandage and Berry (2001, pp.228-230), the fundamentally interpersonal basis of forgiveness may be pivotal in our evolving understanding of forgiveness's underlying dynamics. According to my experiences, I am strongly suggesting that superego instances have an important role in starting and evolution of the forgiveness dynamics, feelings of guilt, and especially the feelings of shame. Forgiving restores equilibrium in superego structures by helping them to resume their regulating functions regarding inner and outer relationships.

In *Studies on Forgiveness,* Day and Maltby (2005, pp. 553-555) wrote that recent authors have suggested that positive psychology presents an adequate theoretical context within which to examine that concept (Snyder & McCullough, 2000; Yamahure-Thompson & Snyder, 2002). Positive psychology tends to emphasize increased well-being and adjustment resulting from resolving interpersonal situations through intrapersonal reflection and positive interpersonal relationships (Lopez et al., 2002). Similarly, forgiveness is seen as a process in which there is a continual engagement through intrapersonal reflection and developing and maintaining social relationships within the context of interpersonal transgression (Yamahure-Thompson & Snyder).

The same authors wrote that typically, these predictions are made around forgiveness of others, and for the most part, research into forgiveness centers on the role of forgiveness of others. However, within the forgiveness literature, there is a three-dimensional model of dispositional forgiveness (Yamahure-Thompson & Snyder, 2002) that, aside from forgiveness of others, identifies forgiveness of oneself (forgiveness regarding one's own previous transgression against others) (Urlic, 2004) and forgiveness of situations (a tendency to accept and seek closure around a negative life event beyond one's control such as an earthquake or illness). There is reason to believe that failure to forgive oneself and situations might be related to social loneliness. Failure to forgive one's own transgression or to be able to cope effectively with a negative life event may lead to concentration on oneself or the negative event and thus lead to a withdrawal from social relationships. I would like to underline the tendency to avoid this more difficult aspect of forgiving and reconciliation processes directed toward oneself, i.e., self-objects and idealized ego states.

This type of approach suggests that forgiveness of another person's transgression is related to a person's social relationship, and the people who tend to forgive others seek to forge stronger social relationships and would tend not to be lonely. The clinical examples will illustrate the dynamics of confronting and overcoming that frustration-provoked loneliness.

Clinical Vignette I

Father and His Sons

The social loneliness of a previously socially very much included war veteran was the most prominent symptom when he was referred to a psychiatrist for therapy. On first encounter, he was complaining of insomnia, depression and lack of possibility to feel any satisfaction. This feeling of lack of energy and blocking of the possibility to unwind thinking, as well as lack of any interest, was making him feel exhausted. The social withdrawal was the way of avoiding strains he was feeling in interpersonal communications. As we got acquainted during the war, he told me that he would like to recount what he was talking about with the priest in the confession.

At the beginning of the war, he was a young father of three sons. His house was near the war-torn zone, and he was among first defenders. The Yugoslav army brought cannons at the edge of hills where across the valley there was his house. As the Croatian army didn't have adequate weapons in that period, his responsibility was to try to incapacitate them for shooting. But, in order not to alarm enemy soldiers, the guardians of cannons had to be silently liquidated.

Years were passing by, his sons had become youngsters, and he started to recollect the episodes when he was strangling enemy soldiers that were young men like his children were becoming. Especially the nightmares were exhausting for him. Some suicidal ideas started to appear as the possible resolution of that situation. Then he started to talk with the priest. The issue of whose guilt the war was couldn't help him because he didn't feel guilt for the war. To his surprise, when we were searching for the right world for his deep inner turmoils, shame was the description he found as the most appropriate. Why shame? Because his beliefs were deeply Christian. When enemies of one time started to assume human qualities in his memories, he found intertwined pictures that made him feel like an assassin. That was absolutely contrary to his morality. On the other side, if the war would start now, perhaps his sons would become defenders and be put in a situation to kill. This idea was totally unacceptable for him.

Then, it was not difficult to understand the emotional turmoils of the veteran, but it required several years of psychotherapy to help him metabolize the difficult feelings caused by war and its consequences. And, in spite of that result, the traits of loneliness have remained as his newly developed behavior.

Many clinical observations of ways of suffering feelings of guilt and/or shame suggest that forgiveness of oneself, and not forgiveness of others or situations, accounts for the unique variance in social loneliness scores. This finding is perhaps surprising, given the emphasis that forgiveness of others has on repairing social relationships. In interpreting this finding, it is important to note that there are two interpretations based on the correlation. First, if forgiveness is treated as the causal variable, this behavior suggests that people are unable to forgive themselves and tend to withdraw from social relationships, feeling they are unworthy of forgiveness. Second, if social loneliness is treated as the causal variable, people who are lonely might feel that they have fewer social relationships and assign more importance to their own transgressions because they are unable to forgive themselves.

However, the finding that forgiveness of others was not significantly correlated with social loneliness suggests no evidence for the prediction derived from positive psychology that people who forgive others will tend to be less socially lonely. Consequently, the sentiment of positive psychology that forgiveness of others might reflect positive relationships with others is not supported. Nevertheless, the findings suggest the need for further examination of the relationship between forgiveness of oneself and social loneliness within the context of withdrawal and the perceived seriousness of one's own transgressions, as it was shown in above-mentioned clinical case and experienced in many others.

McEwen (2002) hypothesizes that self-condemnation may impair self-care, produce depression and anxiety, and demotivate coping. That might result in more immediately apparent negative health consequences than would forgiveness of others, which probably exerts most of its influence by being a coping mechanism for the chronic stress of unforgiveness.

Olga Botcharova, after leading many conflict-resolution training programs in Bosnia and Herzegovina, Croatia and ex-Yugoslavia, writes: "These victims have allowed themselves to feel the pain, to stay with it in order to be able to leave it later... Forgiveness begins for the victims when they make themselves look at the 'ugly gaping wound' caused by loss and confront the secret shame and guilt that accompany the damage to their sense of self-identity" (2001 p.287-288). My therapeutic experiences fully support this point of view.

Whereas most forgiveness research has addressed the granting of forgiveness, one study examined the effects of forgiveness on those who receive it (Witvliet et al., 2002; Cohen et al, 2006). Part of this study compared imagery of (a) receiving an unforgiving response from one's victim, with imagery of (b) receiving forgiveness and (c) experiencing reconciliation. Forgiveness and reconciliation imagery each prompted improvements in basic emotions (e.g., sadness, anger) and moral emotions (e.g., guilt, shame, gratitude, hope), with reduction in negative emotions and increase in positive emotions. A very interesting finding is indicating that, while reconciliation is often valued, contemplating making a reconciliatory gesture can provoke stress reactions. In many clinical examples, this stressful approaching of forgiveness and reconciliation is readily observable.

Various authors promote a "discovery-oriented" position that contrasts with "decision-based" views (Engel, 1989; Hill, 2001; Patton, 2000; Simon & Simon, 1990, cit Legaree et al., 2007). They argue that for forgiveness to happen, it does not need to be actively pursued by the offended person...Engel (1989) asserts: "Forgiveness is not a voluntary act but is something that may or may not spontaneously occur as part of the recovery process" (p.203).

The analysis of the therapy literature revealed a third dimension with distinctive positions with respect to who is to benefit from the act of forgiveness. The question is whether forgiving goes beyond the cessation of negative emotions of resentment, anger, and desire for revenge, to include positive emotions toward the offender such as compassion, mercy, empathy, and perhaps even love (ibid.,p.204).

The benevolence viewpoint places a clear value on humanness, mercy, and community. This is apparent in Freedman's statement: "When one forgives, he/she recognizes that the injurer is a complex human being who deserves love, respect, and compassion, regardless of his/her actions" (2000, ibid. p.89).

After having reviewed the most important considerations and research results about forgiveness, it might be said that further studies of forgiveness could be done in the frame of social sciences, medicine, political sciences, theology, and education. Forgiveness can be applied to the individual, families, neighborhoods, entire communities, and perhaps even to nations. Forgiveness casts a wide net. Forgiveness is not an exclusive solution to human misery; yet, the latest philosophical analyses and social scientific research suggest that forgiveness deserves its place in effecting healing. Otherwise, what might replace that process and therapeutic aim on the way of reconciliation with oneself and other(s)?

Forgiveness and the Role of Mourning Process

Through several clinical examples, I already tried to expose the difficulties in mourning losses and in elaboration of difficult feelings, especially these of guilt and shame. In these circumstances, the essential question arises of how to approach the loss, how to recover from pains, flashbacks, nightmares, the feelings of deep personality and behavioral changes. This pertains especially after losses of family members, fellow soldiers, friends, or even "inner innocence," i.e., previous and/or ideal image of self.

Herman J.L. (1992, p.33-95) writes about three stages of unfolding of psychological recovery process from psychic trauma. First, it is necessary to establish the atmosphere of safety, followed by remembrance and mourning. The third stage gives space to reconnection with ordinary life. The process itself is inherently turbulent and complex. However, according to the author, in the course of a successful recovery, it should be possible to recognize a gradual shift from unpredictable danger to reliable safety, from dissociated trauma to acknowledged memory, and from stigmatized isolation to restored social connection.

Mourning is an inevitable reaction to the actual loss of or the threat of losing meaningful objects (Volkan, 2004, pp. 77-102). In war situations, as well as in various civil traumatic occasions, before thinking or deciding about forgiving, it is necessary to enable the process of mourning to develop.

According to this author, when a loved one dies, an adult goes through various phases of mourning, which can be divided into two categories (Pollock, 1989; Volkan, 1981): initial mourning and the work of mourning. The initial mourning includes responses such as denial, shock, bargaining, pain, and anger, which eventually lead to the beginning of an emotional "knowledge" that the deceased is gone forever. Under normal circumstances, the initial mourning process lasts for about three or four months. Before it is completed, however, the "work of mourning" (Freud, 1917) begins. This second category of mourning involves a slow process of revisiting, reviewing, and transforming the mourner's emotional investment in the mental representation of the lost object. In other words, the work of mourning refers to an internal encounter, and its effects between the images of the lost object and the corresponding self-images of the mourner. There are three major avenues (or a combination of them) that the work of mourning can follow: "normal" mourning, depression (melancholia), or perennial mourning:

The adult perennial mourners may chronically utilize linking objects. A linking object is a tangible, externalized version of the introject, a mental point between the mental representation of the deceased and the corresponding self-image of the mourner. According to Volkan, these linking objects may be a personal possession of the deceased, gift or symbolic farewell note, something the deceased used to extend his/her senses or body functions, realistic or symbolic representation of the deceased, "last-minute object," and created linking objects.

Inspired by Volkan's (1981) concept of linking objects, research was done regarding their role in the process of mourning for sons disappeared in war in Croatia from 1991-1995. By the year 2001, out of 3,052 persons who disappeared during that war, 1,529 persons had been exhumed from 126 mass graves, whereas 1,523 persons were still missing. The case study of disturbed mourning included 26 mothers of Croatian soldiers from Croatian Osijek-Baranja County who went missing in war or whose remains were recovered and identified long after they had gone missing.

Mourning for a disappeared person can be seen as a specific form of pathological grief. The manner of the grief is influenced by the circumstances of death, which determine whether the bereaved will accept the death or not. In our research (Jurčević & Urlić, 2001), out of four of Volkan's groups of linking objects, we identified the objects belonging to the first three. Those were 1) objects that had been worn by the deceased (clothes, wristwatch, ring, or glasses), (6/26); 2) objects that could be viewed in the psychoanalytic sense as an extension of the body of the disappeared or dead person (such as a camera) (4/26); and 3) objects with realistic or symbolic resemblance to the deceased (usually a photograph) (8/26). None of the examined objects belonged to the fourth Volkan's group (objects at hand when the news of the death came or objects present at the funeral, things that could be considered "last minute objects," i.e., related to the moment when the deceased was last seen alive). However, 8/26 objects formed a new hitherto undescribed group. Mothers used such objects to create a "memorial shrine" to their sons. A photograph of the missing person or person whose remains were identified long after he had gone missing occupied a central place at the shrine, and was surrounded by other symbols of the Catholic iconography (Virgin Mary, crucifix), flowers, and candles. The memorial shrine to the beloved son who disappeared was always located in the room where the family spent most of their time and/or where guests were received (living room or kitchen). This could be viewed as an expression typical of Christian, mid-European, Croatian culture tradition.

Slowly, it was understood that the linking object is more than a simple symbol. Unconsciously, these linking objects, or protosymbols, are an "actual" meeting place between the mourner and the dead. There are beneficial aspects of these items. While linking objects are utilized to postpone and freeze the mourning process, they can also be employed to initiate mourning. When circumstances are right, the mourner may go back to his/her linking object, internalize its function, and begin his/her mourning process as if the loss had just happened.

When seen in connection with the healing process for the victim, forgiveness may be looked upon as an intrinsic, positive part of mourning the passage of revenge. Freud, in "Mourning and melancholia" (1959, p.256), described mourning as "detaching the libido bit by bit," and it is this very process that characterizes forgiveness, in the true sense of the word. In a previous work, Volkan ( ) addressed this issue in stating that the ongoing process of forgiving... (is) a process that takes time, often protracted time, and that requires immense effort on the part of the forgiving one. This effort may comprise a major portion of the process of the work with the narcissistically wounded person, and... is akin to the work of mourning...Relinquishing vengefulness means forfeiting pride or malice, and perhaps also letting go of an unhealthy attachment. In the psychological sense, forgiveness is not an act that takes place when anger or hurt or revenge are spent. Rather, it involves the introduction of a leavening agent, an amalgamation resulting in something new: a solution. I am suggesting that to reach the solution (whatever it might be), the process of mourning should represent its most important part.

Some clinical examples will illustrate the above-mentioned features of forgiveness and mourning processes as mirrored in various therapeutic and psychosocial interventions, when not only individuals or groups, but entire communities were threatened by consequences of psychological traumatisation.

Clinical Vignette II

In the group of war veterans, after the war, the members were commenting on lack of public recognition and even on despising they have to bear from time to time. Then Zoran told his dream that he had dreamed several days before that he, without any reason, killed with his pistol a three-year-old girl, the daughter of his cousin. He said: "Such a stupid dream. To shoot on the front line, that is one thing, but this…Such an innocent creature…" he added, shaking his head.

Filip said that some days ago, he was dreaming that he was driving a jeep, and that he ran over one small girl of about four to five years of age. Some other group members were commenting that they often had those kinds of stupid dreams.

After shorter silence, the therapist was interpreting that the "innocent creatures," like small children, are probably their "innocent parts" that would like to be playful like small children, but they can't be because of anxieties, fears and loss of ideals.

After some silence, there was low-voice talking in the group about difficulties to adjust to the actual life, about idealizations and fancies of some years ago, and about their difficulties in changing their idealized projections into very simple realities.

Through the process of group psychotherapy in the homogenous group of war veterans, its members become more and more able to understand the symbolic language and its meaning and perceive more fully the wounded parts of their inner selves. It might be said that their "inner innocence" was "killed" by the facts of war and has changed them profoundly. There is the possibility to work on reparation but not on complete restoration of their good inner objects. The group was slowly becoming aware of the difference.

Our researches are showing how difficult this aim is to attain. Results of the first research cited here (Britvić, Urlić, et al., 2006, 2007a, 2007b) represents the prospective study of 70 war veterans suffering from complex PTSD that have completed a one-year trauma-focused program that had included even group psychotherapy. Our study didn't find a significant reduction of the PTSD symptoms but showed an increase in problem-oriented coping and in coping by avoidance. No change, or only some reduction of depression, was found in comparison with the level from the beginning of treatment. Observed improvement can be explained from the viewpoint of resolving the process of pathologic grief but also the positive effects of other therapeutic factors during the group treatment (Urlić, 1999, 2004, 2005). Psychotherapeutic interventions enabled patients to re-live the emotions of guilt and shame in a new context of the group setting. Revealing and working through the traumatic events facilitated a gradual ending of the process of pathologic grief, which resulted in a reduction of depression. Other therapeutic factors (altruism, giving hope, cohesion and acceptance, leading and directing, developing social skills, discovering and understanding oneself) undoubtedly contributed to the achieved therapeutic effects.

Results of the second research (Britvić, Urlić et al., 2006, 2007) were showing that after long-term dynamic-oriented group psychotherapy of PTSD in war veterans, the intensity of PTSD symptoms was reduced. After the treatment, predominant defense mechanisms were projection and displacement. None of the symptoms or defense mechanisms present at the beginning of the treatment changed significantly after two or five years of treatment. The number of diagnosed major depressive episodes, which increased after the second year of psychotherapy, decreased by the end of treatment. We concluded that psychotherapy, even after five years of treatment, can reduce the intensity of PTSD symptoms, but that the changes in the personality of veterans with complex PTSD are deeply rooted. Traumatic experiences lead to the formation of rigid defense mechanisms, which cannot be significantly changed even by long-term group psychotherapy. Nevertheless, in contrast with the mentioned finding, the social adjustment attitudes were showing improvement. And, probably the most important, there were no auto- or heteroagressive behaviors registered. I am suggesting that this indicates the centrality of the mourning process in healing deep narcissistic wounds.

Clinical Vignette III

The possibility of speaking about aggressive feelings and deeds was very much present in the group, together with feelings of guilt, sometimes even of shame, and the sense of the absurd, and all of that very often ended up in horrifying feelings and breaking of the sleep. It might be said that the process of mourning has many specific features in patients affected by PTSD. The appearance of a grieving process will be shown in a following sequence of three sessions.

Session 1

New patient-member of the group, brings his anxieties, aggressiveness and problems with intimacy.

Stipe, e.g., confessed to the group that five years ago, he was playing Russian roulette, willing to kill himself. Since then he has an ill time with himself...at one point, he was joking with dum-dum bullets in the group. Then the bullets were passed onto Vinko, he was playing an expert in weapons, then he gave the bullets to me, and Nada explained something about them: "The entering wound is like needle punch, but the reverse side wound is as big as such (showing two fists together)."

I returned bullets to Stipe and said: "Like the wounds of war, it seemed diverse during the war and after. They still seem to bleed and many of them can't become scars, like... (examples from the group process)...."

After that interpretation, I could perceive more sadness in the group and in myself. I was feeling pity for these young people.

Session 2

Mira tells the group that she is feeling worse than a year ago. She has no job. Nobody needs her. With thoughts like this one, she goes to bed and gets up every day. She is receiving some compensation money but doesn't feel independent anymore. She is coming home with these heavy feelings, especially for not being able to contribute, as she used to.

Traumatic experience disrupts attachment to the extent that the social world fails to serve its evolutionarily designed protective function for the individual. Disruption of attachment schemas, expressed through the medium of emotional modulation in one generation, are perpetuated through the ongoing parental and familial bonds into the next generation and do not automatically self-correct. If not recognized and analyzed and worked through, the unelaborated traumas have the potential for transgenerational transmission.

Session 3

There is a talk in the group about difficulties in exposing personal feelings and experiences that are repressed because they aren't for the public; nobody could understand them (Dinka, Toni, Mira, Nada).

Marko brings two dreams.

First dream: He was driving the motorbike. Everything was perfect. All of a sudden, two children ran out onto the street, and he ran over them. He awakened with terrifying feelings...

Second dream: Five men were stamping, each on only one foot. He was looking at them like one big eye, like teleobjective. Then one of them was lying on the table, and an enormous man was approaching him. He was directing the ax. He awakened again with terrifying feelings. He associates spontaneously that lately, when he is chewing food, he very often bites his tongue or his mouth.

Trauma survivors must grieve, and the consequences for not grieving are enormous. Unresolved grief prevents recovery from both the psychological and the physical problems that result from exposure to a traumatic experience (Bloom, 2002). The first great difficulty for a psycho-traumatized person or group represents the confrontation and re-living of the traumatic event(s). That is how the mourning process appears—through rage, sadness, unrest, sleeplessness, loss of will and wish to avoid all contacts. The forgiving idea might then appear as a liberating possibility.

Clinical Vignette IV

Neven's third session started with him being silent. In the group, the members were teasing Josip. He was complaining of spinal and neuralgic aches and had hopes in physical therapy. "Physical" becoming "sexual," they were laughing and teasing each other, starting to look around to remember who was married and who was still a single, "promising boy." Somebody started to sing the Beatles' song "Love is all you need." It turned out that those who were married were much more satisfied, thinking of their wives as being of substantial support for them; nevertheless, they were at times very aggressive toward them. The single ones said they were longing for some "good female creature" able to bear them, especially when they were bad tempered.

The atmosphere was becoming more anxious. In that moment, Neven felt it was the right time for him to say that without his wife and children, he wouldn't have any reason to continue to live....

He started to tremble. Encouraged by the therapist, he began to talk.

The war was already over. He was with one of his best friends in the unit that was serving as frontier guards. The atmosphere was uneasy, and they were always prepared for intervention. That day, Neven was cleaning his weapons, including his father's pistol. One of his best friends and neighbours from the village approached him. It was a peaceful day. All of a sudden the bullet "was shot" from his pistol. Looking around, he found his friend lying on the floor. Trying to help him, his friend uttered "you killed me" and remained senseless. Two hours later, he died.

Then Neven continued: "Everybody was trying to console me, but the shock was horrible... (He started to cry).... There was a funeral and I wanted to assist. During the Mass, the widow was staying at one side and myself on the other in the first row. Nobody was coming to take me to her, to give me the possibility to express my condolences. The Mass continued. When the priest said to give peace to each other I decided to approach the widow and to give her the hand, saying: 'I'm so terribly sorry, it was by accident, it was not my fault.' She was looking down to the floor. I offered out my hand, seconds were like hours, I was sweating, people in the church were staring at us. Finally, she raised her hand and shook mine without lifting her eyes.... I did what I could.'"

There was deep silence in the group. Some were very tense, leaning slightly forward. Many said he succeeded to manage the impossible situation with great dignity. "It was not your fault, you are innocent," many said.

Neven remained confused, searching for the eyes of the others to console him.

"Last month I was 'celebrating,' my sentence was over, one year of jail, under condition that in three years, I do not break any law. The father of my late friend was sitting near me. We meet often in the pub, and I always offer him something to drink. And, every Sunday morning, I visit the grave of my late friend and bring him flowers and a candle...."

There were many recollections of similar situations by others, fortunately without such consequences. Many described their feelings listening to Neven. And he said: "I'm feeling so grateful to you. Believe me, this situation is taking my best energies to find the force to continue to live."

One of the very fundamental strategies in coping with trauma is, according to my experiences, naming of the feeling that oppressed a war veteran. By finding the true name of the condition and by being no longer imprisoned in the wordless condition of the trauma, a veteran can start the process of mastering the problem or, as van der Kolk put it: "No pain is so devastating as the pain a person refuses to face, and no suffering is so lasting as suffering left unacknowledged." Everybody is encouraged to find the words in which to frame the meaning of their personal experience.

There was to be a language for every bit of experience, for every "unspeakable" episode. In the group of war veterans, there would be resonance ascertaining that others have similar emotional burdens locked up within their souls. Very slowly, the traumatic memories started to unfold and to find ways of "detoxification" by working them out with the help of the group.

The most difficult task of the therapist, which is paralleled the difficulty of the problem of war veterans, concerns the process of mourning. Sometimes the fantasy of magical resolution through revenge, forgiveness or compensation confronted the multiple losses, especially the attachment bonds. Patients often asked how long such a painful process would last. The next move was towards the creation of one's future.

But, before that, as Hopper (2003) puts it: "All loss must be mourned. Not only the dead. Not only the perfect breast. Not only the good enough mother. The loss of self-esteem, of certainty, of group charisma, a physical power, of the rights and privileges associated with a particular phase of life…must all be acknowledged. Only then is it possible to form a more or less realistic appreciation of what has been lost, and to integrate into the core of the self the psychic representations of their most desirable aspects. In this sense, all growth and development involve the mastery of depressive anxieties associated with the metabolism of prior identifications" (p.62).

Bouza and Barrio (1999), writing about the mourning process, consider that "the normal working out of the loss requires going through all the stages, which takes about one year on average. In order for the process to take place without major problems, the stage of anger and its venting are absolutely necessary, as well as re-linking with reality" (pp. 27-28). They consider that the pathological mourning can stop at any stage, usually in the loss denial, and/or an exaggeration of the expected symptoms, and /or the appearance of altered forms of behaviour that may be dangerous for the physical health of the patient, e.g., imprudence or attempted suicide. Denying the loss and the repression of feelings are the main aspects of bereavement pathology.

Treatment of pathological mourning has four main goals (Bouza & Barrio, 1999):

1. Preventing repression: to enable the patient to remember and relive the events.

2. Emotional support: to compensate for helplessness.
3. Social assistance: an apprenticeship in coping with life events and problem-solving skills.
4. Reconstruction: establishment of new bonds.

Although some research data does suggest that the short group psychotherapy may be effective for soldiers suffering from psychic traumas (Moro et al., 1995, p. 419), I believe that a longer course of psychotherapy is required to re-establish their connections with everyday life. (According to research data from our results exposed earlier, Britvić, Urlić et al., 2006, 2007).

And in her book about trauma, Garland (1999, p.17) wrote: "Mourning is always immensely hard work, even when the relationship was relatively straightforward. The individual may feel he simply does not have the internal resource to do this work in the context of feeling that his own personal world is in pieces. Some of that mourning, as has often been pointed out, must be for himself — for his own lost world, his own pre-trauma life and identity."

The achievement of these goals pre-supposes that the process of working through was successful enough. In the case of psychotherapy with war veterans working through of past trauma(s), of possibilities and impossibilities to get in touch with diverse parts of oneself, one's own needs and wishes, as well as with others in a more durable and intimate way, has the meaning of an important form of mourning process. In that context, the "inner innocence" might be seen as longing for simple self-actualization and its loss as an expression of deep traumas, splitting, denial, repression, projection and projective identification that are keeping up the withdrawal tendencies and loneliness of war veterans and otherwise deeply wounded persons.

The Healing Potential of Forgiveness and Compassion

The forgiving process, according to Enright and Fitzgibbons (2008, p.19) follows several phases: uncovering, decision, work and deepening phases, the latter leading to the new uncovering phase with new offense and/or situation. The same authors, taking into consideration the meaning of forgiveness (pp. 22-24), wrote that forgiveness is centered in morality, which in its simplest form is concerned with the quest for the good. When people seek the good, they do so in relation to others. Thus, morality has an interpersonal sense about it. Whether one examines the idea of forgiveness within the ancient religious traditions or modern philosophical or social scientific fields, forgiveness implies transformation, as well as re-direction of feelings and thinking from judgmental to understanding, from resentful to loving, from anxious to relaxed, from conflicted to cooperative.

The work of forgiveness, as in any work that opens old wounds, can very often increase anger, sadness, or anxiety in the short run. Forgiveness is always a choice that one is free to try or to reject. I suggest that for these shifts to occur on their way to sublimation levels, the mourning process has central place.

Forgiveness seems like a coping strategy as well. The person who forgives focuses on survival and improvement under difficult circumstances. Enright and Fitzgibbons in their book *Helping Clients Forgive* (2008, p.55) describe six styles of forgiveness: revengeful forgiveness, restitutional or compensational forgiveness, expectational forgiveness, lawful expectational forgiveness, forgiveness as social harmony, and forgiveness as love. If we take the process of mourning as basic for forgiving and reconciliatory processes to develop, then all these facts of forgiving might become the expression of various phases of the work of mourning, and whether it is developing or is showing an arrest at a certain level.

Regarding dynamic conceptualization of forgiveness during psychoanalysis, Siassi (2007, p. 1423) writes that "since Akhtar (2002) introduced forgiveness into the analytic literature as a complex emotion with unconscious as well as conscious roots, the field has become more open to exploring the psychodynamics of such other complex concepts as grievance and complaint, vengeance, and reconciliation ...When a process of mourning for losses can be completed, the individual is confronted with a choice regarding the fate of the failed relationship: does he wish to refuse its further intrapsychic significance, or does he wish to reinstate the relationship despite past failures, in the light of his expanded awareness of its limitations? When the bond is intrapsychically significant then there is a wish to reinstate it and so reconstitute a damaged narcissistic equilibrium. At such times of decision, forgiveness is an unconscious expression of the need for human relationships and of the preference for quality over quantity in the experience of life. The lessening of anger and the lowering of primitive defenses that follow successful mourning allow for a softening of the superego—this is both a prerequisite and a consequence of forgiveness. Ultimately, forgiveness allows for the renewal of an accepting and potentially more loving relationship with oneself and the world, as well as the other. It is this restitution of the narcissistic balance of personality through the realignment of internal relationships that gives forgiveness its psychodynamic importance and its potential for developmental gain. Thus, forgiveness, by aiming for narcissistic self-stabilization, holds a unique place in the analytical context. It goes beyond acceptance and reconciliation in uniting and binding the self with previously lost or discarded internal objects whose absence or negative presence was disruptive to the sense of self."

Based on this dynamic conceptualization of forgiveness, Siassi (2007) concludes that the ending of any successful analysis is marked by three possibilities regarding the patient's relationship to significant others and his traumas: (1) in cases where an intimate relationship was marked by minimal expectations, one simply learns to "accept the wrongdoer" without ever feeling the need for forgiveness; (2) in cases where a relationship was marked by high expectations, the patient can learn to "accept the trauma" without the will or need to forgive its perpetrator; and (3) even with the painful frustration of high expectations in an intimate relationship, the patient can come to "forgive" his wrongdoer if there remains enough of a positive internal bond to be salvaged.

He proposes that these different outcomes, especially the last two, raise important developmental questions at the end of analysis/psychotherapy that, if carefully explored, may elevate the role of forgiveness (heretofore implicit in the working-through phase of analysis) to a more central and perhaps explicit place. Furthermore, little systematic distinction has been made among forgiveness, acceptance and reconciliation. There are two decisive variables in the choice between forgiveness and acceptance. One is the severity of the trauma; some wrongs seem to preclude the possibility of forgiveness. More important, however, is the nature of the bond with the wrongdoer, as shown in several clinical vignettes.

Bearing in mind all that was exposed so far, I would like to emphasize the centrality of the work of mourning in "preparing the soil" for further development of psychic life in a more mature way, i.e., the reassessment of internal objects and their reassessment meanings. The same pertains even to therapists, i.e., to their understanding of trauma(s) and its/their consequence(s), because without creating the internal space for forgiving processes, their psychotherapeutic work will be affected by the possibility or impossibility to choose that aim as possible resolution of traumatic situation, leading to reconciliation with oneself and the other(s). At this point, some considerations about counter-transferential issues when treating PTSD might be helpful.

On Some Countertransferential Issues Treating PTSD

As I previously wrote (Urlić, 1999, 2004, 2005), speaking from experiences of my own and those I was working with in this field, the war and its aftermath was not only affecting those who became patients, but those who entered the role of therapists as well. In the war situation in the therapist, countertransference was continuously between stressful life events and secondary traumatization during the therapeutic process. Or, as Tansey and Burke (1989, p.60) said, between projective identification and empathy. It results that secondary traumatization and countertransferential reactions may be intertwined under particular circumstances.

As it is well known, Freud introduced the term countertransference in 1910. From that period until 1948, there were four decades of silence on the issue. M. Klein with her concept of projective identifications and the works of Racker, P. Heimann and Winnicott provoked the eruption of interest in countertransference. In the 1960s, there was the second hiatus in countertransference theory. Kohut (1959) and Greenson (1960) were writing about empathy. From the 1970s on, there is a new interest created in understanding countertransference. Beres and Arlow (1974) described a shift from thinking and feeling with the patient to thinking about the patient, and Schafer (1976) referred to a movement from the experiencing ego to the observing ego.

Empathy is typically related to a therapist's skillful functioning and projective identification and is commonly associated with countertransference turmoil. The processes of empathy and projective identification are intimately related in a way that is critical for deep understanding of countertransference responses to virtually all patients. The strongest and most obvious link between empathy, projective identification, and countertransference is that all three involve the arousal of an identificatory experience—whether transient or enduring—on the part of the therapist.

The "creative regression" in the therapist, which is necessary for the empathic "trial identification" to be aroused, remains controlled and temporary.

The therapist's capacity to entertain various "trial identifications" is correlated with his tolerance for what may be difficult self-experiences. Klain (1998, pp. 162-163), writing about coutertransference in a broader sense that concerns the caretakers, talks about a spectrum of emotional reactions like: observer guilt, feelings of helplessness, rage, shame, sadness and mourning, narcissistic vulnerability, some cultural determinates, and so called "colonial" countertransference.

Countertransference as phenomenon was relatively slow in entering the therapeutic scene; it requires some specific attention when the PTSD is in question, primarily because of the specificity of basically two types of countertransference that this disorder provokes: avoidance and over-identification. And—speaking of experiences of many of Croatian therapists—the arousal of an identificatory experience because of the total war situation and dangers the therapists and their patients were submerged alike. That was emerging especially during supervision.

Writing about countertransference and empathic problems in therapists/helpers working with post-traumatized persons, Klain and Pavić (1999, p.466) said that "due to the fact that patients with post-traumatic stress disorder (PTSD) have suffered one or more horrible experiences, countertransference in their therapists is differently stimulated than in other psychopathology therapies. PTSD patients also tend to have dangerous and terrifying reactions; their reality is very harsh and their destructiveness can be felt almost bodily. From the very beginning of therapy, they have great demands from the therapist. It is quite often that the therapist cannot endure this situation, allowing thus the countertransference to break out. This is then felt by the patient as a proof of the therapist's incapability and disinclination. Lack of confidence is one of the major characteristics of PTSD patients and is highly frustrating to the therapist's narcissism."

Empathy is both similar to and different from countertransference; but it is different from compassion, too. Empathy and countertransference have in common that they are both emotional categories emerging in the relationship with the patient in the here and now situation. They primarily help the analyst, but also the patient, to understand emotionally the analytical process and to interpret it both to himself and to the patient. In this way, both empathy and countertransference contribute to the mutual development of both participants in analysis. Wilson and Lindy (1994, cit. Klain and Pavić, p.467) say that empathy, identification, and countertransference are interrelated processes. On the other side, feelings of compassion may bring about countertransferential enmeshment.

The transference-countertransference sequence is an interactive process and may stimulate reactions (e.g., emotional states, memories, fantasies, and creative insights) in both the patient and the therapist. As noted by Winnicott (1971), the interactive processes of treatment makes countertransference inevitable, including objective and subjective forms of reaction. Transference unfolds in conjunction with the countertransference. From an interpersonal perspective, the countertransference can be as important as the transference, and the person of the therapist can be almost as important as the person of the patient. The issue of merging of two or more personalities and personal experiences should be held under constant critical survey from the therapist.

However, the countertransference process may become unhelpful and even noxious for the patient. It is critical for the patient that the therapist is able to control his own reactions in order to obtain a therapeutic stability. In order to feel stable, the therapist has to confront his/her own vulnerability to catastrophe. Becoming close to his/her patient may be a challenge to his/her own moral attitudes about aggression and killing. The transgenerational transmission of emotions and myths is not to be neglected in that respect, too. Then he/she has to overcome doubts and fears about the intensity of his countertransferential reactions—guilt, over involvement, and enmeshment, or phobic avoidance and burnout in a sensitive position. This is especially important when deep narcissistic traumas are in question and when therapist's vulnerability is under heavy strain to contain it and transform in a useful manner.

The alternations in the therapist between wanting to do more and more and at the same time restricting emotional responses are reflective of the response of the society at large (as exposed previously in some clinical examples). The therapist may feel the representative of the society in taking care of patients suffering from a war that nobody wants. The integration of inner changes in war situations, despite all scars, and the complexities of this specific therapeutic setting and their use in progress for the patient rest on this capacity to recreate humanity out of destruction.

"The complexity of what is at stake between the psychotherapist and a traumatized patient," according to Perret-Čatipović (1999, p.498), "requires the ability of the most experienced clinicians to accompany the patient in the traumatic re-opening of the agencies of his mind." The issue becomes even more complex when both—the patient and his/her therapist—are submerged in the same political/social situation.

Writing about the black hole of trauma, van der Kolk and McFarlane (1996, p.3) expose that traumatized people often are incapable of finding flexible and adaptive solutions; the trauma keeps them rigidly fixated on the past, making them fight the last battle over and over again. However, since it is generally assumed that as long as memories of the trauma remain dissociated they will be expressed as psychiatric symptoms that will interfere with proper functioning, helping people avoid the past is not likely to resolve the effects of the trauma on their lives. Treatment needs to address the twin issues of helping patients a) regain a sense of safety in their bodies, and b) complete the unfinished past. It is likely, though not proven, that attention to these two elements of treatment will alleviate most traumatic stress sequelae.

Sylvia Amati wrote that psychological problems are able to arrest the growth of a child (1989, p.108). It seemed that patients, as exposed through clinical vignettes, suffered from such an arrest and even regression due to the chronic traumas and multiple especially traumatizing stress situations and losses that invested them during the active participation in the war. The countertransferential issues in that way are able to activate some kind of "arrest" even in the therapeutic relationship.

It seems that the continuous closest relationship with many faces of death, killing and sudden changes of values resulted in substantial personality changes. The conscious life couldn't accept all these changes. But, the dreams, behavior, mood and values changes, attitudes, and especially continuous high levels of anxiety, tension and proneness to aggression were disclosing inner strifes. Bruno Bettelheim said that what cannot be put into words cannot be put into rest. The resonance of the group, and its constant mirroring inside ever more defined boundaries and inner structures, contributed to enable the veterans—its members—to start to express their deep feelings and traumas, thus approaching the phases of mourning and adaptation described by Volkan (1979) as 1) denial of loss, 2) anger and 3) the process that goes from "disorganization to reorganization in which the loss is accepted as an irreversible event… the forward movement is not without some back-and-forth fluctuation."

What kind of loss is in question? As I already described elsewhere (Urlić, 2004), the members of the group explained that it was loss of ideals that was connected with the ongoing interpersonal relationships and changes in the army, the administration and rapidly changing society, as well with the actual political and economical situations that were disconnected with the ones intergenerationally transmitted about independence of the homeland. At the same time, they were able to perceive loss of their "innocent parts," which seemed to be the most dramatic personal issue—delineating the whole spectrum of personality changes. There might be an important question: in times of high tensions and dramatic events, how could therapists preserve their "neutrality," i.e., not just sympathy but remain in the domain of empathy?

In the search for good parenting to compensate for the important losses and frustrations, the transferential-countertransferential issues appeared to be of utmost importance. Enormous anxieties and aggressiveness were projected together with idealizations.

Describing the atmosphere during the group process, I would like to quote one group member that was commenting in a cynical way that the war has three phases: First phase: patriotism, second phase: adventurism, third phase: interests. It seems obvious that veterans were recognizing themselves mainly in the first phase that was significantly marked by intergenerational influences. The second phase was the expression of "adrenaline addiction," while they felt excluded from the third phase, which was considered shameful. There is the question of how the therapist can remain critical regarding distinguishing sympathy from empathy?

Rodin (1984, p.581) wrote that the tendency to idealize authority figures is especially prominent in persons who have had difficulty maintaining self-esteem and have relied on "powerful others" in order to feel secure. First, the group members had to transfer the need for idealization to the conductor and to the group-as-a-whole. The process of disillusionment is tolerable when it is gradual and when it is associated with a more realistic perception of the therapist and a greater ability to maintain self-esteem without such external support.

The patients may be filled with rage and a sense of hopelessness when their expectations prove unrealistic. The idealizations of such patients may need to be interpreted and clarified early in treatment in order to minimize traumatic disillusionment.

During group psychotherapy with war veterans in the aftermath of war activities, it was the period for boundaries and the structure of the group to be established, enabling slow but constant disclosures of deep inner traumas and conflicts to emerge. During that process, some features have become clearer (Urlić, 1999, p.492):

- Due to the processes of identification across generations, the ideal ego and the ego ideal tended to fuse and confuse between one's own ideals and values and those transmitted by ancestors;
- The persecutions, humiliations and losses of one generation are readily transmitted onto new generations, often in a way to stimulate very vivid images;
- These images and emotions, connected with values and beliefs, become incorporated in fantasies of persons, so the whole personal development can organize around that traumatic nucleus;
- During the first phase of group process, it seems easier to expose ideals and disillusionments than feelings of guilt, and even more so feelings of shame, especially those connected with changed context (war-peace);
- The group arena offers itself as a transitional space for fantasies and external reality to be shown and discerned, enabling analysis of what was transmitted and what represents the authentic metabolized parts of each person's identity;
- The main difficulty in the therapy refers to the narcissistic nature of traumas and the massive use of immature mechanisms of defense (splitting, avoidance, denial, projection, projective identification, primitive idealization and devaluation), because patients try to protect themselves from painful memories and affects, but these defenses actually interfere with, rather than enhance, functioning.

Writing about transmission of horrible situations through generations, Ulriksen-Vignar (1989) says that genocide and persecution disorganize the parenting capacity and function and that children take on themselves psychic conflicts that belong to the reality lived by their parents... Political ideals anchored in a system of values and identifications enable narcissistic affirmation, the recognition of an inclusion in social tissue whether participating through similarity or opposition.

In situations of permanent persecution and instability, it is essential to maintain the continuity of being and to affirm the unity of endangered self. The person relies on ego ideals that should be preserved at all costs. That narcissistic need to preserve one's identity creates the national identity, independence and prides the image of all-powerful and ideal mother. That ideal mother may easily become idealized. Unfortunately enough, the process of reworking of massive projections and intergenerational transmission of beliefs and emotions in that regard had to pass in Croatian experience through the war, the woe of human nature, including not only those that had assumed the role of patients, but the therapists as well.

As I already underlined, the mourning process is very difficult to unfold during psychotherapeutic process, individual or group one, and to bring about working through of deep wounds. It requires time, containing and empathic capacities, as well as the constant eye on social realities that are probably a more important issue when treating PTSD than any other psychic disorder. And, as one patient from the group said, talking about wounding with dum-dum bullets, the entering wound is like needle punch, but the reverse side wound is as big as a fist. The vivid picture of cause and consequence has very high symbolic strength, as well.

The problems of severe psychic traumas primarily consist in tendencies at "encapsulation" of emotional damages and the disturbances in functioning of one's personality on intimate and relational levels. What is emerging with ever more consistent impact is the questioning of real and attainable therapeutic goals that should be appropriate to the occasion, because re-traumatization caused by re-emerging of very traumatic recollections brought regularly about as complaints of patients. Many were complaining that just when they succeeded in forgetting, the therapist re-opened the worst wounds. From the countertransferential side looking, who would like to be perceived like a torturing, pitiless parent?

Besides, the trifold dilemma emerges when dealing with the persons that killed another human being: on realistic, emotional and ethical levels, severely bearing upon therapist's moral convictions and judgments. This is giving ground to many countertransferential features that have to be recognized and resolved inside therapist's superego structures and empathic and containing capacities (Urlić, 2005, p.254). The possibility to envisage forgiving and reconciliatory processes as desirable therapeutic aims emerges as the only "real" possibility in attempting to overbridge inner splittings and other defensive maneuvers. The wish to forgive is motivated by a healthy, unconscious narcissistic need—a need of the ego, not the superego—to reconstitute the personality by reestablishing the lost bonds. The supervision is necessary to foster this attitude, and to contain it inside adequate possibilities.

ON COMPASSION, EMPATHY, AND SPIRITUALITY DURING PSYCHOTHERAPEUTIC PROCESS AND IN SOCIAL TISSUE

The human condition, together with expressions of uncontrolled human aggression, includes the heightened feelings of compassion, empathy and religious beliefs and practices that I would prefer to place in the area that human beings feel as the place for spiritual experiences. In my opinion, spiritual shouldn't be considered as equal to religious and should encompass the transcendental aspects of thinking human existence. In that frame of reference, "spiritual," I understand primarily as the capacity to believe, to believe in God, in humanness, in humans, in some values...to believe. Under the impact of uncontrolled aggression, the dialogue between a human being and the forces of the universe that we are feeling inside ourselves as well are questioning time and again about the sense. Some new points of view might arise from these considerations. I'll try to illustrate it happening on personal, group and social levels, growing as a very delicate plant that should be protected and helped in growing from the very beginning.

Clinical Vignette V

Eight years after the war, the homogenous group of war veterans was undergoing the psychological psychodynamically oriented treatment, whose important part was group psychotherapy. The group consisted of nine members and the conductor. We will follow the course of that treatment in order to be able to follow-up the creation of space among members and inside each group member.

Session 10

The talk goes about the political situation in the country, then about their social position, and finally about the need to disclose some difficult experiences and fears of disclosing them.

Ivo was feeling uneasy and started to blush. He then started to describe his preparing for joining the army. After preparing his luggage, he took his pistol, went out of house and killed his beloved dog. He was thinking that by doing that, he killed one part of himself... going to the war for him was like entering the ring.

Session 11

After a long silence, there was talk in the group about injustice practiced towards Croatian soldiers after the war, while Serbian war criminals were freely walking though the town. They are protected. Marko, the group member, said: "We are good people, we know how to forgive."

Session 12

The same group participant, Marko, said that between the two sessions, he was on the island, reading the book about the drama of a blind man. He was blind for 30 years. After surgery he could see again. Then he committed suicide... He was commenting about the necessity to accept misfortune ...

The conductor tried to connect the example with the feelings of war veterans after the war. The group participants were expressing many changes they were observing and feeling inside them. Some were feeling like being in another world during the war, and some said that they were numb; they couldn't get in touch with their feelings. Lovre said that his friend perished nearby him and that even now, he is able to hear his friend's voice: "Lovre, help me..."

Session 15

Rainy day. Vinko was thinking on bereavement. Dogs mourn more than men. He was recollecting memories from the battlefield. He saw a dog that didn't leave his master's corpse for three days. He remembers the horrifying roaring of an ox mourning the cow. The roaring was horrible; he can't forget it. He was feeling sad, not being able to mourn like an animal. He added that three of his friends perished, but he is still unable to mourn them.

Another group member was remembering how a cow was mourning her calf. He was recollecting hens pecking corpses. Vinko ended the session remembering sadness in the eyes of a child during the war. He didn't deserve to be sad; he didn't wish the war.

The mourning process was showing itself through hypersensitivity, proneness to paranoid interpretations, and ways of avoidance of new challenges of the adjustment to everyday life. On the other side, there were feelings of being unprotected, threatened, together with the symptom of numbing, indicating inner dissociations.

The following sessions were characterized by expressions of bold aggression, indicating even transgenerational transmission of aggressive behavior. Fears were alternating with fantasies: if there hadn't been war, what they would become in life? What followed was the expression of interethnic hatred and tensions, dramatic feelings and catastrophic foreseeings. More and more critical regarding difficulties in regulating their emotions, many participants' group members were complaining about the impossibility to express themselves and ending up bursting. Nenad said: "Sometimes I feel two personalities in myself that can't get together, like two rejecting poles."

Session 39

The session before the last one, the group members were comparing their feelings at the beginning and approaching the ending of their treatment. They were feeling much better. After a short silence, Nenad said that some days ago, he went to pick up his son from school. When he realized that his son was hit by another boy, he couldn't control himself and hit that child. He was sorry and associated the death of one innocent boy that was killed by one strayed bullet. Then he associated the death of his son during the time he was in trenches...Before the episode in his boy's school, he was having nightmares with lively feelings that someone was cutting his throat, he was feeling blood that was flowing down his throat, and the intensive feeling of sickness. Then he was vomiting ... He had the feeling of puncture ... then he woke up ....

After these recollections, he said peacefully: "We should forgive."

One of the most prominent features from the exposed developmental line of the group-therapeutic process was that among remembering war atrocities that provoked complete changes in lives of war veterans, the notion of forgiveness was mentioned only twice during the 40-session treatment program, in the 11th and 39th sessions. The asphictic atmosphere filled up with war dramas and very regressive levels of emotional functioning of war veterans was passing through specific mourning processes, working through of insights, opening up towards better understanding and the possibility for forgiveness.

After this clinical example, I would like to draw attention to another point connected with human uncontrolled aggression.

The Bosnian film director Jasmila Žbanić's film, "Grbavica," obtained the Golden Bear at Berlin film festival. It is a story of the worst possible war atrocities—the destiny of raped women and consequences on the next generation. Even 16-year-old girls were raped and released from concentration camps only in advanced phases of their pregnancy. There are still no confirmed numbers of raped women in Bosnia-Herzegovina, but their number was estimated between 2,000 and 20,000. Many of them feel so ashamed that are not willing to expose themselves to new shame and humiliation in front of themselves and their social worlds. Some brought their children with them, but the majority of them left these babies. Those crimes were consciously planned in order to humiliate people and to break all bridges among various ethnic groups and individuals. It might be asked what was their guilt that deserved that much hate. The young director of that film put an open question, in her TV interview, what kind of personality and what kind of society is the one where men experience erection out of hate?

After the war, it is possible to feel the more or less repressed pain. I remember autumn 1995, going to besieged Sarajevo in Bosnia-Herzegovina. There were no more shootings and the Serbian army was withdrawing. Some parts of the town were destroyed, some others were severely damaged. Only two main streets were lit, and the town was sunken into darkness every night. It was looking like ghost town. I was asked to help reestablish the University teachings. The hall was filled with students who either couldn't stop talking or were obviously very distracted. I realized that the special situation was asking the adequate approach. And I said to students that I have come to Sarajevo to talk to them but being there, I realized that I'll be better first to listen to them. They were very eager to share with me some of their wartime experiences, and they were pointing out many nice and touching moments between going and coming from battle lines, finding friends and family members again, or staying in couples the whole night embraced with just one bottle of plum-brandy and having fun and feeling closeness and happiness. As a matter of fact, they were in constant death peril. Life was very cheap then, and the joy of survival immense. Then we made an agreement: I'll lecture according to our program and after, we will take two hours time to talk in the group. The third day, the space among us was created as well as inside us. That evening, space had become a very friendly encounter, able to stimulate and to contain horrible but even very intimate personal stories.

One town, two absolutely different experiences. Some citizens of the town were attacking and destroying it, while the other part was defending it. It was depending on the way of approaching, either from the side of hatred and despise or of love and humaneness.

Somehow, it was a similar experience I had from the therapeutic setting. Many times, the unconscious reparatory processes were finding their ways of expression first through dreams.

Clinical Vignette VI

At the end of his psychotherapy, the war veteran Ante, originating from the small town in mountainous region in Croatia, was expressing his astonishment with dreams he had one night after another before coming to the session. He joined the army when he was 17 and passed many extremely difficult and dangerous war situations. During the war, he saw many wounded and dead soldiers. After the war, he developed post-traumatic stress disorder, complaining mostly on his startling responses and difficulties in regulating his emotions and reactions, as well as on nightmares. Many times, he was recollecting his dead and wounded war companions. He was dreaming about shooting, shelling, being under threat, and the ambience was most of the time the realistic remembering of his war experiences.

The first dream he reported was that he was seeing a naked woman lying down. Everybody knew that she was dead already for some time. He was approaching her, but all of a sudden a great number of people started to run after him as he were guilty of something ...

In his next night's dream, he was seeing himself being on the "other side," with the enemies. They were sitting calmly nearby him. He was somehow afraid, but nothing unusual was happening. All of them were waiting for the meal ...The meal was brought and all of them were eating together ...All was calm, they were talking then ...

He awakened with the feeling of astonishment.

In his book, *Forgiveness*, the greatest healer of all, Jampolsky (1999, p.18) writes that "to forgive is to feel the compassion, gentleness, tenderness, and caring that is always within our hearts, no matter how the world may seem at the moment. Forgiveness is the way to a place of inner peace and happiness, the way to our soul...Somehow, there is a part of us that believes we can get the peace of mind we seek by holding onto hatred, or anger, or pain. There's a part that says that we must protect ourselves and that we can achieve happiness and peace of mind by being attached to hatred and seeking revenge. There's a part of us that says we must withdraw and withhold our love and our joy because we have been hurt in the past...Forgiveness can free us from the imprisonment of fear and anger that we have imposed on our minds. It releases us from our need and hope to change the past. When we forgive, our wounds of past grievances are cleansed and healed...Forgiveness is letting go of all hopes for a better past."

It might be said that the process of working through hatreds, transmitted emotions and beliefs, actual conflicts, and the opening up of spaces for more humane and more just encounters should pass through mutual compassion, empathy and work through of all deeds and beliefs, in order to create the possibility to use these spiritual, emotional and cognitive spaces we deserve for our survival in the twenty-first century. Or, otherwise said, the stable insight is not possible to attain without passing through the process of mourning. This situation may even represent an opportunity for development of new culture of compassion.

True security cannot be firmly established with guns or money but only with trust between individuals, and their organizations, among organizations and between societies. Revaluing relationship and rebuilding trust between nations and their citizens is the necessary rehabilitation work of the twenty-first century (Bloom, 2002 p.11)

The Croatian independent news magazine *Nacional*, in the issue of March 7, 2006, recounts the life story of former self-proclaimed premier of s.c. Republic Srpska Krajina, the territory detached from Croatia and occupied by Serbian rebel forces, and one of leaders of the uprising of Serbs in Croatia after Republic of Croatia proclaimed independence from ex-Yugoslavia. That person transformed his beliefs from Serbian ultra-nationalist to penitent Serbian citizen. At the International Court of Justice in The Hague in 2004, he declared: "I am begging my brothers Croatians to forgive their brothers Serbs. I am begging Serbs that leave the past ..." His wife was telling that he was screaming during sleep, that he had nightmares, and that he was suffering from insomnia. He committed suicide in his prison cell, March 15, 2006. Several days after his suicide, his political mentor and protector, Serbian leader Slobodan Milošević, was found dead in his cell in the same prison in Scheveningen, Holland. The commentary is questioning whether the penitence of Babić was sincere, due to newly gained insight, or just revenge ... but, anyhow, the notion of forgiveness was highly unlikely to be heard from that man during wartime when he was in power.

Gartner (1992, cit. Durham, 2000, p.107) has stated: "Mature forgiveness is an integrated realistic view that contains both good and bed aspects of the self and others."

Talking in terms of collapsed space under the impact of violence of war (or some other extreme or long-lasting traumatic event), it is important to become aware of the loss and its meaning. While understanding space in terms of relationships, Winnicott has seen this kind of space, a space "between," as vulnerable, easily invaded and destroyed.

On the other side, Grainger (2003) thinks that the idea of social space includes functional ambiguity. Space includes and excludes at the same time. He wrote that because we depend on being together and apart, individual and corporate in ourselves and for others, and because these things depend on space ... the quality of our relational space is vital to our existence as people.

Bondi (2005), examining spatial terminology and geography, is conceiving the space as relational and as performative. Building on conceptualizations of space being absolute and relative, she put forward the idea that space is "relational." According to her, thinking space is continuously "produced" through the dynamic interconnections between and among places and social relations (pp.137-149). Many of my experiences from the wartimes in Croatia and in Bosnia-Herzegovina confirm that it is necessary to foresee the space for relationships to be offered again. My point is that the phenomenon of the collapse of time is the consequence of excessive violence that overwhelms the coping mechanisms that result in "asphyctic pressure" on social and intimate levels. Anxiety might become of "palpable" consistence in these situations. It is the mourning process that represents the precondition for the space for relationships to be recreated, and hopefully filled with forgiving and reconciling dynamics.

The psychologically minded politicians and politically minded psychiatrists, psychologists and other professionals and paraprofessionals from mainly humanistic fields should bear in mind that creating the space, real and relational, should be one of the primary goals in the processes of overcoming conflicts. Winnicott would say that the potential space acts as an introduction to real space. Canceling even the potential space seems to be conducive to suicidal behavior in one's own cell.

The definition of forgiveness expresses the ideal. People are imperfect, rarely reaching the ideal. Yet, the definition of genuine forgiveness presents a goal for everyone. Surely it is a goal many will not reach; but without that goal, forgiveness is likely to degenerate into meaning whatever any given client (or clinician) wishes it to mean. Such relativism must be resisted, otherwise where reason may have prevailed, there is chaos, as well as lack of the possibility to believe.

Forgiveness as Part of the Healing Process: Mourning Revisited

Examining effects of a Group Forgiveness Intervention on Forgiveness, Perceived Stress, and Trait-Anger, (Luskin et al., 2006), the goal of the study was to evaluate the effects of a six-week forgiveness intervention on three outcomes: (a) offense-specific forgiveness, (b) forgiveness-likelihood in new situations, and (c) health-related psychosocial variables, such as perceived stress and trait anger. Participants were 259 adults who had experienced a hurtful interpersonal transgression from which they still felt negative consequences. They were randomized to a forgiveness-training program or a no-treatment control group. The intervention reduced negative thoughts and feelings about the target transgression two to three times more effectively than the control condition, and it produced significantly greater increases in positive thoughts and feelings toward the transgressor. Significant treatment effects were also found for forgiveness self-efficacy, forgiveness generalized to new situations, perceived stress, and trait-anger (pp.715-733).

But between deciding to forgive and the reconciliation with oneself and the others, as I am pointing throughout these chapters, it is necessary to pass through the mourning process. Those dynamics might take normal and pathological directions, as shown on the table below:

Normal and Pathological Reactions to the Psychical Trauma

NORMAL REACTIONS		PATHOLOGICAL REACTIONS
	TRAUMATIC EVENT	
GRIEVING Fear,grief, anger, fury		REPRESSION of emotions
		PANIC OR NUMBNESS
DENIAL Negation, non-acceptance, repression of remembrance,or total failure to recollect		FLIGHT INTO DEPENDENCE (alcohol, drugs, - as ways of resolving painful feelings)
RE-EMERGENCE OF TRAUMATIC EXPERIENCES in thoughts and feelings		OVERFLOODING with traumatic events and experiences – re-experiencing of trauma, and imposing traumatic throughts and feelings
WORKING-THROUGH confrontation with trauma (wound is becoming scar)		PSYCHOSOMATICS due to psychic tensions: hypertension, gastric and/or duodenal ulcer, headaches…
NORMAL INCLUSION IN LIFE – without unfavorable psychic consequences		CHARACTER DISORDERS personality disorders

It is important to stress that the sequence of normal reactions, or pathological ones, may be arrested or diverted in the opposite directions. That is a great threat for the equilibrium of mental functioning of psychologically deeply stressed people that require psychotherapeutic intervention from individual to social levels, as well as through understanding of their dynamics. The mourning process appears to represent the key issue in the process of forgiving and reconciliation with oneself and other(s). The impossibility to attain it, or to complete it at least to higher, advanced degree, prognosticaly, is not favorable. In that case, the therapeutic aims should be reframed.

War stress exerts influence on every individual and provokes different reactions in each community member and in the community as a whole. Response to stress depends on three essential factors: (1) the characteristics of the individual, his/her world of inner objects, and acquired strategy for resolving stress situations. In other words, once successfully overcome, stress can provide a good basis for overcoming stress situation in the future; (2) the characteristics of the stress, which substantially influence the response to it; (3) support of the surroundings can help to overcome stress. Solidarity, loyalty, empathic reaction, including help in finding coping mechanisms, are the ways to overcome the reaction to experienced trauma.

As well as emotions, there are facts, with their strength and weight. That is the reason why it is not enough to work through stressful experiences but to develop consciousness about the past and the present as well, through confrontations and working through as parts of the mourning process. In that sense, to quote Bion's concepts of establishing relationships between an individual person and the group, he considered that love, hate, but also knowledge ("K") are intrinsic emotional links between two objects and that this is essential for a relationship to exist at all. The attitude called "knowing" is the activity through which the subject becomes aware of the emotional experience and can abstract from it a formulation that adequately represents this experience. The process of abstraction is essential to the emotional experience of the K-link, because the abstracted elements can be used for learning from experience and for understanding (Bion, 1962, cit. Fonagy and Target, 2003, p.121)

The emotional condition in which the factors "K" are reversed was called the "minus-K-link," where "the meaning and emotion are actively denuded from vitality and sense so that discovery and development become impossible" (cit. Urlić 2004, p. 462).

The holding of the group brought about lowering of defences that were arisen under the impact of traumatic events, which like in Neven's story, enabled mirroring and approaching reality with parallel development of mourning process on different levels. Holding attitude is appropriate and essential if we are to prepare the therapeutic ambience for forgiveness and reconciliation to unfold.

REFERENCES

Akhtar S (2002). Forgiveness: Origins, dynamics, psychopathology and technical relevance. *Psychoanal Q*. 71:175-212.

Amati S. (1989) Recuperer la honte. In J. Puget (ed) *Violence d'etat et psychanalyse*. Paris: Dunod.

Beres, D., Arlow, J.A. (1974). Fantasy and identification in empathy. *Psychoanalytic Quarterly*. 43(1):26-50.

Berry, J.W. and Worthington, E.J., Jr., O'Connor, L.E., Les Parrott III, Wade, N.G. *Journal of Personality*. 73:1, February 2005.

Bloom, S.L. (2006). Community Works, USA. Neither liberty nor safety: The impact of fear on individuals, institutions, and societies, Part IV, *Psychotherapy and Politics International*. 1(4),4-23.

Bondi, L. (2005). Troubling space, making space, doing space. *Group Analysis*. 38:137-149.

Botcharova, O. (2001, pp. 287-288). In: Wang, S. Revenge and forgiveness in Laramie, Wyoming. *Psychoanalytic Dialogues*. Hillsdale: Jan/Feb 2005, Vol. 15, 1:1.

Bouza M. F., Barrio J. A. E. (1999). Brief Psychodrama and Bereavement. The International Forum of Group Psychotherapy. Budapest, Hungary: *Proceedings of the IAGP Board Meeting*, pp.

Britvić, D., Antičević, V., Kekez, V., Lapenda, B., Urlić, I. Psychodynamic aspects of adaptation and treatment of psycho trauma: Study results: Druš.Istraž.Zagreb, 2007a, 3(89): 497-513.

Britvić, D., Antičević, V., Urlić, I., Dodig, G., Lapenda, B., Kekez, V., Mustapić, I.: Psychotherapeutic Treatment Program for Post-traumatic Stress Disorder: Prospective Study of 70 War veterans. *Group Analysis*. 2007b, 40(4):507-522.

Britvić, D., Radelić, N., Urlić, I.: Long-term dynamic oriented group psychotherapy of post-traumatic stress disorder in war veterans: Prospective study of five-year treatment, *Croat. Med. J.* 2006, 47: 75-83.

Clark, A.J. Forgiveness: A neurological model. *Medical Hypotheses*. (2005) 65, 649-654.

Cohen, A. B., Malka, A., Rozin, P., Cherfas, L., Religion and unforgivable offenses. *Journal of Personality*. 74:1, Feb 2006, Blackwell Publishing, Inc.

Day, L. and Maltby, J., (2005). Forgiveness and Social Loneliness. *The Journal of Psychology*. 139(6), 553-555.

Durham, M.S. (2000). *The Therapist's Encounters with Revenge and Forgiveness*. London and Philadelphia, Jessica Kingsley Publ.

Enright, R.D. (2008). (9th Ed). *Forgiveness is a choice. A Step-by-Step Process for Resolving Anger and Restoring Hope*. Washington DC: American Psychological Association.

Enright, R.D., Fitzgibbons, R.P. DC (2008). (7th Ed). *Helping clients forgive. An Empirical Guide for Resolving Anger and Restoring Hope*. Washington DC. American Psychological Association.

Faulkner, W. (1926). *Mayday*. South Bend, IN: University of Notre Dame Press, 1977.

Fonagy, P., Target, M. (2003). *Psychoanalytic Theories. Perspectives from Developmental Psychopathology*. London and Philadelphia, Whurr Publishers.

Garland C. (1999b). Thinking about trauma. In *Understanding Trauma. A Psychoanalytical Approach*. London, New York: Karnac.

Herman, J.L. (1992). *Trauma and recovery*. New York: Basic Books.

Hopper, E. (2003). *Traumatic Experience in the Unconscious Life of Groups*. London, New York: Jessica Kingsley.

Jampolsky, G.G., (1999). *Forgiveness, the greatest healer of all*. Hillsboro, Oregon: Beyond Words Publishing, Inc.

Jurčević, S., Urlić, I.: Linking Objects in the Process of Mourning for Sons Disappeared in War: Croatia 2001. *Croat. Med. J.* 2002; 43(2): 234-239.

Jurčević, S., Urlić, I., Vlastelica, M. Denial and Dissociation as Coping Strategies in Mothers' Postmortem Identification of Their Sons. *American Imago*. 2005, 62 (4): 395-417.

Klain, E. (1998). Transference and Countertransference in Psychoanalytic Psychotherapeutic Approach to War Victims. In: Arcel L.T., Tocilj Šimunković, G. War Violence, Trauma and Coping Process. Armed Conflict in Europe and survivor responses. International Rehabilitation Council for Torture Victims, Copenhagen.

Klain, E., Pavić, L. Countertrasference and Empathic Problems in Therapists/Helpers Working with Post-traumatized Persons. *Croat Med J*. 40(4):446-472, 1999.

Knight, J.R., Hugenberger, G.P. On Forgiveness. *Southern Medical Journal*. Vol. 100, No 4, April 2007. Special Section: Spirituality/Medicine Interface Project.

Legaree, T.A., Turner, J., and Lollis, S. Forgiveness and therapy: A Critical Review of Conceptualization, Practices, and Values Found in the Literature. *Journal of Marital and Family Therapy*. April 2007, 33 (2):192-213.

Luskin, F., Norman, S.B., Standard, S., Bruning, J., Evans, S. Thorensen, C.E. (2006). *J Clin Psychol*. 66:715-733 VAA Palo Alto Health Care System and Stanford University.

McCullough, M.E., Pargament, K.I., Thoresen, C.E. (2001). *Forgiveness. Theory, Research and Practice*. New York, London: The Guilford Press.

Moro, Lj., Frančišković, T., Varenina-Novaković, G., Urlić, I. War Trauma: Influence on Individuals and Community. U: Tata Arcel L. i sur. War violence, trauma and coping process. Copenhagen: IRCT; 1998:86-92.

Moro, Lj., Varenina, G., Beitović, G., Frančišković, T., Urlić, I.: Evaluation of Short Group. Psychotherapy of Soldiers Suffering from Psychical Traumas. *Coll. Antropol.* 1995, 2(19):413-420.

Newberg, A.B., d'Aquili, E.G., Newberg, S.K., deMarici, V. The Neuropsychological Correlates of Forgiveness. In: McCullough, M.E., Pargament, K.I., Thoresen, C.E.: *Forgiveness, Theory, Research, and Practice*. (2001). New York—London: The Guilford Press.

Orathinkal, J., Vansteenwegen, A., Enright, R.D., Stroobants, R. Further Validation of the Dutch Version of the Enright Forgiveness Inventory. *Community Mental Health Journal*. Vol. 43, No.2, April 2007.

Pargament, K.I., Thoresen, C.E. (2001). *Forgiveness. Theory, Research and Practice*. New York, London: The Guilford Press.

Perret-Čatipović, M. Psychoanalytic Psychotherapy with Migrant War Victims: Transference and Countertransference Issues. *Croat Med J*. 1999., 40:498-502.

Rodin G.M. (1984). Psychotherapy of Patients with Chronic Medical Disorders. In H.H. Goldman (ed) *Review of General Psychiatry*. Los Altos, California: Lange Medical Publications.

Schafer, R. (1976). *A New Language for Psychoanalysis*. New Haven and London: Yale University Press.

Siassi, S. Forgiveness, acceptance and the matter of expectation. *International Journal of Psychoanalysis*. London, Dec 2007, Vol. 88, Part 6, pg. 1423.

Toussaint, L., Webb, J. R. (2005). Gender differences in the relationship between empathy and forgiveness. *The Journal of Social Psychology*. 145(6),673-685.

Tansey, M.J., Burke, W.F. *Understanding countertransference. From projective identification to empathy*. Hillsdale, NJ: Hove and London; The Analytic Press; 1989.

Ulriksen-Vignar M. (1989) La transmission de l'horreur. In J. Puget (ed). *Violence d'etat et psychoanalyze*. Paris: Dunod.

Urlić, I. (2004). *Trauma and reparation, mourning and forgiveness: The healing potential of the group*. Group Analysis, 37,453-471.

Urlić, I. Recognizing Inner and Outer Realities as a Process: On Some Countertransferential Issues of the Group Conductor. *Group Analysis* 2005, 38 (2): 249-263.

Urlić, I. Aftermath of War Experience: Impact of Anxiety and Aggressive Feelings on the Group and the Therapist. *Croatian Med J.* 1999: 486-492.

Urlić, I. Recognizing Inner and Outer Realities as a Process: On Some Countertransferential Issues of the Group Conductor, Special Issue: Article. *Group Analysis.* Copyright 2005 The Group-Analytic Society (London), Vol. 38(2):249-263.

Van der Kolk, B.A., McFarlane, A.C. (1996). The black hole of trauma. In B. van der Kolk, A. McFarlane, L. Weisaeth (eds). *traumatic stress: The effects of overwhelming experience on mind, body, and society.* New York: Guilford Press.

Van der Kolk, B.A.(1993). Groups for Patients with Histories of Catastrophic Trauma. In: A. Alonso, L. Hillel, I. Swiller (eds) *Group Therapy in Clinical Practice.* Washington D.C., London: American Psychiatric Press.

Volkan, V.D., (2004, pp 77-102). After the violence: The internal world and linking objects of a refugee family. In: *Analysts in Trenches.* ed.: Bruce Sklarew, Stuart W. Twemlow, and Sallye M. Wilkinson. Hillside, NJ: The Analytic Press.

Volkan V.D. (1979). Cyprus—War and Adaptation. *A Psychoanalytic History of Two Ethnic Groups in Conflict.* Charlottesville, USA: University Press of Virginia.

Volkan, V.D. (June 2004). Individuals and Societies as "Perennial Mourners": Their Linking Objects and Public Memorials. Chapter for a book on death, endings and mourning to be edited by Rebecca Curtis and Lori Bohm.

Wang, S. Revenge and Forgiveness in Laramie, Wyoming. Forgiveness, retaliation, theater, psychoanalysis. *Psychoanalytic Dialogues.* Hillsdale: Jan/Feb 2005. Vol. 15(1): 1.

Webb, M., Call, S., Chickering, S.A., Colburn, T.A., Heisler, D. Dispositional Forgiveness and Adult Attachment Styles. *The Journal of Social Psychology.* 2006, 146(4), 509-512.

Wilson, J.P., Lindy, J.D. (1994). Emphatic Strain and Countertransference, in Wilson, J.P. and Lindy, J.D. (eds). *Countertransference in the Treatment of PTSD.* New York: Guilford Press (Klain and Pavić, 1999 p.467).

Winnicott, D. (1971). *Playing and Reality.* London: Penguin Books.

Worthington, E.L., Van Oyen Witvliet, C., Pietrini, P., Miller, A.J. (2007). Forgiveness, Health, and Well-Being: A Review of Evidence for Emotional Versus Decisional Forgiveness, Dispositional Forgiveness, and Reduced Unforgiveness. *J. Behav Med.*

Worthington, E.L., Sandage, S.J., Berry, J.W. (Eds). (2001). Group Interventions to Promote Forgiveness. What researchers and clinicians ought to know. In: McCullough, M.E., Pargament, K.I., Thoresen, C.E. (2001). *Forgiveness. Theory, Research and Practice.* New York, London: The Guilford Press.

Chapter 9

On the Culture of Forgiveness as Essential for Reconciliation

Ivan Urlic

I have returned
From a world beyond knowledge
And now must unlearn
For otherwise I clearly see
I can no longer live.
(Charlotte Delbo (1995), Auschwitz and After)

On Reconciliation

Speaking about psychotherapy with war veterans, with refugees and with displaced persons, there is always possibility to become overwhelmed by blood, tears and rage, as well as enthusiasm that we have to deal with. To uncover such experiences, to name them, and to work them through, means at the same time to open up the possibility to mourn the losses and to encounter many new realities. Writing about therapy, van der Kolk (1993) opens up his experiences that "disclosing the trauma, expressing related feelings, and establishing a trusting relationship with another person allow these individuals to explore emotions, to retrieve memories, and to understand current behaviors as reactivations of past experience" (p.293).

The physician or mental health worker or helper in over-bridging controversies are finding themselves time and again confronted with questions about the possibilities, ways and aims trying to help people suffering from consequences of severe PTSD. From clinical experiences, I summarized through time three possible developmental lines after occurrence of severe trauma, caused by war deeds or otherwise:

To continue to live with one's enemies;

To understand in depth (adequately to the situation) the nature of the conflict and loss of those involved in it, and to offer help on psychosocial level; and/or

To develop the deep understanding of the conflict and loss of those involved in order to create the space for the culture of forgiveness to develop, aiming at the reconciliation on three levels: intrapsychic, interpersonal and social.

I am advocating the point of view that there is a continuum of human relatedness, from living with internal and/or external enemies to developing deeper comprehensive understandings. In order to reconcile with oneself and with the others, it is necessary to re-establish containing capacity of the personality through the mourning process. The reconciliation itself as a therapeutic aim and the achievement of results are attainable only through previous development of the culture of forgiveness.

Clinical Vignette I

Some Experiences from Bosnia and Herzegovina

1995, the end of the war, Sarajevo was giving the picture of an entirely devastated town. It was still besieged, but there were no shootings anymore. The organization for psychosocial help "France Libertés" was helping in organizing the University activities and was establishing a small network of Centres for psychosocial help. At that time, it was the much-needed initiative, because the whole social life was ruined by a thousand days of siege and waves of refugees coming from other parts of Bosnia and Herzegovina. It happened that in one of those Centers, one young man activated a hand–bomb, wounding himself and endangering lives of two helpers of the Center, one young man and one young woman. They were so scared that wanted to leave the psychosocial work immediately. I was asked to try to help them, as well as the whole Center, to overcome the trauma by working it through, if possible.

When we met in the Center for the first time, I was told by the whole team that they were not intending to proceed with their work because their lives were threatened. But, they accepted my proposal that I would talk individually about experiences with every member of the team, and that we would have group meetings of the whole team, together with French helpers and organizers, in order to understand better their work and motives for it, as well as their fears. The proposal was accepted. In the meantime, the young woman was re-traumatized by encountering the aggressor in the Court of Justice. At our final group meeting, the whole group was able to work through the trauma to the point that they promised, regarding leaving their psychosocial helping activity, to think it over and to say their final decision in two days time ... They decided to continue with their helping activities in the Center.

It might be said that some work on reconciliation with the threat and uncertainty was done by all members of the Center. But, in order to attain the possibility for reconciliation, especially under very difficult circumstances, the process of forgiveness had to take place, and some grieving for the loss of some earlier idealizations of themselves and their aims. There are limits for everyone and for everything, they had to admit.

To understand the concept of reconciliation, one must first understand the issue of large group identity and everything associated with it. The fourth of the deepest levels of communication, as stipulated by Foulkes, is the primordial level, representing the collective unconscious and the collective myths, archetypes, language, etc., within it (Klain et al., 2002, p.11).

In *The Sublime Objects of Ideology*, Žižek (1989) writes: "Every historical rupture, every advent of a new master-signifier, changes retroactively the meaning of all tradition, restructures the narration of the past, makes it readable in another, new way ... in the symptom, the repressed content is returning from the future and not from the past." This consideration reminds me of the event from the town of Coventry that impressed me deeply when I entered the destroyed cathedral.

During the World War II, Hitler's army, with its missiles V1 and V2, was especially targeting industrial cities, and Coventry was the most destroyed one. One night, the gothic cathedral was hit and destroyed. The fire was swallowing what was wooden. People managed to save what remained of the cross and knelt to pray for those who did it. Today, there is the bronze cross shaped upon the burned one, and citizens of Coventry carved in the church wall: "Father forgive."

Another recollection from 1992: By that time, Croatia was flooded by new waves of Bosnian refugees and all that could be done or organized for these unhappy people seemed so little. Then I heard a story about Mother Theresa of Calcutta. When she obtained the Peace Nobel Prize, she was surrounded by journalists. They praised her for her unique activity in organizing with her nuns the aid for the poorest of ill and abandoned people. But, they said, it is only a drop in the ocean of human needs. Mother Theresa agreed and said: "Yes, it is just a drop in the ocean, but a drop of goodness. Who knows, perhaps someone else will add his drop ..." I believe it is worthwhile to make it as simple as such and to act in that direction.

It proves to be relatively easy at the level of small groups, or even larger ones, if one believes in the psychoanalytical culture based on psychoanalytic discourse and understanding. Parker (1997) stated: "The personal meanings of each citizen of the modern state have given way to fragmented experiences that cannot be interpreted to reveal the truth of the human condition. Humanism was the secularized translation of religious belief in the Enlightenment, but this now dissolves into hedonism or a feeling of resignation. We are offered 'intensity' of experience instead of the possibility of understanding what an experience might mean." The intensity instead of space for understanding and metabolizing is probably one of the prominent signs of the culture of narcissism in which we live in these postmodern and post-postmodern times. Perhaps even the ethnic groups are driven by intensity and not by ratio, because we are witnessing in many wars and clashes the strong component of emotional/religious affiliations and prejudices.

"The relationship between psychoanalysis and post-modernity has been explored in two main ways; either by using psychoanalysis as a modern Enlightenment system of thought to understand developments in this new postmodern culture that is breeding forms of narcissistic pathology, or through using postmodern ideas to rework psychoanalysis to make it compatible with the changed state of things. The positive aspect is that there are always deeper meanings to be discovered, and Kleinian theory is seen as able to respond to the feeling of produced because it theorizes the threat as being inside the self. The feelings of threat are the feelings of the destructiveness (death instinct, paranoid-schizoid position, envy), which can be overcome by making reparation." (Parker, 1997, p. 163)

Making reparation, restorative justice, and/or forgiveness requires the wrongdoer to undergo certain stages—a cognitive stage of recognizing that he/she has done wrong, an emotional response of regret or remorse, and a stage involving the determination to change or to make amends. Together, these three stages constitute the process of repentance.

The assumption based on Al-Mabuk's and Freedman's findings that most people need to be taught about forgiveness to begin forgiving is in contrast with Patton's (1985) articulate challenge that most people discover the idea of forgiving on their own (p.52) (as shown in some clinical vignettes from my experience).

Forgiveness and reconciliation are sometimes equated (Hargrave, 1994; Lauritzen, 1987). Forgiveness is one person's individual choice to abandon resentment and to adopt friendlier attitudes toward a wrongdoer. Because forgiveness is a free choice on the part of the one wronged, it can be unconditional regardless of what the offender does. Reconciliation always involves at least two people—the offender and the offended. Reconciliation, when there has been a serious moral breech, should be conditional on the offender's willingness and ability to change the offensive ways. Reconciliation is dependent mainly on the ability of the individuals involved to reestablish trust, that is, a sense of safety in their relationship. Because of that, forgiveness is an internal process, while reconciliation is an overt, behavioral process of two or more people working out an existing difficulty. Forgiveness is a necessary condition for genuine reconciliation, but a willingness to reconcile on the offender's part is not a necessary condition for forgiveness. But, as said before, the precondition and unifying stream of that dynamic represents the work of mourning.

Forgiveness is an active struggle to reduce the resentments. When we forgive, we tend to remember in new ways, thus opening up to the process of reconciliation. In that case, the mourning process is already well on its way, and confrontation with the most traumatic aspects of events was at least in a considerable way re-worked in cognitive and emotional ways.

Creating the Space for Forgiveness

Forgiveness as a process and as an achievement appears to be a very difficult topic. The citizens of Dubrovnik (as described in Chapter 8) were expressing their bitterness about being put in the position of victims. The feelings and vengeful fantasies in that moment were the only possibility left to relieve the situation of impotence and immediate threat (as Avi Berman and Miriam Berger elaborated in their chapters). According to the experience accumulated so far, it is very difficult to talk about forgiveness and possibilities of reconciliation in the situation when the country is in war, or exposed to terrorist attacks, or in some other situations called "no war no peace,," or in any other threatening situation. It is generally considered that under these conditions, the potential space for more constructive solutions is collapsed. This phenomenon of "collapsed space"' usually doesn't permit going beyond the level of feelings of being victims and of vengeful fantasies and plans. The potential space where past, present and possible future might be intertwined in more constructive ways is the topic I will move on to after having talked about conflicts due to uncontrolled aggression and the difficult mourning processes that take time to develop, many times disguised and not easily recognizable, that help to complete them in order to open up the previously collapsed space. In that way, some traditional wisdom shaped as fables might prepare our emotional and spiritual spaces to get closer to the forgiving and reconciliation processes to shape some potential space. The first one is:

The Magic Eyes. A Little Fable

In one village of Friesland, there lived a baker named Fouke, a righteous man, and his wife Hilda. Her soft roundness seemed to invite people to come close to her. One morning, having worked since dawn, Fouke came home and found a stranger in his bedroom, laying his head on Hilda's round bosom.

Hilda's adultery soon became the talk of the tavern and the scandal of the village congregation. Everyone assumed that Fouke would cast Hilda out of his house, so righteous was he. But he surprised everyone by keeping Hilda as his wife, saying he forgave her as the Good Book said he should.

In his heart of hearts, however, Fouke could not forgive Hilda for bringing shame to his name. Whenever he thought about her, his feelings toward her were angry and hard; he despised her as if she were a common whore. When it came right down to it, he hated her for betraying him after he had been so good and so faithful a husband to her. He only pretended to forgive Hilda so that he could punish her with his righteous mercy.

But Fouke's fakery did not sit well in Heaven.

So each time that Fouke felt his secret hatred toward Hilda, an angel came to him and dropped a small pebble into Fouke's heart. Each time a pebble dropped, Fouke would feel a stab of pain.

Thus he hated her the more; his hate brought him pain, and his pain made him hate. The pebbles multiplied. And Fouke's heart grew very heavy, so heavy that Fouke began to wish he were dead.

One night, the angel came to Fouke and told him that there was one remedy for the hurt of a wounded heart. Fouke would need the miracle of the magic eyes. He would need eyes that could look back to the beginning of his hurt and see his Hilda, not as a wife who betrayed him, but as a weak woman who needed him.

Fouke protested. "Nothing can change the past," he said. "Hilda is guilty, a fact that not even an angel can change."

"Yes, poor, hurting man, you are right," the angel said. "You cannot change the past; you can only heal the hurt that comes to you from the past. And you can heal it only with the vision of the magic eyes you can get by desiring them. And each time you see Hilda through your new eyes, one pebble will be lifted from your aching heart."

Soon Hilda began to change in front of Fouke's eyes, wonderfully and mysteriously. The angel kept his promise; he lifted the pebbles from Fouke's heart, one by one, though it took a long time to take them all away. He invited Hilda to come into his heart again, and she came, and together they began again a journey into their second season of humble joy.

"The story of Fouke and his unfaithful wife is not only a story of hurt but of humiliation, and the picture of a heart weighed down with stones is a moving one,," writes Lord Alderdice in his response to my Foulkes lecture in 2004. He told similar story from Ireland.

The Story of a Disobedient Son

In that story, a father takes his recidivist son to the side and explains how his repeated disobedience leaves the father hurt and grieving for the loss of the good relationship that there could be. The father, to convey this to the son, takes a plank of wood and each time the son offends, he hammers a nail into the plank. After some weeks, the plank is full of nails, and the son begins to realize extent of his malign effect on his father. They agree that for each good deed, a nail will now be removed and, with some delight, the father, after only a month or so, shows the son that every single nail has been removed. The son, however, remains dismayed, and when the father asks him why he is still unhappy, the son points out that the holes—the imprints of the nails—remain. He had learned an important lesson. Lord Alderdice was commenting that "even after all the work of healing there are still scars—and sometimes more than scars. For many people damaged by their own violence or that of others, even putting things into words and dealing with the feelings still leaves a profound difficulty in returning to everyday life. The over-stimulation of their experiences of extreme violence, as perpetrators or victims, leaves a legacy that is hard to manage" (p.475).

The two stories are complementary but do not convey an identical message. The first one is idealizing the very achievement of forgiving—the attaining of reconciliation as an ideal aim, while the second story is pointing out how there is not imaginable healing process after suffered violence without scars left. But, both stories put on common denominator the painfulness of the forgiving process itself and of worth of the achievement of the true, deep forgiving feeling and reconciliation.

Forgiveness could be seen (Durham, 2000) as a cancellation of blame and resentment, while others think of it in terms of a slow truce-making. "The Forgiveness Movement holds a positive view of forgiveness. In other quarters, forgiveness is seen as a symptom of weakness, or as a surrender. Many clinicians are cautious about approaching the subject. The issue of forgiveness, with its religious associations, seems to lie in an area where many would prefer not to tread. And yet, forgiveness is clearly in the air with all its ethical and religious elements, which I consider as complementary, nevertheless not necessarily identical. In what ways, then, can the therapist best integrate this ancient and modern component into the work of psychotherapy?" (p.68).

Or, put in another way, it might be asked how far is healing actually possible? I agree with the approach that Smedes (1996, p.2) described as four H stages process—Hurting, Hating, Healing, Honesty. Lord Alderdice was commenting on my considerations in this respect in the following way: "'In this fourth stage, he points out that revenge is a flawed attempt at a magical resolution rather than the honest, painful mourning and renunciation of vengeance that is necessary for forgiveness and the healing of relationships. Here, he moves (thinking again on my standpoint), perhaps somewhat controversially, to spirituality and the transcendent, referring back to the mechanism of the scapegoat that is, of course, such a central feature of traditional religious thought and practice as well as the law and culture. Is this where the notion of Truth and Reconciliation Commissions enter in? Do they somehow bring together the spiritual, legal and cultural elements that can facilitate the re-growth and growth that Volkan calls 'the process that goes from disorganization to reorganization'?" Here, Lord Alderdice's point regarding spirituality and the transcendental is somehow a skeptical one. As I already mentioned, mine is the one that considers the capacity to believe to be central, essential in this process.

Deep hurts we never deserved flow from the past into our living present. W. Faulkner, the well-known American writer wrote that past is never dead, it is not even the past ...

The great Jewish philosopher Hannah Arendt (1970) toward the end of her epochal study on The Human Condition shared her discovery of the only power that can stop the inexorable stream of painful memories: the "Faculty of forgiveness"—or, as G. Kaufmann put it, the courage of forgiveness.

Smedes (1996, p.71), writing about forgiving and forgetting, states that "we are discovering that the only way to get over the misery of resentment for remembered wrongs is to forgive the people who did them. Only when we heal ourselves can there be a healing between us and the person who did the wounding."

But, thinking on the process of forgiving, the experiences and observations are showing that (according to Smedes, 1996, pp. 94-121) people forgive:

- Slowly!
- With a little understanding!
- In confusion
- With anger left over!
- A little at a time!
- Freely or not at all
- With a fundamental feeling

Along these lines, Monbourquette (1997) explains twelve relevant steps that the authentic forgiveness includes:

1. Decision not to revenge, and stop with attacking;
2. Recognition of one's own injuries and inner poverty;
3. Sharing of one's own injuries with someone;
4. Identification of one's own loss in order to renew the mourning process;
5. Acceptance of one's own anger and wish for revenge;
6. Forgiving oneself;
7. Beginning to understand a person that was injured;
8. Finding of the sense of one's own wounds in one's life;
9. Recognition of dignity to be forgiven and already pardoned;
10. Not wishing to forgive at all costs;
11. Opening to the grace of forgiveness;
12. Decision to end a relationship or to renew it.

The psychological work in frame of exposed stages of understanding and resolving hostilities and preventing warfare would open up the perspective of human relationships, what Virginia Satir (1978, cit Urlić, 2004, p.469) summarized as: respect of differences, transformation of conflicts, development of possibilities, ability for undertaking the responsibility for one's own life, health, work and relationships.

I believe that the process of reparation should unfold and promote *the culture of forgiving, leading to reconciliation*. In the course of a successful recovery, it should be possible to recognize a gradual shift from unpredictable danger to reliable safety, from dissociated trauma to acknowledged memory, and from stigmatized isolation to restored social connection.

In the process of closing down psychosocial activities all of us—helpers, mostly dealing with groups of refugees and IDPs—were asking them about the most important element of our work in helping them through years. Their answers might have been summed up as *our presence and availability*. The explanation was that our presence on regular basis was ascertaining them in their existence and being important to someone again. It was like we were witnessing their bare existence. Our respect for them was exchanged for their respect for us. And, as they put it, they were absolutely sure in our availability at any time. Because of that, they were very rarely asking for some additional intervention. We were asking ourselves whether presence and availability were not the essential features of good enough mothering. Once, André Malraux asked his lifelong friend who had become priest what he could say from his experiences about the core essence of a human creature. The priest answered: "Man is a little scared child, and very unhappy." So, feeling the presence and availability of the mothering element is of primary importance when planning the help for refugees and displaced persons or taking care of people that had to pass through severe stresses and traumatic situations and eventually developed PTSD in its many forms.

In conclusion, I would like to underline that the path to reconciliation leads through the process of forgiving (Urlić, 2004, p.469). To heal the undeserved wounds on personal, social and ethnic-national levels, there is a path that I understand as the *five stages process* that should unfold on both sides in conflict:

1. Becoming conscious of the problem complexity (confrontation with many diverse realities and experiences);
2. Developing deeper understanding of its manifest and especially latent contents (the mourning process);
3. Working through the newly gained insight;
4. Renouncing vengeance and making forgiving possible;
5. Creating the space for reconciliatory processes to unfold, with oneself and other(s) (i.e., restoration of the capacity to believe).

The first three stages correspond to the well–known, usual psychoanalytically informed attitude/work. The fourth and fifth stages, besides rational and emotional components, include ethical, philosophical and spiritual/religious contents, the contents based on belief.

I suggest that the process of reparation should unfold intertwined with the mourning process and promote the culture of forgiving, leading to reconciliation, and to enlargement of the space of relationships. The containing capacity results re-established and deepened.

There are really incredible situations when traumatic stress and hatred do transform in forgiveness through deep human understanding. One patient of mine, a war veteran with severe PTSD symptoms, discontinued his psychotherapy and, before committing suicide, wounded three of his best friends and fellow soldiers. When I visited them in the hospital, one of them told me: "I have already forgiven him because the war has taken his soul away!"

So, between the "chosen trauma" and "chosen glory" (according to V. Volkan's concepts), there is another way that opens up with the help of culture of forgiving and the psychoanalytic culture in general, the way of reconciliation with oneself and with the present times, in order to open up possibilities for a more humane future to be created for us and for those that will follow us.

Considering the above-mentioned attitudes toward forgiveness, it is interesting and somewhat puzzling that forgiveness as a concept and as a process is beginning to be reconsidered from a more positive perspective on personal, group and social levels, leaving aside some ethical/religious/philosophical questions about its deep meanings and contents, recognizing its necessity alongside the dynamics of usual emotional and cognitive functioning.

And Curle (1997), writing about hatred and reconciliation in the frame of reference of public mental health, wrote that in today's often crazily chaotic conflicts, it is particularly important to consider the aftermath of direct violence. Although a ceasefire may have been arranged—or imposed as in Bosnia and Herzegovina—the emotions of anger and hatred may still dominate the minds of most people (as shown in a clinical vignette). It is, therefore, vital to pay great attention to the process of reconciliation as seminal for opening up to the future.

On the Way of Reconciliation: Forgiveness and Mourning Processes Revisited

On the architrave of Saint Jerome's church from the 14th century in Stari Grad on the Croatian island of Hvar it is written: "Who would like to enter this house of prayer, first has to reconcile with the one and only God and with his neighbors."

And Jampolsky (1999, p.24) in his book *Forgiveness*, wrote: "Imagine the peace that could come to our planet if all the people of the world would let go off old grievances with their neighbors. Imagine what could happen if we would all let go off centuries-old battles over racial differences, religious differences, and past injuries to one another." The same idea, the same need, goes over centuries as the expression of deep personal and societal wish. It looks like everlasting tension between two poles, the libidinal and the aggressive ones.

Researching in order to trace roots of reconciliatory behavior after violent attacks, much ethological research has been done in last several decades, bringing about very interesting and indicative insights.

Writing about resolution and distress alleviation in monkeys and apes, de Waal and Aureli (2000, p. 360) have found that research on nonhuman primates has produced compelling evidence for reconciliation and consolation, i.e., post-conflict contacts that serve to respectively repair social relationship and reassure distressed individuals, such as victims of attack. This has led to a view of conflict and conflict resolution as an integrated part of social relationship, hence determined by social factors and modifiable by the social environment.

There is another way to address old/new wounds. It pertains to the unavoidable approach of Archbishop Desmond Tutu (1998, p.201) in his efforts to achieve a free, nonracial South Africa through the creation of the Truth and Reconciliation Commission. He addressed issues of justice, vengeance and forgiveness as they relate to apartheid, asking perpetrators of racial atrocities to confess their crimes in return for amnesty. In his famous book, *No future without forgiveness*, he wrote that: "The real reconciliation can take place only by uncovering real feelings: Feebleness, violence, pain, humiliation ... the truth. Sometimes things might worsen. It is a dangerous endeavor, but at the end is worthwhile because only confronting with reality one can obtain the real healing. The false reconciliation can only bring about the false healing."

When we talk about forgiveness and the possibility of reconciliation, it doesn't mean that something should be forgotten. On the contrary, it is important to remember in order not to repeat the misdeeds. To forgive doesn't mean to condone what was done. It means to take seriously what had happened ... In order to do this operation, it is necessary to put oneself in the role of guilty ones and try to understand what might have induced them to behave like they did. The penitence and the confession from the guilty one are the necessary condition for the victim to become able to forgive.

With shame and guilt feelings, something important is lost. In the clinical vignettes and in reports from the social, political and cultural ambiences, it was described how the processes of confrontation with traumatic events, sometimes incredibly violent ones, represent a retraumatisation that brings about avoidant behavior and sets in motion repressive, dissociative and projective mechanisms. But, all losses have to be mourned.

The achievement of forgiving and reconciliation with oneself and others pre-supposes that the processes of mourning and working through were successful enough. In the case of psychotherapy with war veterans and other victims of trauma and war, working through of past traumas, of possibilities and impossibilities to get in touch with diverse parts of oneself, one's own needs and wishes, as well as with others in a more durable and intimate way, has the meaning of an important form of mourning process, as it was already pointed out.

When the mourning process could develop with considerable intensity, the process of working through of such difficult feelings like shame can take place. In the same time, there is a constant danger of falling into the countertransferential trap of over-identification or avoidance, the classical features of countertransference when working with heavily psychotraumatized person(s) or societies. I believe that many traumas, "chosen" and "forgotten" ones, are exerting lasting pressure that bear upon relationships even on the level of societies, religions and states. The group arena, or otherwise therapeutically created space, might be seen on a metaphorical level on large scale from individual to social.

Writing about the "anti-group," i.e., destructive forces in the group and their creative potential, Nitsun (1996) told that we should become aware of perception and projection. "As human beings, we have a particular way of making sense of our lives. We have memories for everything that has ever happened to us, almost since the day of our births, and maybe before. If we have fearful or hurtful things happen to us when we are young, we not only remember them, but we tend to cling to them for judging the present and the future." Here, we might trace the roots of transgenerational transmission of emotions.

On a more fundamental level, the containment, if not resolution, of the anti-group relieves participants of the anxious preoccupations engendered by a destructive group process. This paves the way for a freer use of imagination, thought, and feeling, and, in particular the exercise of play, in both a symbolic and an actual sense. Winnicott (1971) himself noted that play leads to group relationship, but as was shown in some examples, the containment of destructive tendencies is necessary in order for the group to play. Or, put in other words, to help recreate the space that was collapsed into the places for exposing and overcoming conflicts.

Large-group regression after a society has faced a massive trauma—involving drastic loss of life, property, or prestige, and sometimes humiliation by another group—reflects the efforts of a group and its leader to maintain, protect, modify, or repair their shared group identity. As in individual regression, many survivors in a traumatized society continue to function like mature adults in some ways, even as they are experiencing regression in others. Regression is not an all-or-nothing experience and is typically accompanied by attempts to adapt. Sometimes, these efforts to cope with the trauma will take the shape even of artistic creativity.

Reconciliation with Oneself and the Present: The Re-Emerging of Hope

During the mourning process, as well as during the whole therapeutic process with war veterans and otherwise psychotraumatised people, one might let him/herself be guided by the advice R. M. Rilke wrote to a young poet:

"Be patient toward all that is unsolved in your heart, and try to love the questions themselves like locked rooms and like books that are written in a very foreign tongue. Do not now seek the answers, which cannot be given because you would not be able to live them. And the point is, to live everything. Live the questions now. Perhaps you will then, gradually, without noticing it, live along some distant day into the answer." (Italics are underlining of mine.)

In terms of group relations, one could say that when war is in question, it pertains to a conflict reaction of a large group towards small groups or individuals. War treats an individual or a group of people in such a way as to activate or create archaic defenses towards the collective in us. The ancient dilemma between the collective and the individual is evoked and activated in the course of war, sometimes to the extent that the recognition of the individual is overshadowed. During war, a formation of archaic defenses appears and constitutes an archaic survival shield. The encapsulation of traumatic events might represent the survival maneuver, as well. The defenses do not correspond to the usual defenses of a person but serve to arrest reinforced demands from the environment. In this case, we speak of regressive states. They might be seen in reaction after all traumatic events that are bearing heavily upon each individual, too. A central question remains what this actually implies in the frame of individual or group psychotherapy.

For those affected by war, or any other type of severe psychotrauma, the continued close relationship with the many faces of death, killing and sudden changes of values have resulted in substantial personality changes. Their conscious life could not accept all these changes. But, their dreams, behavior, mood and values change; attitudes, and especially continuous high levels of anxiety, tension and proneness to aggression disclose inner strifes.

Bruno Bettelheim said that what cannot be put into words cannot be put to rest (Bettelheim, 1986). According to some examples from group psychotherapy, the resonance of the group, and its constant mirroring inside ever more defined boundaries and inner structures, contributed to enable the veterans—its members—to begin expressing their deep feelings and traumas, thus approaching the phases of mourning and adaptation described by Volkan as: (1) denial of loss, (2) anger, and (3) the process that goes from "disorganization to reorganization in which the loss is accepted as an irreversible event… the forward movement is not without some back-and-forth fluctuation" (Volkan, 1980).

What kind of loss is in question? As the members of the group expressed themselves, it was loss of ideals in part that was connected with the ongoing interpersonal relationships and changes in the army, toward the administration and toward rapidly changing society, ideals that were disconnected with the ones intergenerationally transmitted about independence of the homeland. At the same time, they were able to perceive loss of their "innocent parts," what seemed to be the most dramatic personal issue—delineating the whole spectrum of personality changes.

The patients may be filled with rage and a sense of hopelessness when their expectations prove unrealistic. The idealizations of such patients may need to be interpreted and clarified early in treatment in order to minimize traumatic disillusionment. During the group therapeutic process experiences (as exposed in previous chapters), some bitter feelings of disillusionment were shown, as well as a deep confidentiality developed toward conductor and other members of the group.

In situations of permanent persecution and instability, it is essential to maintain the continuity of being and to affirm the unity of endangered self. The person relies on ego ideal that should be preserved at all costs. That narcissistic need to preserve one's identity is created out of the national identity, independence and pride in the image of an all-powerful and ideal mother. The ideal mother easily becomes idealized. Unfortunately enough, the process of reworking of massive projections and intergenerational transmission of beliefs and emotions in that regard had to pass in Croatian experience through the war. On a more intimate level, the mourning processes enabling the culture of forgiveness to unfold bringing about the reconciliatory dynamics to develop towards oneself and other(s) have all characteristics of personal, group, as well as larger social unities maturational development.

The Alternative Way: The Culture of Forgiveness

During the training in group analysis, one trainee said: "It is not just to forgive if first you didn't untie your internal knots. It's false. It is only formal."

The notions about splitting of or non-integration of good and bad objects and the ensuing archaic mechanisms of defense, connected with awesome prejudices, mistrust and hatred, in these personalities are playing the central role.

As pointed out previously (Clark, 2005, pp. 652-653), other processes are conflated with forgiveness. One of those is reconciliation, defined as the restoration of a trusting relationship between victim and perpetrator.

Finally, a quote from de Waal in his book *Peacemaking among Primates* is appropriate (1989, p.270-271): "Forgiveness is not, as some people seem to believe, a mysterious and sublime idea that we owe to a few millennia of Judeo-Christianity. It did not originate in the minds of people and cannot, therefore, be appropriated by an ideology or a religion. The fact that monkeys, apes, and humans all engage in reconciliation behavior means that it is probably over thirty million years old, preceding the evolutionary divergence of these primates... Instead of looking at reconciliation as a triumph of reason over instinct, we need to begin to study the roots and universality of the psychological mechanisms involved. It is time for science to enter the scene."

This suggestion, coming from ethological studies, opens up the new perspective when aiming at reconciliation with oneself and the others in psychotherapeutic and larger social ambiences. It puts the reconciliatory strivings as deeply rooted in human core essence. In that way, looking along human developmental lines, it can be reactivated either spontaneously or due to psychotherapeutic or psychosocial engagement.

Gruchy (2002, p. 26) writing about reconciliation restoring justice wrote that in a world torn apart by conflict in so many places, reconciliation is a theme that demands constant consideration in ways that relate to context in which we live, taking into consideration social and political consequences, as well as some more obvious interpersonal ones.

There are interrelated ways in which we will speak about reconciliation, each of which refers to the overcoming of a relationship of enmity and alienation. The first or theological refers to reconciliation between God and humanity and what this means in terms of social relations. The second or interpersonal way of speaking about reconciliation refers to relations between individuals, as, for example, in restoring a marriage relationship or the relationship between a victim and a perpetrator of crime. The third or social refers to reconciliation between alienated communities and groups at a local level, such as the healing of race relations in a housing estate or at a school, especially in the wake of an outbreak of violence. The fourth or political refers to projects such as the process of national reconciliation in South Africa, the overcoming of sectarianism in Northern Ireland, or the achievement of sustainable peace in the Middle East.

Irrespective of whether we speak about reconciliation theologically, interpersonally, socially or politically, we need to recognize that we are invariably talking about a sequential process. Reconciliation is a way of dealing with and overcoming past alienation, enmity and hurt. But it is also a way of relating to the "other" in the present, and the goal that is always ahead of us in the future however much we may experience it here and now (ibid.p.27). This present and future, without the previous thorough mourning of all losses, might appear as a result of only superficial forgiving and reconciling, letting aside the most bitter aspects of the wrong done.

Reconciliation might represent a journey from the past into the future, a journey from estrangement to communion, or from what was patently unjust in search of a future that is just. The goal of reconciliation might be achieved at various stages along the way following estrangement and even divorce, when a restoration of relations is reached. But reconciliation as a final achievement is, in a sense, always beyond our grasp. It is, if you like, a gift that we experience and live by even now, but for most of us, nations included, it is always something ahead of us. It is work in progress, a dynamic set of processes into which we are drawn and in which we participate. So it is important to recognize the relationship and distinction between reconciliation as an event, a process, and a goal, and not to confuse our ultimate hopes with realistic possibilities even if they are connected.

Creating space is critical, irrespective of the nature of the reconciliation we seek. The process of reconciliation begins through the taking of what might appear to be small and often tentative step such as meeting and listening to the estranged "other." But it is a critical first step involving both parties. The "other" is initially experienced as a barrier, someone who stands in the way of us getting our own way. This implies a respect for the "other," as a human being no matter how much we may disagree. Whether we see the "other" as a threat or as a partner in the search for reconciliation, our response will determine whether we are able to make the second choice.

As a matter of fact, the literal meaning of the New Testament Greek word for reconciliation, "to exchange," derived from meaning the "other." In that sense, the "mutual acknowledgement" work (already mentioned in this book) aimed at getting closer Israelis and Palestinians, is showing how difficult task it is to understand the "other" and to make oneself understandable to the "other." The most difficult task represents transforming, blaming and anger into mutual acknowledgement, respect, forgiving, and possibly to reconciliation as a realistic perspective, at least partially. Time has not the most important role in achieving that goal. It is not possible to prescribe or to exactly predict the time needed for maturational processes to complete, but what we are able is to facilitate them to appear and develop.

Reconciliation begins to become when, without surrendering our identity, who we are, but opening up ourselves to the "other," we enter into the space between, exchanging places with the other in a conversation that takes us beyond ourselves. In doing so, we find ourselves in vicarious solidarity with, rather than against, the "other," only what we would want them to do to us. Furthermore, in the process, our self-understanding begins to change. If and when it occurs, reconciliation always does so within a particular context and with regard to a particular set of interpersonal or social relations. The dynamics of the process will, therefore, vary, even though there will also be constants and, while similar, it will be different, depending on whether it is at the level of interpersonal or social relations. Reconciliation is about building bridges, about allowing conflicting stories to interact in ways that evoke respect, build relationships and help restructure power relations.

In our Croatian experience, not even 14 years after the war, the rebuilding of trustful relationships process does not seem to be fully developed. On a more personal level, the wish to repair a damaged bond through forgiveness is also a wish to reconstitute the personality by regaining the ruptured narcissistic balance and to restore the damaged trust, meaning and hope in relationships, a loss even more significant than that of an important object.

One of the fruits of forgiveness is a "forgiving attitude" (which is also a developmental accomplishment allowing some people to be more forgiving than others) vis-à-vis oneself and the rest of the world. As the process of mourning carries a person from anger to sadness, the superego softens. The work of forgiveness further continues this softening as the residual narcissistic anger in the relationship gives way to understanding and a longing for rapprochement—to make good the lost relationship. I am suggesting that the whole process might be described in four stages: confrontation—mourning—forgiveness—reconciliation. The working through in each phase can be slowed down, or arrested, but with facilitation can be accomplished, giving a feeling of emotional maturation and restoration of inner peace.

The knowledge or fantasy that the hurtful other wishes to be forgiven begins a process of empowerment, as the erstwhile victim ponders the choice between empowering himself through the exercise of (pseudo-)control by not forgiving, and the wish to empower himself through empathy and love. One clinical vignette might offer an interesting point of view regarding standpoints in considering good and evil.

Clinical Vignette II

The Exhibition of Snakes

There was an exhibition of snakes in the city. This theme was brought into the group:

> Nada was at the exhibition, and her mother told her that she has always been doing something foolish.
> Zoran said that where he is living, snakes kill people. Toni said that some snakes suck milk. Vinko said: "We had one milk-sucking snake in our headquarters at the battlefield. We gave it milk on a plate. The snake was well behaved; we liked to have it around."

Therapist: "So, the snake, the evil, was put under control... Humans have their drives, even to suck milk or blood, as well as other drives..."
Toni: "We are able to think and to govern our drives."
Therapist: "In the war situation, too?"
Toni: "Chetnics (Srebian ultranationalists) were premeditating the evil."
Therapist: "Not as animals that are driven by their drives?"
Toni: "No, they premeditated all this, and therefore they should be condemned."
The group agreed that the evil should be condemned, and all the evil was projected towards the enemy and premedication.

It seems that premeditated aggression brings about traumatic hatred more than any other cause. However, in the imagination of the group members, snakes could represent something malign as well as benign. The animals' behaviour is justified by their drives, which is understandable and forgivable. The violent actions of humans cannot be justified in the same way. Instead, it enters into the picture of traumatic hatred mirrored in the group process (as well as in individual psychotherapy), destroying humans and humanity.

When the extent of trauma is not so great as to preclude the possibility of forgiveness, either choice can be legitimately justified (as this clinical example is illustrating). The distinction and understanding of the real meaning of traumatic event(s) on personal and social levels should be recognized in order to process it/them further in the inner world spheres. However, in such cases, opting for forgiveness puts an end to the vicious cycle whereby the victim can re-empower himself only by "acting out" his anger. In coming to empathize with the wrongdoer or to imagine his remorse, the erstwhile victim is empowered in a real way. The balance that is re-established in the relationship as a result of this reversal becomes narcissistically fulfilling at another level because it creates the kind of tit-for-tat situation that appeals to the unconscious and archaic mind. As an act of transcendence, forgiveness replaces judgment with understanding, the quest for power with a quest for love; in enabling the healing of a ruptured bond, it further promotes the psychological well-being of victim and wrongdoer alike. But, always after mourning was set in motion as a profound feeling.

The concepts of the "good breast" and the "bad breast" are a useful metaphorical foundation for the forgiving or unforgiving attitudes. When a child's bond with the maternal object is "good enough," he can let go of the "bad breast," that is, forgive it for its unavailability on command and so avoid a sadomasochistic engagement with it. This allows the child to recognize the satisfactory qualities of the metaphorical milk, be grateful for them and make reparation for his destructive wishes at moments of frustration or disappointment. As reparation and gratitude (Klein, 1957) become familiar modes of interaction with the world, hope that quality can indeed be found in relationships is increasingly engendered. Thus, the root of the depressive position, whose outcome is gratitude, is forgiveness. The nurturing milk survives the destructive projections of the forgiving child, who can appreciate its overall goodness. This is an important step towards acceptance of the reality principle—that the world is as it is, and not as one would wish it to be. That pertains to the inevitability of psychotraumatized people to confront ego ideals and ideal ego with larger social realities.

So, paradoxically, the angry fixation upon the bad breast destroys any sense that there is any good milk to be had—it becomes impossible to take in the very desideratum that is so longed for. The pain of frustration and emptiness may be further idealized in a reaction formation whereby pleasure is derived from the refusal to forgive. Trapped in his venomous feelings towards an all-bad object, with no recourse but to project them outwards, the child cannot forgive. But, brought in an atmosphere of therapeutic confrontations and exchanges, like in group psychotherapy setting, the "child" could be compelled to overcome such developmental arrest and open up towards new insights and syntheses of feelings and mindfulness.

Consequently, the waiving of forgiveness is a form of acceptance when one puts him/herself to a higher code of conduct and morality, whereby even legitimate expectations from significant others are minimized and turned upon oneself in order to maintain one's narcissistically charged status of "holier than thou." Once more, we are witnessing the significant role of expectation as a protagonist in the dynamic of forgiveness: namely, how turning expectations from others to oneself can set the person in the position of waiving forgiveness from others no matter how brutally one is treated. To forgive, therefore, reveals and supports newfound strength and a willingness to take the risk of intimacy.

Dynamically conceived forgiveness always occurs in the charged zone of a relationship filled with expectations. "Non-dynamic" forgiveness—such as "I forgive you, stranger, for stepping on my toe or for screwing up my car-insurance application"—is not really forgiveness at all, but the word is used as part of a social formula of reconciliation and getting on. It honors the deed, makes it public and moves on.

The recontextualization of the memory of harm following the willingness to forgive by virtue of softening the superego allows access to heretofore repressed or suppressed memories, leading to a realignment of the internal-object world; this is a sine qua non of the reality principle, thus further enhancing the psychological gains of forgiveness.

The forgiving attitude that is the by-product of self-forgiveness and works against the use of primitive splitting and projective defenses supports a kinder superego and upholds the narcissistic balance. The many internal struggles to achieve this therapeutic aim were exposed in clinical vignettes. According to my experience, aiming in that direction, the therapeutic results were much better than of those who received only psychopharmacological treatment and/or some support.

Following acceptance and also following forgiveness, when it is forthcoming, one is gradually able to make a shift from focusing on the wrongdoer to the wrong, from the criminal to the crime. This is due to the diminution of the narcissistic injury of feeling singled out, targeted and damaged, which modulates the quest for a just world and allows for starting a philosophical outlook on the world. My five-step approach proved to be workable in these situations. The lost narcissistic balance of the personality following the deep emotional wounds is disruptive to one's sense of confidence in the world. The failure of legitimate expectations ruptures basic trust and the recognizable structure of interpersonal relationship. The wish to restore that trust and structure is another driving force towards forgiveness.

Taking into consideration all that was said, it becomes ever more evident that forgiveness becomes a salient psychoanalytic construct in those analyses where patients unconsciously decide that the overall balance of a damaged or ruptured relationship is worth salvaging. This observation echoes Kohut's (1971) description of the restoration of the ruptured analytic bond after inevitable misattunements. Kohut's emphasis on the healing quality in the re-establishment of the analytic bond is also a central issue for the dynamics of forgiveness.

Forgiveness and reconciliation are such powerful experiences that can, under the right circumstances, bring about emotional healing, help the one forgiven, and even heal the damaged relationship. Forgiveness makes possible the reuniting of people torn apart by unfairness and hurt, thus enabling reconciliation with oneself and other(s). Of course, forgiving someone does not guarantee that one will be reunited, if such union is the goal. One can offer only so much. The other has to do his/her part also. The mutuality of acknowledgement of suffering is a key issue here.

Let's look at some of the elements of reconciliation as we concentrate on the possibilities of reconciling (Enright, 2001, pp.263, 264). When people reconcile, they come together again in mutual trust following a division caused by at least one person's unfairness. In my view, giving and receiving forgiveness precede genuine reconciliation, otherwise remnants of resentment can make people stand a bit to one side and not enter into a relationship as before. Those who actively work together on the processes of giving and receiving forgiveness are far along the journey toward reconciliation. Nevertheless, there are several issues involved in rebuilding the relationship beyond forgiveness; trust, open communication while rewriting the contract, and restored justice.

An interesting approach to phenomena and processes we are analyzing was the O'Dea (2008) proposal that perhaps a major change occurs in our understanding of who and what we are and in our sense of how fundamentally interconnected we are with each other. Another more immediate consequence might be a shift in the worldview presently offered by the majority of modern neuroscientists, who suggest that mind is a meaningless side effect of the workings of a purely mechanical brain, that our innermost thoughts and feelings are fully determined, and that free will is an illusion. Whether one prefers to believe that "God made me do it" or "my genes made me do it," the consequences of devaluing personal responsibility can be tragic. What might happen instead if mainstream science began to accept not only that free will exists but also—as is strongly suggested by experiments on anomalous cognition and by the findings of quantum physics—that mind is an active, interconnecting force, deeply entangled with ourselves and the world, and that the true nature of the universe is fluid, self-organizing, and inherently cooperative? Could such an expansive worldview lead to improved moral behavior, a greater sense of compassion, and perhaps a reduced fear of death? The possibility that the answers might be "yes" strongly encourages an open mind and continued dialogue.

If traditional scientists refuse to give up on their exclusively materialist paradigm, then the focus of other researches in the scientific community should be on supporting the development of alternative sciences and models wherever they are taking shape. The emphasis should be on integration, not division, and on expanding our knowledge in an ideologically free way. Eventually, the science that is the most integrative will become the science of the future, perhaps signaling the coming of the age of re-enlightenment (ibid. pp. 41, 42). In that sense, the clinical experiences, as well as social and political realities, have the value of contributing with the direct observations of consequences of psychic traumas, and of healing potential of individuals and groups, be it in spontaneous or organized ways.

All too many times, we have to rediscover what was already preserved in old wisdom of humane genius. Mourning processes and their meanings have been and still are the matter of many disputes of mostly secular or spiritual orientation. All wars finally end when people sit and talk. And, there is no emotional need or rational decision to forgive in order to start a dialogue, or the mourning process completed, or the compulsion to restore justice and to reconcile. My experiences have taught me that it is important to bear in mind the possibility and the need to develop the culture of forgiveness, and to enable and foster the necessary intertwined phases of mourning processes to unwind. What will ensue will be the necessity to reconcile with oneself and the other(s), in order to survive not only existentially but even emotionally and spiritually. And to be able to follow the praise carved in Renaissance times on one Dalmatian house: "*Thank you, Lord, for allowing me to be in this world,*" conveying to us the peaceful and integrated feeling of many facets of life.

References

Alfred, A. Truth and Reconciliation: A Psycho legal Perspective. *Ethnicity and Health.* 5(3/4)2000:1355-7858.

Lord Alderdice, J. Response to Lecture by Ivan Urlic. *Group Analysis.* 2004, 37(4): 472-476.

Arendt, H. (1970). *The Human Condition.* Chicago and London: University of Chicago Press.

Aureli, F., De Waal, F.B.M. (2000). *Natural conflict resolution.* Berkeley: University of California Press.

Bettelheim, B. (1986). *Surviving the Holocaust.* London: Flamingo.

Clark, A.J. Forgiveness: A neurological model. *Medical Hypotheses.* (2005) 65, 649-654.

Cozolino, L. The Neuroscience of Human Relationships. *Attachment and the Developing Social Brain.* W.W. Norton & Company, New York—London, 2006.

Day, L., Malbty, J. Forgiveness and Social Loneliness. *The Journal of Psychology.* 2005, 139(6), 553-555.

De Waal, F. (1989). *Peacemaking among primates.* Cambridge, MA: Harvard University Press.

Durham, M.S. (2000) *The Therapist's Encounters with Revenge and Forgiveness.* London and Philadelphia: Jessica Kingsley Publishers.

Enright, R.D., Forgiveness is a choice. *A Step-by-Step Process for Resolving Anger and Restoring Hope.* Washington D.C. 2001.

Enright, R.D., Freedman, S., Rique, J. The Psychology of Interpersonal Forgiveness. In: Enright, R.D., North, J. (Eds.) *Exploring for Forgiveness.* The University of Wisconsin Press, 1998.

Gruchy, J.W. de, *Reconciliation. Restoring justice.* Minneapolis 2002: Fortress Press.

Harris, A.H.S., Luskin, F., Norman, S.B., Standard, S., Bruning, J., Evans, S., and Thoresen, C.E. Effects of a Group Forgiveness Intervention on Forgiveness, Perceived Stress, and Trait-Anger. *Journal of Clinical Psychology.* Vol. 62(6), 715-733 (2006).

Jampolsky, G.G. (1999). *Forgiveness, the greatest healer of all.* Hillsboro, Oregon: Beyond Words Publishing, Inc.

Kaufman, M.E. The Courage to Forgive. *Isr J Psychiatry Relat Sci.* 21(3)1984:177-187.

Klain, E. (1998). Transference and Countertransference in Psychoanalytic Psychotherapeutic Approach to War Victims. In: Arcel L.T., Tocilj Šimunković, G. War Violence, Trauma and Coping Process. Armed Conflict in Europe and survivor responses. *International Rehabilitation Council for Torture Victims.* Copenhagen.

Klain, E., Pavić, L., Psychotrauma and Reconciliation, *Croat Med J.* 42(3):126-137,2002.

Klein M (1957). Envy and gratitude. In: *Envy and gratitude and other works.* 1946-1963. London: Hogarth, 1975.

Kohut H (1971). *The analysis of the self.* Guilford, CT: International UP.

Lauritzen, P. (1987). Forgiveness: Moral prerogative or religious duty? *Journal of Religious Ethics.* 15:141-150.

Legaree, T.A., Turner, J. And Lollis, S. Forgiveness and therapy: A Critical Review of Conceptualization, Practices, and Values Found in the Literature. *Journal of Marital and Family Therapy.* April 2007, Vol. 33, No.2 192-213.

Milivojević, Lj., Urlić, I., Szonyi, G. *Shadow of War Experience:* The Economy of Interethnic space, Panel-EGATIN.

Monbourquette, J. (1997). Kako oprostiti (How to forgive)? *To forgive in order to heal, to heal in order to forgive.* Zagreb: Oko 3 ujutro.

Nitsun, M. (1996). The Anti-Group. *Destructive forces in the group and their creative potential.* London and New York: Routledge.

O'Dea J. Toward a New Scientific Synthesis. *An Age of Re-enlightenment?* The Institute of Noetic Sciences Petaluma, CA 2008.

Parker, I. (1997). *Psychoanalytic culture. Psychoanalytic Discourse in Western Society.* London, Thousand Oaks, New Delhi, SAGE publications.

Rilke, R.M. (1920/2000). Letters to a young poet. In: Clarkson, P. (Ed.). *Ethics: Working with ethical and moral dilemmas in psychotherapy.* London: Whurr.

Rosen I (2007). Revenge: The hate that dare not speak its name. *J Am Psychoanal Assoc.* 55:595-620.

Satir, V. (1978). *Peoplemaking.* London: Souvenir Press, 1983.

Smedes, L.B. *Forgive and Forget. Healing The Hurts We Don't Deserve.* San Francisco: Herper, 1996.

Tutu, D.M. (1999). *No future without forgiveness* (Translated in Italian), Milano 2001, Feltrinelli.

Urlić, I. *Trauma and reparation, Mourning and Forgiveness: The Healing Potential of the Group. Group Analysis.* 2004, 37 (4): 453-471. Foulkes Lecture.

Urlić, I., Recognizing Inner and Outer Realities as a Process: On Some Countertransferential Issues of the Group Conductor, Special Issue: Article, Group Analysis, *The Group-Analytic Society.* (London), Vol. 38(2):249-263. .

Van der Kolk, B.A. (1993). Groups for Patients with Histories of Catastrophic Trauma. In: A. Alonso, L. Hillel, I. Swiller (eds) *Group Therapy in Clinical Practice.* Washington D.C., London: American Psychiatric Press.

Van der Kolk, B.A., McFarlane, A.C. (1996). The black hole of trauma. In B. Van der Kolk, A. McFarlane, L. Weisaeth (eds). *Traumatic stress: The effects of overwhelming experience on mind, body, and society.* New York: Guilford.

Volkan, V.D., Individuals and Societies as "Perennial Mourners." *Their Linking Objects and Public Memorials.* Chapter for a book on death, endings and mourning to be edited by Rebecca Curtis and Lori Bohm, 2004.

Winnicott, D. (1971) *Playing and Reality.* London: Penguin Books.

Wohl, M.J.A., Don Kuiken and Noels, K.A. Three ways to forgive: A numerically aided phenomenological study. *British Journal of Social Psychology.* (2006), 45, 547-561 © 2006. The British Psychological Society.

Worthington, E.L. Jr., Witvliet, Van Oyen Witvliet, C., Pietrini, P., Miller, A.J. Forgiveness, Health, and Well-Being: A Review of Evidence for Emotional Versus Decisional Forgiveness, Dispositional Forgiveness, and Reduced Unforgiveness. *J Behav Med DOI.* 10.1007/ 10865-007-9105-8.

Žižek, S. (1989). *The Sublime Object of Ideology.* London: Verso.

Author Index

H

J

K

L

M

N

O

P

R

S

T

U

V

W

Z

SUBJECT INDEX

A

B

C

D

E

F

G

H

I

J

K

L

M

N

O

P

R

S

T

U

V

W